EXECUTIVE PROTECTION

THE NEXT LEVEL

Richard Hardaker

Shield Crest

© Copyright 2017 Richard Hardaker

ISBN   978-1-911090-84-7

MMXVII

A CIP catalogue record for this book
is available from the British Library

Published by
ShieldCrest Publishing Ltd
86 Springhill Road
Grendon Underwood
Buckinghamshire,
HP18 0TF
England
www.shieldcrest.co.uk

Dedicated to Elisabeth and her beautiful and loving family who inspired me to finish this book.

Richard Hardaker joined the Military Police in 1974 and then specialised in Close Protection in 1986.

Having provided Close Protection whilst seconded to the Foreign Office and assignments at NATO, Cyprus and the first Gulf War Richard has a vast wealth of knowledge and experience within the CP sector.

He left the military in 1997 and continued CP within the civilian sector in positions as Team Leader and currently is the Head of Protective Security Detail(CP) Operations to the head of a wealthy Arab (UAE) state, a position he has held since 2004.

FOREWORD

In writing this book, Executive Protection – The Next Level I've provided information, which would be useful to those deployed in non-hostile areas in posts as a PSD (CP) Ops Manager, Regional Team Leader or a Localised Detail Supervisor as part of an Executive Close Protection Team. This book is intended as useful reference material for such an appointment. The current standards of the CP industry in some areas are lower than they should be given the level of responsibility vested in the CPO. A different approach needs to be made if standards are to be raised. Moving upwards to the next level from being a Team Member or Supervisor and taking on the added responsibility can be daunting for some and needless to say, some may be ill-prepared for the supervisory challenges which lay ahead. This book aims to fill in the gap analysis to make your team better tomorrow than they are today.

There is no intention in writing this book to show tactical drills or procedures and nor is it intended to replace recognised courses of instruction. The fact remains however that you only get the chance to get it right once and hopefully this book will help you to maximise the potential of all through the rigorous processes of identifying the right staff and then ensuring necessary disciplines featured within this book are applied.

The first topic in the book is to do with teamwork as without this you'll have nothing to supervise except trying to calm the chaos and mayhem when the team structure has broken down. Getting this right in the early stages can pave the way to a successful team profile and mission outcome.

Other aspects look at the more in-depth topics that are inherent to CP Operations and likely to enhance the basic knowledge of those aspiring to be either Regional Commanders (Team Leader) or indeed Managers. The more knowledge you have can only be beneficial to you and not only as a Team Member but for those who one day will be followed by others. This in effect will be the evolution of future leaders.

The mandate of operational tactics for CP very rarely changes around the globe other than being specific for each theatre locale in which you may be deployed but there is an ever changing picture that you will see on a day to day basis as you go about your operational duties. You need to be ready and prepared to absorb these changes in order for you to fulfil your contractual obligations to protect and secure your client by whatever means necessary. Regional Commanders and Localised Detail Supervisors play a pivotal role in ensuring that their teams are well prepared to maximise their own and indeed an overall collective performance and effort. Managers and team leaders must lead from the front and should always be better prepared to offer advice and guidance. There can be no margin for error.

A Detail Supervisor in some operations may become the operations Regional Commander (Team Leader). However, what follows is useful to both.

CONTENTS

Chapter 1

Teamwork

Maximising Performance

1. **Introduction**

In the corporate world of Close Protection (CP) there could be many teams within a group and each team is allocated a Detail Supervisor, in order to run the day-to-day activities. A Protective Security Detail (PSD) Team Leader is the link between the deployed personnel and management with the group being led overall by a PSD (CP Ops Manager) for command, control, operational and technical direction and guidance. A PSD team in whatever theatre of operation can never succeed without the full cooperation and support of everyone involved and with clear and concise guidelines in place. This includes those who work in the background and in the shadows of others as it is the focus of the back room staff that keep the front line active, but never share the credit for a successful mission outcome. It should be remembered that no one person in a team is any more or less important than the next and every team person must know this from the outset. Regardless of whether the role is Managerial, Team Leader, Detail Supervisor or a Team Member, it is important that each role is valued and their work is positively praised if you are to maximise commitment and performance. Everyone is a cog in an ever-spinning wheel; if one of those cogs breaks then so too can the operation. Most ops will hinge on a cohesive effort from top downwards and the team will only be as good as the weakest link and will be judged accordingly.

Delegation from the hierarchical chain is crucial to the performance of personnel. Added responsibility to Team Members will allow them to aspire to the challenge and become a more effective operative with a far better contribution to the ethics of the operation. Equally, having responsibility makes them involved and may release ideas that could ultimately be shared with others and Manager's alike and then adopted in either a raw or abridged version. If you don't involve them then you could in effect be stifling some great ideas, which could be a missed opportunity and the loss of a potential leader.

Teamwork is all about a collective contribution and not just a single act. The latter may become detrimental to the operation by having a single agenda not shared or viewed by others. Those single-minded operatives are not team players and will struggle to become a cohesive asset to the larger group. Unless they can be lead in the right direction they will become a liability and a threat to the mission and will ultimately be the weakest link. This link unfortunately will be judged as to the performance and effectiveness of the whole team. It's important therefore that this link is severed, nurtured or eradicated in the early stages to avoid a complete mission failure with the loss of your client, team members or both.

The correct selection of the team in the first place is crucial to the success of the team's well-being and mission status. Dynamics of a team are the behavioural relationships between team members who are assigned connected tasks within the operation and are affected by the roles and responsibilities of each contributing team member.

The nature of the industry and the massive responsibilities placed on the shoulders of each and every team member requires the best and most accommodating team to be formed through experience, knowledge and skills that are pertinent to that particular operation. Equally, the psychometric balance of an operative is just as important as skill sets if we are to minimise liabilities and risks from within.

2. **Management of Team Performance**

The definition of Team Management is:

'The administration of a group of people assembled to work on a particular task or to perform a particular function within a PSD operation.'

Team management typically involves setting team priorities and performance objectives, reviewing performance and methods employed and spearheading the team's decision-making process.

The correct management of people dictates the overall results displayed by team members. Managers have to strike a balance with regards to tracking performance at both individual operative and team level. On one hand, the manager must ensure that each team member is responsible for and accountable to a particular key result and set of targets. On the other hand, managers must see to it that each of the individual deliverables is aligned with the overall team goals. Having teamwork therefore is imperative and managers must create an environment to strengthen the working relationships between and amongst all members to eliminate isolation.

3. **PSD Team Leader/Detail Supervisor**

Definition of a Leader/Supervisor is:

'A team member who has more authority than other members, but is appointed to;

    a.   *Represent the whole team to the next higher reporting level*
    b.   *Make decisions in the absence of a consensus*
    c.   *Resolve conflict between team members*
    d.   *Co-ordinate team efforts*

PSD Supervisors are those individuals in a group who have been deployed to achieve mutual goals that will inevitably and almost immediately begin to share their thoughts on how the team should go about attaining the goals. It is often the case that management will recognise a leader characteristic and appoint, or promote certain people to assume a leadership role. Often though, but not always, it will be a team member that has more experience in the field than others who is appointed as Supervisor though they are not, for whatever reason, management material.

When the CP Ops Manager appoints, promotes or hires a Detail Supervisor, the objective is to guide the outcomes of the team's results through effective leadership and dynamic approach. The role of Detail Supervisor normally carries some of the same responsibilities as that of a team member, with additional higher-level duties added. Creating reports, monitoring each team asset and directing the flow of day-to-day tasks are often these extra duties. All are commensurate with the functionality of the team's structure.

4. **Effective Regional Commanders (Team Leaders)/Detail Supervisors**

The most effective Detail Supervisors will know the strengths of each team member, their challenges and motivational hot spots. This could be supported with an overview of CV's or indeed the Graphology triggers. By having this information, the Detail Supervisor will be able to guide the outcome of any client interaction even when not physically present with the end result being goal orientated results, increased performance and all the other good news that allows their managers to sleep well at night. Most of the client appointment positions are decided upon in advance by the PSD (CP Ops Manager) giving due consideration to the expectations of the client and the type of individual who would be best suited for the appointment. This could be linked to the individual's skill set, languages, presentation etc.

A Detail Supervisor cannot be considered effective if he is unable to motivate and mobilise the entire team or if he had to do all the work himself. Effective Detail Supervisors maintain open and transparent lines of communications with their team members to ensure that everyone knows what he is expected to do, and that each member understands how his role contributes to the overall mission goal. In addition, Detail Supervisors become effective when they set a good example themselves to their Team Members and when they immerse themselves in the actual work instead of just delegating all responsibilities. A hands-on leader gains more respect than one who shirks his own responsibilities and gives little praise for the team effort, but takes it all for himself. That is not a workable option in a team environment but most will accept it as part of the hierarchical chain.

Supervisors must be acutely aware of time management and how long it is likely to take to complete a task so that he can use his assets more effectively. It is an important leadership skill that will allow the supervisor to prioritise and organise work in order to guarantee delivery of results. As a good supervisor, if you're not mindful of how it's possible to utilise time and the way to keep others motivated with better time management, you'll fall behind and will struggle to catch up. It is hoped at this point however that teamwork will keep it together otherwise you'll create an issue where your leadership will be challenged.

Apart from everything that has been mentioned before, effective decision-making capabilities are irreplaceable. A good supervisor needs to take fast calls as specified by the nature and demands of your employment. The picture is ever changing and reactions to events need to be as quick and as responsive as you can be. Our future is unpredictable, however an effective Detail Supervisor should be able to control the level of doubt with the implementation of the correct choice of action at the time and to be able to stand by their justification.

Inter-personal and communication skills are an important way of boosting the power of different leadership traits. It must be realised however that without such communication skills, the meaning of leadership will be lost.

5. **How to Lead a Team**

To successfully lead a team, the Detail Supervisor must first know what the team is for and why it was set up in the first place. We know that it'll be a protective detail since that is the nature of who we are but this has to be quantified further in terms of the type of protection required. Is it satellite surveillance with a protective responsive element? Is it a closed box formation with immediate responsive measures? From here, the team leader can establish specific targets and success parameters against which the team's performance will be evaluated.

It would be useful for the Detail Supervisor to come up with a gap analysis (tasks) with the team to ensure that the operational strategies they come up against will be addressed and met successfully. If there are any shortfalls then these will need to be addressed at the earliest opportunity. Once the analysis is completed, the Detail Supervisor should then translate the strategies into individual tasks and items to action, assigning roles that are appropriate to each member's capacity, ability and willingness to work. It should not be assumed that every team member is capable of performing the same task. A good Detail Supervisor will soon know the capabilities of each member of their team. Negatives should be turned into positives however for some it's an uphill struggle and often the stubborn ones are unwilling to change for the good and are generally in a rut and set in their ways. A team should never run with a weak person on board, they become liabilities, are constantly monitored, unpredictable, off-focus and a risk to the whole team's survival effort. You end up having to carry a burden. This person should be off-loaded at the earliest opportunity to protect the team, the client and ultimately the whole operation.

Of course, teamwork is not an exact science. Conversations can fall off-topic, team meetings can turn into mere social gatherings and disagreements can lead to stalemates and individuals can refuse to cooperate. These reasons, along with others are the reasoning behind having a Detail Supervisor in the first place to minimise any chance of this happening in the first instance.

Detail Supervisors often don't have the opportunity to choose the people they wish to work with as they are selected by management. Detail Supervisors have to be able to work with a mixture of personalities that can be diverse at times, have varied experiences and skill sets. Utilising these can strengthen the position of the Detail Supervisor and indeed the team by embracing the modern operative.

It is imperative that a Detail Supervisor knows the type of leader they are and what style they have. There are several which will work in different circumstances and to each personality. It is possible that several of the following may be appropriate in given situations but the end goal is to maximise the employability of your team members.

a.   Transactional leadership
b.   Autocratic leadership
c.   Bureaucratic leadership
d.   Charismatic leadership
e.   Democratic/participative leadership
f.   Laissez-faire leadership
g.   Task-oriented leadership
h.   People/relations-oriented leadership
i.   Servant leadership
j.   Transformational leadership

In order to gauge which leadership style you fall into, the following short description of the above should be sufficient to form your own judgment and style:

a.   *Transactional Leadership*:   This is probably best known as managerial leadership, which focuses on supervision, organisation and performance. It is also a type of leadership in which leaders promote compliance by followers through both rewards and punishments.

b.   *Autocratic Leadership:*   By its very name, this style of leadership is authoritarian and is characterised by taking control over all decisions and has little input from team members. This type of leader will make choices based upon their own ideas and judgments and will rarely accept input from others.

c.   *Bureaucratic Leadership:*   This is a management led style of leadership based upon fixed official duties under a hierarchy of authority with little or no flexibility outside of the set rules.

d.   *Charismatic Leadership:*   This style of leadership tends to inspire and motivate followers to perform to higher levels and to be committed to the good of the operation and team alike. Having this style gives inspirational motivation to others.

e.   *Democratic/participative Leadership:*   This style, as the name implies involves participation from the team who take a more participative role in the decision making process. Each member of the team are given an opportunity to contribute and to share ideas where discussions are encouraged.

f.   *Laissez-Faire Leadership:*   This style is where leaders are hands-off and allow team members to make their own decisions. In other words, leaving things to take their own course without interfering. This style of leadership has been known to create the lowest morale and job productivity as there is no guidance, direction or structure.

g.   *Task Orientated Leadership:* This style could be classed as goal orientated which has a behavioural approach by the team leader in order to achieve a certain performance standard.

h.   *People/Relations-Orientated Leadership:*   By inspiring team members to meet or exceed the role specific goals and for staff to feel much better about themselves and positive about the career they have chosen. Can also be referred to as emotional leadership.

i.   *Servant Leadership:*   Where the leader becomes primarily the servant and wishes to serve as well as to lead.

j.   *Transformational Leadership:*   This style of leadership is where the leader has a vision and has identified the need for change and then works with the team to execute the change in a collective and timely manner.

6.   **Detail Supervisor Role – Stages of Team Development**

Having an awareness of what teamwork is and the stages of development will help you to respond in the most effective way:

a.   ***Forming***

The selection and criteria in identifying suitable team members includes the necessary skills and diverse backgrounds to encourage a healthy debate. As a Detail Supervisor or Team Leader, it is your job to start discussions, share a vision, and discuss what outcomes are needed and how you can all work together to achieve them. Team members will cautiously explore the boundaries of acceptable group behaviour. They will search for their position within the group and test the leader's guidance. It is normal for very little team progress to occur at this point.

b.   ***Storming***

This is probably the most difficult stage for the group. At this stage, you need to face issues that come up in an assertive way so that you can describe your needs and wants but also to listen carefully to what is said by the team members. A calm approach is essential and if you can keep the atmosphere from becoming too tense this will help you to move forward more quickly. Members often become impatient about lack of progress, but are still inexperienced with working as a team.

c.   ***Norming***

As the team begins to work together, make sure that you revisit goals regularly and encourage creativity. Communication is important as well as regular feedback on progress. Your job is to facilitate, encouraging rather than directing the team. Emotional conflict is reduced at this stage as relationships become more cooperative. Teams are able to concentrate on their work and start to make significant progress. And contribution.

d.   ***Performing***

At this stage you need a more hands-off approach. You need to watch for conflict issues and look for ways to improve and motivate. At this stage the team have discovered each other's strengths and weaknesses and learned what their roles and expectations are. Team satisfaction is running high, as is their loyalty. Your job is also to celebrate the success of the team. A simple 'Thank You' can go a long way! Look for opportunities to share results so that others are aware of the team success. Clients however will always expect results and they don't want to see or hear about any issues that go on behind the scenes.

Note that it is often the small things that people do or say which contribute to the effort and can make all the difference in building a cohesive, productive and enjoyable team.

7.   **Teamwork**

It is the basic analogy where 'Two heads are better than one' and often by sharing a problem to seek out solutions, you open the floor to others who offer a new insight based on their own experiences, knowledge and skills. Delegating tasks will alleviate you having to do everything so that you can concentrate on leadership. In some situations, teamwork can prevent you from reinventing the wheel as it is possible that someone else may have come across the same problem on another assignment and was able to resolve it thereby saving you hours of time and resources that could otherwise be put to better use.

Teamwork can help people to become smarter not harder. Creative ideas can receive immediate feedback and there is less chance of someone being stuck with the problem, as more people will be thinking of a solution to the problem and with more strategies to try.

Another benefit of teamwork has to do with health of employees. Having a level of support from management through their supervisor can offer new inspiration and energy. Having due regard for OPSEC, the talking of previous assignments, projects or problems leads to less isolation for the team member who shares these experiences and therefore won't be left in situations all alone.

8.   **Teamwork Skills**

In order for teamwork to succeed, more than the Detail Supervisor needs to be on-board. People who are working as part of a team must be willing to talk openly and listen to opinions of others without getting defensive. In many cases, people must be willing to make changes to how they work to accommodate team strategies that may not be their own. Teamwork may take a while to foster therefore people must be willing to give time and effort to allow the process to succeed. Detail Supervisors must also allow time for a settling in period for new team members to adjust, but up to a point whereby you don't end up carrying that particular person. This matter would then need to be addressed with management if it reached this point.

As teams grow larger, the skills and methods that people require grow as more ideas are expressed freely. Detail Supervisors must use these to create and maintain a spirit of teamwork change. The intimacy of a small group is lost, and the opportunity for misinformation and disruptive rumours grow.

The following are characteristics of effective teams which mean overall that they are cohesive and led with ideal leadership and knowing what the end game is from the beginning.

a.   ***The team must have a clear goal.*** Avoid fuzzy, ambiguous and impractical statements. Team goals should call for a specific performance objective, expressed so concisely that everyone knows when the objective has been met.

b.   ***The team must have a result driven structure.*** The team should be allowed to operate in a manner that produces results and is commensurate with the operational mandate. It is often best to allow the team to develop the structure and best working practices.

c.   ***The team must have competent team members***. Given the skill set and knowledge that an operative has this part means that the problem given to the team should be one that all members can tackle given their level of knowledge.

d.   ***The team must have unified commitment.*** This doesn't mean that the team needs to agree on everything. It means that all members must be directing their efforts towards the goal. If an individual has a personal agenda, then other members should confront this and resolve soonest.

e.   ***The team must have a collaborative climate.*** It is a climate of trust produced by honest, open, consistent and respective behaviour. With this climate, teams perform well and without it they fail.

f.   ***The team must have high standards that are understood by all.*** CP teams must know what is expected of them individually and with mutual support collectively.

g.   ***The team must receive external support and encouragement.*** Whilst a team member will work hard it is essential that they are praised for work well done. This is a motivation factor and may increase creativity and performance. It also inspires a great deal of confidence.

h.   ***The team must have principled leadership.***   A team usually needs someone to lead the effort. Team members need to know that the Detail Supervisor has the position because they have good leadership skills and are working for the good of the team. Team members will be less supportive if they feel that the supervisor is putting himself/herself above the team, achieving personal recognition or otherwise benefitting from the position at the expense of others. Resentment could creep in.

The following is an appropriate, suitable and effective acronym in today's modern working environment:

T	-	*Together*
E	-	*Everyone*
A	-	*Achieves*
M	-	*More*

Chapter 2

Use of Graphology for PSD Selection

1. **Introduction**

Graphology has been around for centuries starting possibly with Suetonius, a Roman Historian through scholars like Shakespeare and Walter Scott who believed that people's personality is reflected through their style of writing. The scientific part began as early as the 17th century. The bases on which today's methods are used were set down during the 19th and early 20th centuries which makes graphology a relatively new science. It currently has wide ranging usage such as education, recruitment and HR to criminal psychology and illness diagnosis. This chapter is not designed to teach you the art of Graphology nor to fully grasp the concept of reading a sample piece of writing, it is merely to give you a better understanding of how to use this tool and what you are likely to get back in return. As a person in a position of responsibility, whether it be a detail supervisor, team leader or manager you may be asked to select and recruit CP staff over time and to know that you have a tool at your disposal is invaluable.

In order to select a suitable operative for a PSD deployment, there are various selection criteria that need to be met in the first instance. Whilst having a SIA CP front line license is the first, there are several others which should be considered as necessary prior to selection confirmation which will be commensurate with the type of deployment being considered for. If time allows, basic selection criteria should include a physical assessment, academic assessment, in-depth interview process to name but a few.

Many large corporate entities use Personality Profile Assessment (PPA) to find suitable candidates to fill their vacant posts but this method is not suited to everyone and is often not as in depth enough to truly gain an understanding of a potential operative. As a manager you will need to understand the inner workings of a member of your team(s) to see what makes them tick and the PPA won't provide you with that information to allow you to make the correct judgment call. PPA's are not personalised, as they are computer generated and several people could quite easily have the same print out. Whichever system you decide to use the returns you get need to maximise the results for you to make an informed assessment of candidates suitability. Don't be swayed to just one idea because it's seen as the choice of your company.

By using graphology correctly it will supplement your decision making process and you will be surprised by the results and how real these observations are to the candidate's own personality. They reflect the individual in a way that nothing else will come close. Graphology can also be used for internally promoted candidates from within your teams to ensure they fit the necessary profile for the post on offer and that there are no surprises later on.

It is essential that the right balance be made when selecting teams to ensure that you minimise conflict when the teams come together. If you use graphology correctly and interpret the data and information that it produces then it will hopefully help you in making the right decision.

As a graphologist is an expert in their field, it is likely that the reading of information provided by candidates will be out-sourced at a cost to you or your company. This will be money well spent in ensuring that a balanced team is deployed. It is important that you use every practical tool available to you to select the right people for the right job especially given the responsibility vested in the team. After all they are there to protect the client and the last thing you want is one who goes rogue.

The core competencies of an ideal PSD member, Team Leader or supervisor are explained and detailed towards the end of this chapter. There is a greater expectation today for the CP operative to be everything to all people and his skills and knowledge base far surpasses any of our fore fathers. This is a whole new ball game and selecting the right caliber of individual is imperative. Intelligence over brawn is critical in today's high profile executive protection. Selecting the wrong person may just jeopardise the whole mission and compromise the client and team alike.

You may also lose your lucrative contract by the actions and attitudes of some that could've been identified, prevented and dealt with in the early stages.

2.   **What is Graphology?**

A good handwriting analysis can give an accurate and realistic description of a personality – a description that could be difficult to acquire in any other way e.g. PPA. The formation of letters, words and spacing reveals information about the hidden personality of the writer. A page of handwriting says far more than the actual contents of a letter. Just like a picture can paint a thousand words.

Written movements recorded on paper are in some respects like a cardiogram that describes the condition of the heart or an encephalogram that reflects the activity of the brain.

Attitudes and feelings influence the formations of handwriting and the translation of these formations into language will best describe the nature of the personality concerned.

At its most complex, graphology is a large and dynamic subject. At its basic level however, it is relatively easy to understand and to begin to apply. Using graphology as a simple guide, it can provide useful indicators to the writer's personality.

Spoken words can be manipulated to hide real thoughts and feelings, but genuine emotions and attitudes inherent in handwriting that forges those words cannot be falsified. Written words take shape on paper in spontaneous movements that minutely reflect the attitudes and feelings of the writer so that handwriting becomes a fine and sensitive gauge of sentiment.

Graphology can show:

- An understanding of the writers personality
- Can even understand the most difficult of people.
- The hidden feelings and emotions straight from paper
- The signs of conflict and tension
- The real character, nature and sincerity of the writer
- Where rivals are coming from so you can never be taken by surprise
- Generosity and gentleness where you least expect it. There is often a heart of gold in the crustiest of exteriors.
- Intelligence, aggression, confidence and more
- The signs of low-esteem
- Selfishness, inhibition, vitality, energy and many more personal traits

To ensure that there is a far greater degree of certainty in place for candidates who are being selected for a PSD deployment, graphology adds a bonus in that it requires no painful or embarrassing interviews, which a case sensitive candidate may see as an invasion of their privacy. Because of nervousness, an otherwise perfectly qualified applicant may not be able to do justice at an interview. As a result, you may end up with a completely inaccurate assessment of the applicant's suitability for the post. This would be your loss at the end of the day. You will still have the final say no matter what the results are.

3.   **How to Use Graphology**

Graphology should be seen and used as a tool to enhance the selection criteria you should already have in place. Some may see this as more influentially important than say an interview but it is essential that you remain focused on the role criteria. Graphology will highlight certain individual traits that will become known, as 'Flags' and these are the ones that a manager or whoever will be responsible for the final decision will need to take into account and look at in more depth.

It is essential that a fully versed and educated expert be sought to provide the information you seek. It takes years to understand and read handwriting and if it is to be used as a tool in recruitment, then it needs to be taken seriously. The cost will need to be included into any fiscal planning.

In order to narrow down the kind of information graphology can generate, it is essential that the expert in graphology, who will read the handwriting provided by the candidate has some information about what you are looking for in the first place in relation to the type of PSD role. The expert in graphology may not be from a security background and thus some of the words they use to describe certain functions within a PSD may not be the same as we would use but the outcome will nevertheless be the very similar.

Table 2.1 – *Must have and must avoid*

Must Have	Must Avoid
Self-Confidence	Laziness
Initiative	Sex, drug & alcohol problems
Ability to keep secrets	Dishonesty
Respectfulness	Emotional instability
Attention to detail	Tactlessness
Flexibility (but not unpredictability)	Resentfulness
Carefulness	Defiance
Quick comprehension	Stubbornness
Energy	Temper
Ability to observe	Ostentation
Cooperativeness	Slow thinking
Sense of responsibility	Over sensitive to criticism
Objectiveness	Domineering
Organisational ability	
Emotional responsiveness	
Listening ability	
Communication ability	
Memory	
Independence	

Once the expert has been given the above information, they are able to pull out the relevant information from the sample provided by the candidate. There could be a wealth of information that wouldn't ordinarily have any relevance to a PSD operative so it is essential that the parameters are narrowed accordingly when first setting up Graphology with your expert so as to avoid any ambiguity.

Comprehensive detailed Red Flag statements regarding candidates are shown at the end of this chapter, which you may find useful and may wish to use during your own process.

Graphology is unable to state 'this means that' because specific movements need to be considered in context. At the end of this chapter is a list of indicators that could prompt a more detailed investigation. These explanations are a valuable aid in understanding the inner depths of graphology and the personality of your prospective team members.

When analysing a piece of writing it is essential that you are able to identify the main features of the sample writing. These would include:

- Size and proportions
- General layout
- Direction of lines
- Degree of connection
- Regularity
- Rhythm (or evenness)
- Degree of broadness
- Speed of writing
- Form of letters
- Covering of space
- Shading
- Angle of writing (slant)
- Right and left tendencies
- Spacing
- Degree of attention
- Pressure
- Decoration/distortion

4.   **Graphology – The Basic Analysis**

It is important to note that before beginning an analysis, ensure that the author of the writing example has agreed that his or her writing can be analysed and that any comments made by the graphologist can be shown to him or her if requested.

a.   *Is the sample valid?*   That is, has the style of writing been affected by any external influences? e.g., an uneven writing surface, an awkward writing position, or written on the move. You cannot analyse a sample that is not reliable. For the purposes of checking slant and coverage it is more difficult to analyse samples that have been written on lined paper. Plain should be used.

b.   *Size.*   There are many aspects to the size of writing and alone it doesn't indicate many things. Size needs to be considered along with other factors and there are some simple indicators. Small writing is generally a strong indicator of a detailed, technical personality. Large rounded and dominant central case letters indicate a friendly and sociable personality.

c. *Letter-Word Slant.* Check to see if there is a consistent slant to the letters and therefore the words in the given sample by the candidate. Check by drawing lines through the up and downward strokes. Backwards slants indicate an introverted personality (even when the person is left handed) and someone who could be showing some opposition to their environment whereas forward slants are extroverted. An upright slant tends to indicate a person who is independent and not prone to display their feelings. Upright strokes indicate a personality who is motivated by factors other than people. The degree of consistency of the slant (i.e. parallel strokes) indicates the degree of emotional consistency.

d. *Line Slant.* Writing which rises to the right shows optimism and cheerfulness. Sagging to the right shows physical or mental weariness. (This applies to signatures sloping downwards also).

e. *Flow.* This is one of the essential indicators, but like any other factor it is not to be used on its own. Generally restraint is indicated every time the pen leaves the paper and the converse applies. Gushing, eager, impulsive people have a more continuous flow of writing. Flowing writing has linked letters and sometimes linked words. Artistic and conceptual people who like space and time around them will often have completely separated letters. (It follows that pressure at school on some children to 'write joined-up' – because the common view is that to do otherwise is 'not-grown-up' – is unnatural and often counter-productive. In any event, continuity of the flow does not correlate to intelligence).

f. *Spacing.* Space between words indicates social attitude to others. Close words are a sign of sociability. Large spaces between words indicate the person is comfortable alone, and may even distrust others. Spacing between letters represents the time a person is willing to spend evaluating external factors and the way they deal with others, either impulsively or cautiously.

g. *Decoration and Distortion.* Don't confuse the two. Decoration is intended; distorted is malformed and unintentional. Both are different to unfinished letters, which gives a different indicator. Decoration is generally a sign that the writer wishes to be noticed more than he or she is at present. Malformed letters indicate a variety of things that must be dealt with individually. Unfinished words can be a sign of intelligence and impatience.

5. **The Three Zones – Divisions of Responsibility**

An essential aspect to analyse is the bias of the writing towards upper, central and lower zones. The upper case is in the area in which the extended up-strokes are found in the tall letters like **b, d, f, h, l, t,** etc. The central or middle zone is the central region occupied by letters with neither long up-strokes nor long down-strokes, such as **a, c, e, m, n, o,** etc. The lower zone is the area occupied by the extended down-strokes of letters such as **g, j, p, q,** etc.

Idealism
Religion
Philosophy   **Upper Zone**
Imagination

Logic Pragmatism Common-sense Instinct	**Middle Zone**

Animal Appetite Physical Force	**Lower Zone**

The central zone (middle) contains most of the writing. The upper and lower zones are those that extend above and below the central body of each letter. The three zones represent the three aspects of our personality. If it helps you to assess the relative dominance of the three zones draw a horizontal set of tram lines through some lines of writing to mark the division between the three cases. Look at the relative dominance and extent of each of the cases:

- *Upper*   our 'higher' selves, and thinking about religion and philosophy
- *Central*   our mental and social approach to life
- *Lower*   our physical aptitudes and attitudes

Look where the writing is mainly concentrated, and where the emphasis is; this is where the emphasis of the personality is too. Look for any encroachment from upper zone to the line above or from lower zone to the line below – it's a sure indication that the encroachment is dominant. Also, look at the central zone to see if there is an upward or downward pull. An upward pull is best spotted if you see an arched pattern running through the central zone and seeing a pattern of troughs through the central zone best spots a downward pull. The pull pattern in the central zone also indicates the emphasis of the personality.

6.   **Simple Indicators**

- Large broad upper loops are a sign of emotion
- Right pulled lower loops show interest for the good of others
- Left pulled upper case shows a fondness for the past
- Uneven upper loops show changeable satisfaction, or disillusionment
- Full left-pulled lower loops show physical intent
- Closed 'e's and other small closed central loops show secrecy
- 'Stand-alone' or properly formed 's's at word ends show independence.
- Word-end 's' where top of letter is formed into downward right loop shows a yielding or co-operative nature.
- Angular central case is a sign of an interest in ideas rather than people.
- Rounded central case shows interest of people.
- Uncompleted case letters, e.g. 'a's, 'b's etc., (open when they would normally be joined loops) show a casual nature; very open shows propensity to gossip.
- Small writing is generally a sign of technical personality
- Loops in angular writing show potentially difficult character.
- 'T' cross strokes connecting a number of 't's with a single line shows speed of thought (but not a guarantee of correct thinking)
- Omitted 'i' dots and 't' cross strokes shows forgetfulness and carelessness.
- Position and style of 'I' dots show different things:

       o   Directly above, close to and in line means exacting
       o   Ahead means active and thinking
       o   Flicked and wavy could show a sense of humour
       o   Behind shows thoughtfulness
       o   Inconsistent (varying positions) means a distracted mind.

7.   Graphology Reports

There are two types of reports that are available for you to consider and both are briefly explained below. You have to be mindful from the start as to the depth and level of information you actually require and need for you to fulfil your selection and protection criteria. What is acceptable for one person/company may differ greatly for another but your starting point should be a discussion with the graphologist to get the base line addressed. If all you want is an overview then the shorter abridged version may be useful. Both will incur a cost and this will be decided upon from the depth of information that is provided but the choice is dependent on what you are looking for in terms of information to be gleaned. You will either receive a full report or an abridged version (your choice), which highlights the areas of concern. The first of course is more in depth and will go deeper into the analysis. Both reports are very different and the one which you may decide upon will often be the abridged version as this brings out the salient points in a more detailed way in terms of flags and a brief script rather than lots of script. Both examples are added at the end of this section for comparison.

a.   *Full & Completed Graphology Report*

    There will be several headings contained within this report and each will have a lengthy script to answer the heading point. You must bear in mind though that the turnaround for this type of report will take slightly longer than the abridged version.

b.   *An abridged version*

    You will need to discuss with your Graphologist as to how to tailor the information you will require so that it best suits your needs.

    The report you receive under this heading will incorporate the following information. The first page will show an overview of the Red Flags against the candidate number across the top. The second page will include a breakdown of information regarding the Red Flags with a corresponding number greater than [>0]. Where there are blanks then this indicates that there are no concerns within that particular area or against the candidate. The example at the end of this chapter shows that Candidate 5 has several high point Red Flags that should raise questions as to their suitability. Anything >3 should be subjected to further scrutiny.

In the event that you have asked for and received an abridged version and you have doubts about an individual from the information provided, then there are 3 courses of action you can take:

1.   Either accept the comments in the red flag reports and decide not to recruit the individual, or
2.   Request a full report from the graphologist.

3.   Employ the candidate amongst a large team rather than one on one so that you can maintain supervision.

8.   Red Flag Statements Relevant to CP and Discussed with Graphologist

The kind of information relevant to a CP Operative must first be identified if you are to gain maximum use out of the reports.   The Red Flags in which are essential and should be discussed with the expert are set out below. These can be tweaked to suit your own needs. Each flag has a brief description as to what they actually mean.   Looking on the example of the abridged report version at the end of this chapter, the headings named in table 1.2 below are used to score an individual's character. (A score from 1- 10 gives the extent of the characteristic, with a score of 10 being for the most serious issues.)

Table 2.2 *Headings Used in the Abridged Report*

Red Flag Report Headings	Descriptive Meaning
Inattention to Detail (Laziness)	You prefer to see the overall picture rather than getting bogged down with details
Instinctive Issues (problems relating to sex, drugs, alcohol)	Your energy levels are not consistently high
Deceit (dishonesty)	You feel secure when nobody knows you.
Unpredictable Emotional Response (emotional instability)	Your emotional response to situations is not predictable by you or by others around you. You may feel strongly about something and then at a later date feel rather remote.
Tactlessness	You put up a big front. When inside you don't feel so secure.
Resentfulness	You have your guard up to fend off those who would impose upon you.
Defiance	If you feel pushed, you will fight back rather than run. You are not one to take things lying down.
Stubbornness	Even when you are wrong, you won't admit it. This may be a useful defence when you are with someone who is a stronger character than you.
Temper	You react with anger when situations get frustrating for you
Ostentation	You know how to communicate to others that you are different.
Slow Thinking	You like to think things through before starting a plan of action. You believe this will cut down on mistakes.

Over sensitive to criticism	This can be an asset as well as a deficit. It can motivate a person to perform so that the work is above criticism.
Domineering	It is easy for you to tell others what to do.

9. PSD (CPO) Graphology Red Flag Extensions

As mentioned previously, with graphology it is not possible to state 'this means that' because specific movements need to be considered in context. The tables below however, are some indicators that could prompt more detailed investigation. These are expansions of the Red Flag statements above.

Table 2.3

INATTENTION TO DETAIL (Laziness)	
Extension	**Written Observation**
Prone to sedentary preferences and may lack physical follow through.	Stunted lower zone, sometimes squeezed shut (lower zones are the bottom of the letters '*f, g, j, p, q ,v*'
Easily influenced: tends to give in too readily; may take the 'easy way' out.	Dish shaped '*t*' bars
Procrastinates	'*t*' bars and '*i*' dots left of stem
Careless	Missing '*t*' bars and '*i*' dots.
Aimlessness	Short, light pressure, low '*t*' bars
Lackadaisical	Lack of horizontal tension
Dependent	End strokes taper without pressure. Very close word spacing.
Yielding	Soft rounded structures lacking definite formation

Table 2.4

INSTINCTIVE ISSUES (Relating to Sex, Drugs & Alcohol)	
Extension	**Written Observation**
Lack of muscular coordination; can be a sign of drug addiction or alcoholism	Dragging of pen (little dots left on paper)
Tension, physiological or neurological problems	Tremors
Compulsive and uncontrollable urges; excessive indulgence in sensual pleasures	Muddiness (loops filled with ink, caused by writer not pen). Heavy blotting of letters with excessive corrugations (ridged or ruffled) in the stroke
Self-negating	Horizontal stroke crosses out the signature
Subconscious self-destructive tendencies, dislike of self, acting out instead of confronting oneself.	Crossing in script (including cut through signature)
Wants to appear more in control than really is	Patching/soldering
Struggling against feelings of tiredness and possibly negative moods. Suffers from frustration	Words start high off line and then fall down like roof tiles.

Table 2.5

DECEIT – DISHONESTY (See Diagram 11 below)	
Extension	**Written Observations**
Dishonesty can be a result of egotism, arrogance and conceit; or fantasy, boasting and exaggeration; or lack of confidence and shyness. Non-improving amendments	Ambiguous letters (letters looking like other letters). Displaced pressure (e.g. pressure on the up strokes when pressure should be on the down strokes) Illegible signature Signature different from text. Missing letters Circle letters ('a, o, d, g, q' that have extra loops inside

Table 2.6

TACTLESSNESS	
Extension	**Written Observations**
Imposition of will regardless of social consequences. Can represent lack of sensitivity to other people's feelings.	Angles next to round forms
May show little interest in other people's needs	Letters very disconnected
Uncomfortable in large crowds and uneasy in social relationships. Difficulties with people who make demands or cling. Feelings of isolation.	Extremely wide spaces between words and lines
Ill at ease in the presence of others, especially when the situation is unfamiliar.	Final hump in the '*m*' is higher than the first.
Voluble	Lower case letters (such as '*a*' and '*o*') open at the top. Large circle to '*d*'.
Indifference to other people's opinions. Sets own standards; may live lifestyle that opposes authority.	Increasing size of letters in a word

Table 2.7

UNPREDICTABLE EMOTIONAL RESPONSE	
Extension	**Written Observations**
Poor self-esteem, impulsive, unfocused	Weak or unstable middle zone (middle zone letters are '*m, n, a, o*' etc.)
Struggle between wanting to be noticed and wanting to be alone; excitability; easily distracted; inconsistent; moody	Uneven letter size
Tension and frustration. Uncertainty in decision making	Inconsistent slant
Emotions keep getting in the way; lack of internal order.	Tangling of lines
Seeking perfection in order to cover up insecurity and feelings of inferiority. Concern about abilities and performance; defensive	Touch ups in the writing

Table 2.8

RESENTFULNESS	
Extension	**Written Observations**
	Inflexible straight initial stroke from the base line (the imaginary line below the middle zone letters

Table 2.9

DEFIANCE – *(See diagram 3 below)*	
Extension	Written Observations
Hidden Aggression	Jutting strokes below line
Resistance towards authority. Alert to possible injustices by authority figures. Rebellious; fear of losing autonomy.	Misplaced capitals within words. Final buckle of the '*k*' large and out of proportion to rest of letter.

Table 2.10

TEMPER	
Extensions	**Written Observations**
Anger, fear, self-destructive pattern, defensive, critical, eruptive temperament, repressed, impulsive	Extreme or heavy crossing out
Anger, hostility, short fuse	Tics
Inner tension, irritability and temper	Dot grinding
Wants to get on with things. May fly off the handle at the slightest provocation	Right placed '*t*' bars

Table 2.11

STUBBORNESS	
Extension	**Written Observations**
Tenting – inverted '*v*' formations; with firm down strokes at obtuse angle (not right angle) to the base line.	Cut off word endings. (words that end abruptly with no rightward extensions). Stubbornness, repressed anger

Table 2.12

OSTENTATION	
Extensions	**Written Observations**
Could bluff others that they are able to cope when in fact they are unable to follow through.	Very showy-excessive flourishes and decorative strokes (sometimes illegible)
Over compensates for poor self-esteem, narcissism.	Enlarged or elaborated signature. Excessively long end strokes that curve up and back. Excessively tall '*t*' and '*d*' stems. Excessive slant. Circled '*I*' dots

Table 2.13

DOMINEERING – (See Diagram 2 below)	
Extensions	**Written Observations**
Deep inner desire to punish. Upper zone: sarcasm; lower zone: dangerous	Slashes
High tension; may have a brutal streak	Intense pressure

Table 2.14

OVERSENSITIVE TO CRITICISM	
Extensions	**Written Observations**
Will avoid risk taking and need to feel very secure before moving forwards. Apprehensiveness can limit action.	Left tendencies ('*i*' *dots and* '*t*' bars behind the letter stem, etc.)
Sensitive to criticism	All '*t*'s and '*d*'s made with large loops

Table 2.15

SLOW THINKING	
Extensions	**Written Observations**
Could become irritated if forced to deal with a mentally faster person. Minds could go blank under pressure. Lack of spontaneity.	Very slow writing

10.   Hand Writing Examples/Discussions

The following is a hand writing example followed by evaluating notes of an expert on how this person was perceived and viewed based on the script which had been provided for analysis. The depth of information drawn from the example is comprehensive and really alters what was at first a complaint then twists the matter to make the writer the problem.

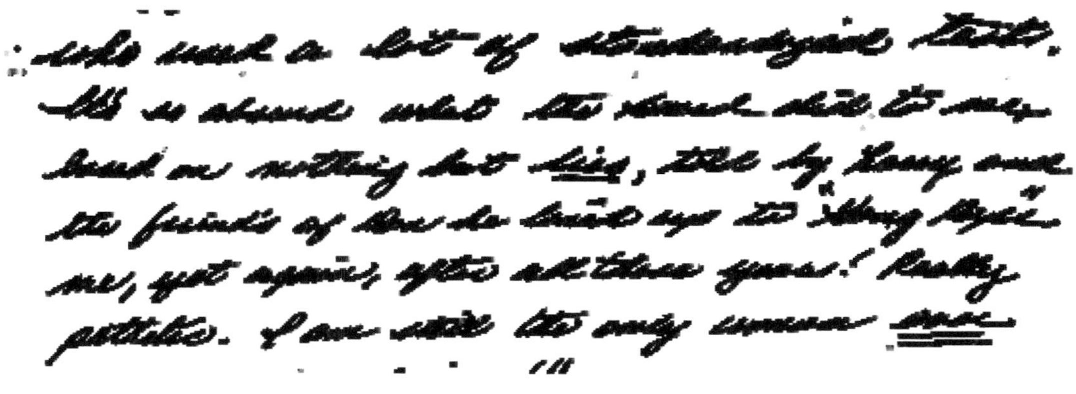

Fig 2.1

a.   **Discussions/Positive points**

This person in figure 2.1 above is capable of coming across as friendly, intelligent, lively and capable of logical thinking (right slant; fluent writing; smooth ink trail; light pressure; fluent connections between letters; very connected writing; methodical irregularity in the height of the middle zones) with a willingness to be helpful (reasonable space between letters; long final endings to words; right slant with loops) and to behave conventionally (American copybook style; connected letters). She has mental enthusiasm (long and high 't' bars; some rising baselines) and determination (reasonably straight baselines; knotted letters; hooked letter endings; straight strokes going down into the lower zone).

b.   **Red Flags**

The writing is, however, masked writing which covers a highly manipulative and invasive personality (angled 'u' structures; narrow margins. She can switch within moments from being friendly to being extremely egotistical, someone who completely overestimates her own importance (enrolled writing). She responds instinctively to people (up strokes have a strong right slant) and she will find it difficult to check her emotional reactions. She dramatises everything she says because she believes others cannot understand the significance of her statements (excessive underlining; final strokes end in the upper zone). She needs to justify her beliefs (squeezed writing with angles at top and bottom of letters) and because she is resentful, mistrustful, very sensitive to criticism (looped 't' and 'd' stems; narrow pen stroke), she feels taken advantage of and will be quick to contradict (straight brace strokes at the beginning of letters; 't' bars becoming thinner and ending in acute points). She suffers tensions in her relationships and feels a need to humiliate others, run vendettas and take revenge (ovals with angles on the base line; parallel strokes; light pressure with angles). She is evasive, tries to conceal things, blames others and lies (excessive looping on ovals; curled in start to some oval structures). She will try to outsmart other people, strike at their weak points (spiky writing) and this may be particularly true in relation to her own family ('shark tooth' constructions of the 'n', i.e. the final stroke collapses into a 'c' structure.)

c.   **Conclusion**

So here is someone who may come across as sociable (curved writing; dominant middle zone; close word spacing), but underneath there are strong feelings of resentment. When she is stressed her behaviour will become increasingly unstable and infantile with a desperate need for attention. Pent up anger (forward 't' bars; downward 't' bars; arrow head 'i' dots; connected right slant writing) may burst out against those people she feels have shown her injustice. For someone who is able to put on a charming front, she can be nasty. She is capable of pathological jealousy and show passionate and very disturbing behaviour. Conclusion: she **will** be trouble.

Shown below are further examples of the type of letter to look out for which would be Red Flagged as a concern. Descriptive comments are set out alongside the relevant letters for ease of understanding:

Example	Description
	The down slanted *t* bar to the right reveals a **Dominant** person who likes to be in control and loves it. The blunt ending signifies dominance, but in a way which doesn't antagonise those around them. The sharp *t* bar signifies domineering, sarcasm, whining, griping and possible cruel behaviour when they don't get their own way.

Fig 2.2

Example	Description
	A large lower case letter, especially a *k* anywhere in the writing can signify **Defiance**. A defiant person can resist another person's authority and this high *k* is often termed as the 'Go to Hell' letter. It is often seen as resentment at being told what to do which may create a rebellious situation by the individual. This stance is of course unworkable in a team.

Fig 2.3

Example	Description
	This kind of writing often shows **Anti-Social** behaviour and is generally seen in the lower loops of *y's*, *g's* and sometimes in *j's*. This kind of person doesn't trust anyone and rarely lets people get close enough for them to really know them. They fear getting hurt emotionally and could be a block for any intimacy.

Fig 2.4

23

Example	Description
	This person will be **Argumentative** which is shown by the breakaway *p* with a high beginning stroke. There exists the possibility that this trait could be increased if the writer is sarcastic, analytical, irritated, stubborn and/or impulsive.

Fig 2.5

Example	Description
	This person has **Sarcasm** and is revealed by the sharp pointed *t* bar. It is like a verbal dagger defending an ego. Sarcasm can have a dual meaning to whatever is said and is often mixed with humour to exacerbate the wit. This kind of person can be infuriating and may cause conflict within the team.

Fig 2.6

Example	Description
	Be wary of this kind of writing. It is written by someone who <u>may</u> like **lying** and everything that this person says must be thoroughly checked. The lying is shown by a combination of loops in the right and left side of the lower case *a's* and *o's*. The crossing of the huge inner loops signifies a person who lies pathologically. If this person is in your team then you will not be able to trust them.

Fig 2.7

Example	Description
	This person is looking for a **challenge** which is shown by the stinger like hook in the middle zones of '*a*', '*c*' or '*d*'. This person could have anger at strong members of the opposite sex whilst only being attracted or would tolerate those who are a challenge. Once this person feels in total control then they will become bored and lose momentum.

Fig 2.8

Example	Description
	Sensitive to Criticism is what this person has and is shown by the looped stem in the lower case '*d*' or '*t*'. The bigger the loop the more painful the criticism will be felt. If the loop appears overly inflated then the person may imagine criticism. The '*d*' loop relates to personal self whilst the '*t*' loop relates to sensitiveness to ideas and philosophies. This kind of person may not be strong enough to hold back a reaction to negative comments.

Fig 2.9

Example	Description
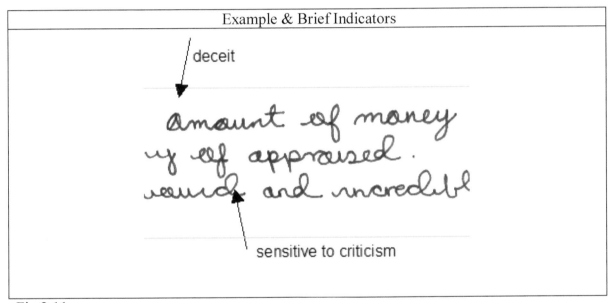	This person is **Stubborn** which is revealed by the '*d*' and '*t*' stems being tent like or an inverted v. The more this letter is braced the more this person is inclined to stick with his or her own ideas. Stubborn people will rarely admit that they are wrong and certainly don't want to be confused with any further information once they have made up their own minds. This makes the person less flexible and is likely to do his or her own thing rather than follow directional protocol.

Fig 2.10

Example & Brief Indicators
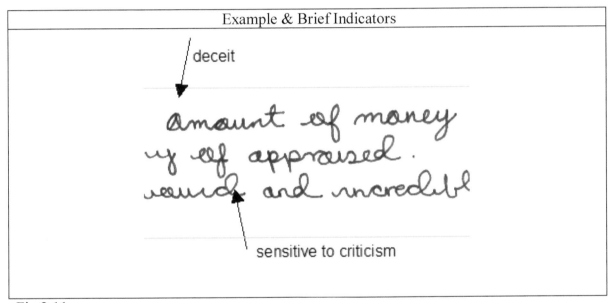

Fig 2.11

11. Frequently Asked Questions

Some general questions about graphology are listed below:

a. Can you tell the writer's sex from a sample of handwriting?

    Generally speaking no, although handwriting does often have the appearance of being either 'feminine' or 'masculine'

b. Does writing change with age?

    Since writing reflects the writer's state of mind at the time of writing, it would be strange if the person's handwriting did not reflect signs of maturity and psychological development as the person ages.

c. Can the potential for violence be seen in handwriting?

Very often yes - Graphologists refer to 'red flags', which can be easily detected in the writing and can reveal whether the writer has violent tendencies. These are great indicators to those using graphology as a recruitment tool for CP deployments.

d.   Can you tell what kind of work the writer is employed in from his/her writing?

No - this does not usually reveal itself, although very often the potential for what he/she can do is revealed.

d.   Can handwriting analysis reveal the future?

No.

e.   Can handwriting analysis reveal what makes us tick?

Yes definitely.

f.   Can graphologists analyse print script and blocked capitals?

Yes – print style writing, like cursive script, has strokes in all three zones (upper, middle, lower) but block printing is limited to the middle zone (with no "tails" below the baseline or strokes rising above the middle zone).

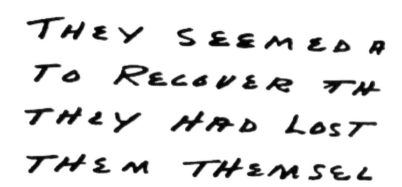

THEY SEEMED A
TO RECOVER TH
THEY HAD LOST
THEM THEMSEL

Fig 2.12

Analysing printed writing presents more of a challenge than cursive script but, using the basic principles of graphology, slant, layout, pressure etc. can ~provide a wealth of information.

g.   Can any language be analysed?

Yes. It doesn't matter which country the writer is from. It is the style that is taken into account

Example of a Full Graphology Report

First Impressions
(Leftward slant – past orientated, keeps feelings hidden, can be self-involved
(Small writing, small capital letters – modest, will work quietly, more introverted
Also, concerns with past, independent and determined
Some letter disconnectedness – ideas person, will talk and listen

Small writing, mainly zonal balance, small capitals – quietly confident, balanced personality

PERSONALITY STRUCTURE

The handwriting shows that XXXX presents himself extremely skilfully and understands the importance of creating a good image. He is also a very observant man who is polite and well mannered, therefore able to maintain contact at every level. He does not antagonise others deliberately and exercises restraint even when others panic, therefore will be useful and helpful in a crisis situation. The small, left slanted writing with wide word spacing suggests that he will give more to the development of inner abilities and resources than to emotional issues. He is emotionally vulnerable and large personalities would over-whelm him. However, there is much warmth to a basically quiet and shy character. The writer has signed with a high sweeping arcade followed by an illegible, but creative image. In this instance, the large, high and covering arcade conceals and protects a personality that wishes to give little away.

XXXX is therefore essentially an introvert and relies on his own inner resources and looks inward to his own subjective thoughts and feelings. He can communicate very well as his handwriting is legible but the past has a strong hold over him and his overall approach is one of caution. The handwriting, however, is of a good form level. The writer is modest and has a healthy respect for boundaries and other people. He is sensible, quietly self-confident and very intuitive.

This is a sensitive man who could be a little shy and inhibited initially, but he hides this well. Although this writer is a friendly and communicative person, he is a person who values his own personal space and time for himself. The writing although slightly irregular in letter sizes shows no dominant zone as upper, middle and lower zone are in reasonable balance indicating a well-rounded personality. The letter irregularity indicates fluctuating confidence and is evidence of some personal strain and anxiety but this is hidden by a polished public persona.

COMMUNICATION SKILLS & SOCIAL ATTITUDE

XXXX is not pushy, boastful or deliberately aggressive as he prefers compromise to argument and would therefore choose not to be deliberately involved in confrontation. However, he may on occasion dig his heels in on a matter of principle, but this attitude conceals some emotional vulnerability.

XXXX is a private person and lacks natural spontaneity for opening up to others and showing his real feelings. Socially, he has the capacity for friendship and can talk and listen but may have a fear of failure in personal, close relationships. He desires interaction with others but feels held back and it is difficult for him to take people at face value. The handwriting is quite legible indicating a genuine personality; one not deliberately intending to deceive, but this person is not a natural, confident communicator. He does not express himself impulsively; decisions and caution will influence feelings.

There is a basic contradiction within the script. The writing is small and left slanted, but the letters are generally broad. This writing denotes a mainly introspective person, one not apt to seek the limelight except when with close friends and people he trusts. The left slant indicates an introverted and contemplative nature where the broadness in the writing signifies an easy going and extraverted character. Extraverted people are often confident while introverts tend to be shy. The character is therefore unsure of which way to react.

WORKING QUALITIES

Work is an important factor and XXXX approach to it will be professional. He is reliable, will take responsibility and tasks will be carried out conscientiously and seen through to a conclusion in a thorough and efficient manner. He will not waste time on unessential or irrelevant matters.

XXXX does not feel comfortable within a large team and is happiest working in a solo situation or a small team with definite parameters, rather than in continual contact with many employees. He enjoys producing results and is independent and determined. He can be decisive, but decisions will be made with careful thought and preparation. He does not like making instant decisions.

XXXX handwriting shows an academic mentality. He is a fluid thinker with a keen eye for detail and he possesses a very good memory. Strengths are: 'public presentation' of himself', intelligence, operating logically, analytically, efficiency, will work quietly, independently and intuitively with a sense of moral conviction, sense of purpose and ability to follow through. Weaknesses are: reserve and limited need for interaction, not a natural communicator, some signs of stress and caution which might be perceived as a weakness, and resistance in accepting fast progress or change.

INTELLECTUAL QUALITIES

XXXX is an intelligent person who can combine the practical with the theoretical. His basic approach is logical and analytical. His analytical mind is coupled with a sharp critical sense. He will make judgments based on careful observation, perception and on the facts of the case, but he also has the power to see possibilities and to make intuitive and time saving leaps in thinking. XXXX uses a curious and keen mind to his advantage and his intelligence is refined and discriminating.

This writer can remain objective and detached in his thinking as he shows little emotional response to evaluating information. He will be a good planner and organiser, as he is a person who thinks decisions through.

To conclude, this writer is gifted with clear, logical thinking and is adept at any form of organisation and, after careful thought, initiating good ideas or new ways of doing things. Planning ability and timing are good and he possesses the follow-through necessary in order to see plans through to their eventual conclusion. This handwriting is not forceful, however it does indicate suppleness, flexibility, adaptability and a co-operative nature. XXXX is mainly level headed with a quick disposition and the energy he has at his disposal he uses efficiently. He has a desire to accomplish his aims and will be able to direct, organise, motivate and administer a small team of people he is responsible for.

Example of an Abridged (Shortened) Report

Table 2.16

July 12, 2xxx	Candidate Number					
Flags	**1**	**2**	**3**	**4**	**5**	**6**
Inattentive						
Instinctive Issues						
Ambiguous					[2]	
Emotional Response	[1]				[6]	[1]
Tact				[2]	[3]	
Resistance						
Defiance				[1]	[2]	
Stubbornness					[2]	[1]
Temper						
Demonstrative	[1]				[4]	
Planning					[2]	
Reaction to Criticism		[2]			[2]	
Dominance					[1]	

Note:

- Not every single flag situation needs to be completed. It will depend on the strength of the writing as to which flags are used.
- The numbers associated with the flags will need some kind of explanation as to what they mean in order for you to use the information correctly.
- The red flag numbers run from 0 to 10, 0 being the best. Generally anything up to and including 3 are acceptable but any results will need to be analysed first before accepting the candidate as you may find that the description given by the Graphologist gives rise for concern.
- Your graphologist will generally prepare a brief self-explanatory report for you as shown in the examples set out below per candidate.
- The Graphologist will never use the name of the candidate when submitting his report as they feel a personal connection. The Graphologist will indicate to you as to which number relates to which candidate.

Table 2.17

Candidate 1	
Red Flag	**Explanation**
Emotional Response [1]	There is an inconsistent slant in words on the same line (a sign of wavering between doubt and certainty), so he does not have a precise hold on emotional problems.
Demonstrative [1]	Some ostentation is shown by the very large initial of the first name (18 mm versus an average of 6mm), which appears to be compensation for some worries about self-esteem.

Table 2.18

Candidate 2	
Red Flag	**Explanation**
NIL	There are signs of an occasional shortage of stamina (falling baselines and not particularly heavy pressure), but no red flags are showing

Table 2.19

Candidate 3	
Red Flag	**Explanation**
Reaction to Criticism [2]	Sudden stroke thickening, open 'd' stems, relatively light pressure, wide word spacing resulting in vertical rivers of white on the sheet (self-doubt and a critical nature, so he does not like to be criticised himself) and the illegible signature with the horizontal ending (secretive) show a sensitivity to criticism.

Table 2.20

Candidate 4	
Red Flag	**Explanation**
Tact [2]	A determined individual who may not suffer fools gladly (left slant, heavy pressure, blunt letter endings, angles in the lower zone) and who may, on occasions, have difficulty in restraining himself in saying what he thinks.
Defiance [1]	He is clearly capable of defiance, but this does not look like a serious issue because the baselines are falling (a sign he is not always in the happiest of spirits) and there are some self-protective strokes (see the 'email' address @ circle around the lower case 'a' of his first name in the signature).

Table 2.21

Candidate 5	
Red Flag	**Explanation**
Ambiguous [2]	Letters look like other letters (many 't's look like 'j's a sign that he resists accepted and legal norms of behaviour. He has some 'shark tooth' structures, which mean he may play on other people's credulity. The signature is illegible
Emotional Response [6]	At the start he tries to stay calm, but most times he responds instinctively to people and situations and may find it very difficult to check his emotional reactions (strong right slant). He reverses the lower zone in

	opposition to the copybook style and some of these are dagger shaped, pointing to emotional blocks. The personal pronoun is a lower case 'i' which means that behaviour may be altered to serve the writer's own emotional needs. Because he feels uncomfortable under emotional stress, he feels he is unable to handle it. He works best when in support of a stronger personality
Tact [3]	Lack of control may cause him to be tactless. Disconnected 'printed' letters suggest intuition, but can also mean an anti-social attitude. Arches and angles mixed together (see the strange 'm's) suggest social immaturity. This person can be torn between soft behaviour (arches) and harsh behaviour (angles) and so he may lack sensitivity to other people's feelings.
Defiance [2]	He is alert to possible injustices by authority figures (capital letters in wrong places, angles in the lower zone, braced starting stroke to the signature).
Stubbornness [2]	There are tented structures in the script.
Demonstrative [4]	The first name of the signature is large (20mm versus 9mm average) so he wishes to be noticed. He also puts a circled 'i' dot on both his names, a sign he wants to be different. The end stroke of some 'n's lift up to the top of the middle zone, another sign of wishing to be noticed. His lower case personal pronoun 'i' means he has self-esteem problems and may compensate by unintentionally trying to get noticed by going 'over the top'. It looks as if he has real doubts as to whether or not he should be in this type of work.
Planning [2]	He procrastinates on occasions ('t' bars to left of stems) and misses out on details. His sense of inadequacy may limit his ability to comprehend a situation.
Reaction to Criticism [2]	He often feels censure when such was not intended (lower case personal pronoun).
Dominance [1]	The thickness of the down strokes compared with up strokes, the strong pressure and some downward placed 't' bars show domineering tendencies and a need for self-assertion. However, the length of the 't' bars is short and the pressure of the 't' bars is light, so this tendency is restrained.

Table 2.22

Candidate 6	
Red Flag	**Explanation**
Emotional Response [1]	Some anxiety is shown by the rewriting that does not increase legibility and the restless right slant of the first initial in the signature
Stubborn [1]	He is intelligent with an occasionally stubborn approach, but he is not likely to force his point (light pressure).

Graphical Representation of Red Flags for <u>Candidate 5</u> above Only
Table 2.23

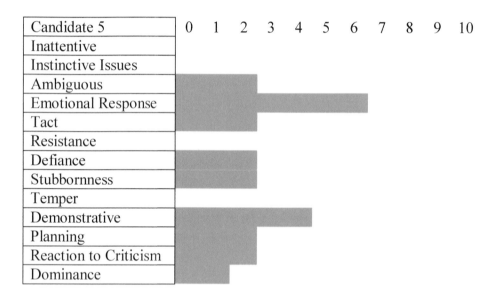

Remember, 0 is best and 10 is the worst case scenario.

Table 2.21 shows that Candidate 5 overall has issues and therefore would not be a valued or suitable team member. He would be argumentative, has doubts as to whether or not he should be a CPO. He also lacks sensitivity to other people's feelings. He is likely to play on other people's credulity. He would be unable to handle emotional stress. He has the basis for challenges to authority, which could undermine the Manager or Team Leader and in the end be disruptive to the team dynamics.

12. **PSD (CP) Core Competencies**

Being a member of a security detail is not just about being there and looking smart and presentable. Today's modern security specialist is a different breed to our forefathers and client expectations of their security personnel enters a whole new level. Shown at the end of this chapter is a list of credentials that an ideal CP operative should ideally have. It is not exhaustive and every operation may have something else to add into the criteria. The shaded areas would ordinarily be outside of the mandate required for that particular specialist's requirements, but is a requirement for the supervisor & team leaders as well as the managerial role for the ops manager. We live in an uncertain world and some of the PSD criteria, which has been drawn on may seem obscure for your particular assignment but the expectation of 'anything could happen' should be where you need to focus so that nothing comes as a surprise to you and that both you and your team are fully prepared for any eventuality. We also live in a technical world and your knowledge skill base in this particular field needs to be acute in order for you to be able to provide the full package to your employers. You'll be expected to use iPads, laptops and smart phones etc. Nothing can really be set in stone since that concept will become too rigid and CP is all about being flexible and adaptable.

The list shown at table 2.24 below could be used as a working guide during your selection process. It could also be included in any Job Description you may have pertinent to a specific role.

Table 2.24

PSD Core & Desired Competencies

Research Skills	PSD Section Member	PSD Section & Station Chiefs	PSD Ops Manager
• Knowledge of sources of information	✓	✓	✓
• Understand and apply basic research principles	✓	✓	✓
• Ability to conduct research on travel, new technology, local events	✓	✓	✓
• Knowledge and ability to operate computers	✓	✓	✓
• Ability to gather operational intelligence	✓	✓	✓
• Ability to develop threat profiles		✓	✓
• Ability in preparing a personal profile			✓

Inter – Personal Skills			
• Ability to network with others	✓	✓	✓
• Skilled in effective communication both upwards and downwards as well as sideways	✓	✓	✓
• Develop independent thinking skills	✓	✓	✓
• Develop team skills	✓	✓	✓
• Ability to conduct interviews		✓	✓
• Knowledge in protocol, dress, personal appearance, manners, conduct and dining etiquette	✓	✓	✓
• Ability to liaise with other organisations	✓	✓	✓
• Ability to effectively communicate over phone or radio	✓	✓	✓
• Knowledge of verbal persuasion techniques	✓	✓	✓
• Basic knowledge of recruiting and selecting personnel			✓

Mechanical Ability			

• Basic protection equipment operation when issued. May include:
   ○ Security Vehicles
   ○ Specialist clothing [When Issued]
	✓	✓	✓

• Understand fire prevention and extinguisher techniques	✓	✓	✓
• Understand basic vehicle repair.e.g.; Changing a tyre	✓	✓	✓

Presentation Skills

• *Conduct training and briefings for client PSDs*	■	✓	✓
• *Understand the basic instructional system design principles*	■	✓	✓
• *Create effective presentations/reports*	✓	✓	✓

Inspections/SAP

• *Conduct physical security surveys as detailed by senior staff to include:*
  ○ *DoP*
  ○ *PuP*
  ○ *ERV points*
  ○ *Access Routes*
  ○ *Liaison*
  ○ *Lay Up points*
  ○ *Evac routine*
  ○ *Client LOCSTAT whilst at event*
  ○ *Client tables if restaurant used*
  ○ *Running time of event*
	✓	✓	✓

• *Check primary & secondary routes for:*	■	■	■
• *Choke points & danger zones*	✓	✓	✓
• *Conduct Risk Assessments for each mission profile*	✓	✓	✓
• *Understand the specialist needs and requirements of clients including recreational needs*	✓	✓	✓

Emergency Medical Care

• *CPR with current updates*	✓	✓	✓

• *Trauma Identification to include*
  ○ *Heart attack*
  ○ *Head injury*
  ○ *Shock*
  ○ *Fractures*
  ○ *Incident related injuries which may include:*
    ▪ *Stab wounds*
    ▪ *Blast injuries*
    ▪ *Gunshot wounds*
	✓	✓	✓

• *First Aid Certificate (Triennial) FAW or FPOS(i) or FREC* ○ *Annual Update certification if necessary*	✓	✓	✓
• *First Aid Certificate (Triennial) Paediatric*	✓	✓	■
• *Health & Safety Issues*	✓	✓	✓

Specialist Security Concerns

• *Terrorism issues & current trend reviews*	✓	✓	✓
• *Violence in the workplace issues*	✓	✓	✓
• *Special function planning; theatre, cinema etc.*	✓	✓	✓

Use of Force Issues

• *Defensive tactics – Countermeasures* ○ *Vehicular or Human intervention*	✓	✓	✓

Technical Security Issues

• Detecting/Recognition of explosive devices	✓	✓	✓
• Understanding bugs and listening devices and how they function	✓	✓	✓
• Understanding sensor (alarm) technology and operations	✓	✓	✓
• Conduct preliminary vehicle searches where necessary	✓	✓	✓

Writing Skills

• Knowledge of Terminology 　○ Legal 　○ CP Ops	✓	✓	✓
• Report/Statement Writing	✓	✓	✓
• Preparing OpOs/plans	■	✓	✓
• Developing Policies & procedures	■	✓	✓
• Be able to prepare advance reports for domestic or overseas travel	✓	✓	✓

Driving Skills

• Be able to perform safe driving techniques	✓	✓	✓
• Develop Evasive Driving Skills	✓	✓	✓
• Be able to master convoy driving skills	✓	✓	✓
• Local and situational awareness knowledge	✓	✓	✓

Physical Fitness

• Maintenance of personal fitness levels [Strength & CV]	✓	✓	✓
• Endurance training levels maintained	✓	✓	✓

Legal Issues

• Knowledge of current UK law in relation to OAPA and your role as a PSD (CPO)	✓	✓	✓
• Be able to prepare case information for legal authorities in relation to actions you may have used whilst protecting your client	✓	✓	✓
• Understand stalkers and the relevant UK law	✓	✓	✓

Crisis Management

• Event planning with contingencies	✓	✓	✓
• Running/Managing an Ops Room	■	✓	✓
• Understand what constitutes an Ops Room	✓	✓	✓

Principal Movement Techniques

• Understand the basic Principal Movement Techniques	✓	✓	✓
• Be able to map read and know local knowledge	✓	✓	✓
• Be able to perform confidently the skills set developed during your CP course and those skills gained with experience	✓	✓	✓

Surveillance Detection Skills

• *Ability to observe/describe/identify people and vehicles for later recall*	✓	✓	✓
• *Understand the surveillance process and what you can do to counter it*	✓	✓	✓
• *Understand the basic surveillance techniques and the MO of known groups*	✓	✓	✓

Chapter 3

Health & Safety for Protective Security Detail (PSD) Operations

1.   **Introduction**

Being in a position of responsibility you will be bound by current regulations within the country you are operating in and you will be expected to abide by this legislation.   Any type of work undertaken here in the UK is governed by legislature under the Health & Safety (H&S) at Work Act. This was introduced to ensure that all reasonable steps had been taken, where possible, to maximize the safety aspect of all employees and all other 3rd parties who may or may not be vulnerable at that time.   Health & Safety has to be incorporated into the working practices of any PSD (CP) mission deployment.

Every action that we take throughout our daily lives is fraught with elements of risk be it walking, driving or simple things like re-fueling a car. Appropriately, re-fueling of a car has an element of risk; does it take petrol or diesel so we consciously think of the correct fuel before inserting the nozzle so as to eliminate the risk of damage to the engine and to avoid a costly bill. The same is applied to people. We consciously prepare our mind at the point we are given a task to complete.   We would think about how the task is to be tackled satisfactorily as well as reducing the element of injury to the PSD or a 3rd party.   So subconsciously, we mentally prepare the safest option regardless of what steps have been taken by an employer.

The above is a common sense approach, which is expected under the Health & Safety Act in that all PSD teams and 3rd parties should absorb a personal responsibility in that everyone takes necessary and reasonable steps to limit a risk. It should never be one sided as each event will have a different approach and outcome so reducing the risk by both sides will greatly reduce any serious consequences overall.

All PSD Localised Supervisors & Regional Commanders have a duty to implement and enforce H & S on behalf of the company you work for and it is essential that it is incorporated into any planning of future and current mission profiles.

Health & Safety is not a subject that can be taken lightly. It has both serious and legal ramifications in the event care and attention has been violated by corporate or individuals and the well being of your staff is just as important as the safety of the client.

2.   **Risk Assessments**

The term ***Risk Assessment*** originally comes from the insurance industry and is one stage in their process of determining and spreading the liabilities they carried. It has since been adopted into Health & Safety and the meaning has been widened to cover a spectrum of activities from the initial identification of a ***Hazard*** to the ***Establishment of Safe Working Conditions***.

The purpose therefore of this chapter is to identify hazards present in any situation or activity and the extent of the risks involved.

To understand the constituent parts of a Risk Assessment, the following definitions are given:

a.	***Hazard***	Something with potential to cause harm
b.	***Probability***	The likelihood that a hazard will cause harm or damage
c.	***Risk***	Compound of the probability and severity of the resulting damage or harm
d.	***Danger***	The state of being at Risk
e.	***Extent of the Risk***	A measure of the number of people likely to be affected & the severity (the consequences)

Risks therefore reflect either the possibility or probability that harm will occur in one form or another and to what extent. This has to be understood by all in order to make the correct judgment in applying it to the working practices of the PSD environment.

Every task will carry an element of Risk and each one is looked at in differing ways. Ultimately though, a Risk Assessment is to identify hazards so that action can be taken to eliminate, reduce or control them before accidents occur where injury or damage is inflicted. How you carry out an assessment differs in many ways too as each task can vary significantly. Nevertheless, a strategy needs to be applied that incorporates the following:

a. Identify the hazards and what would constitute one
b. Eliminate the hazards or reduce to a minimum
c. Evaluate the residual risks
d. Develop precautionary strategies
e. Train all PSD (CP) personnel in new equipment
f. Implement precautionary measures
g. Monitor performance

There are many inherent risks with being deployed on a PSD mission not least that we are expected to provide the ultimate sacrifice to protect our client. This is a high point of a Risk but a lot can be done to mitigate this not least by better, more thorough and robust planning in order to counter such a Risk and then live to be able to evaluate the situation for future missions, but you will never be able to negate fully any potential Risk no matter how in depth your assessments are.

3. **Risks Associated with Employment Category**

Developing Risk Assessments for a PSD is not always straightforward. There is no client who can be considered a 'Zero Risk' case otherwise you wouldn't be employed as a security professional in the first place. Supervisors should ensure at least the following:

a. _PSD (Security Driver)_

 (1) Ensure that you know the characteristics of the vehicle you've been assigned including any expected performance levels.
 (2) Know what fuel the vehicle is capable of taking (Diesel/Petrol)
 (3) Drive the vehicle in order to get a feel of how it drives and its performance in order to become confident and proficient.

(4)   Drive within the confines of the law.

(5)   Only drive the vehicle to the limits of your own confidence and abilities in addition to that of the vehicle itself.

(6)   If the vehicle has to be used to ram a hostile intervention you need to apply the correct drills. This evaluation needs to be achieved in a Nano-second, as there is no margin for error. Unless you can be confident of an outcome, ***do not*** apply the ramming technique as the Risk would be too great and your means of escape has suddenly closed.

(7)   Always wear your seat belt. There is a serious risk of injury.

(8)   Never use your mobile phone whilst driving unless on hands free. The distraction may cause you to lose control of the vehicle.

(9)   Never leave your vehicle unattended. The vehicle could either be stolen or used against you.

(10)   Ensure that all tyre pressures are checked at regular intervals to avoid a blowout, which may result in serious injury to yourself and passengers.

(11)   Never open your car door until first checking behind. This will avoid cyclists and other vehicles hitting yours causing chards of glass to fly or the door to fling inwards trapping you against the doorframe.

(12)   Comply with OPSEC

(13)   Avoid parking your vehicle nose in.

(14)   Ensure that the spare wheel is maintained if you have one. Several top end vehicles generally use run flats.

(15)   Ensure that you have the correct vehicle for the task. No good having a saloon car when you need a 4 x 4.

(16)   Ensure that a first aid pack is carried in the vehicle and kitted out with what you need and what you are trained to use.

(17)   Make sure that the correct type of fluids is used when washing operational vehicles. Keep all fluids separate and identified.

(18)   Protect all classified documents you hold as part of your duties in order to avoid the loss of confidential information.

b.   *PSD (CP) Operative*

(1)   In order to mitigate a risk, be aware of your surroundings.

(2)   Comply with OPSEC

(3)   Never take on an aggressor unless you are confident of your abilities.

(4)   Never ride a horse during operational requests unless you are a competent person.

(5)   During hill walking excursions with your client, ensure that you are adequately dressed and prepared for such a journey with the necessary water and medical kits + comms and maps etc.

(6)   Ensure that all venues you go to as part of your duties that you are familiar with the layout, exits and emergency procedures.

(7)   If a PSD (SAP) is available, request their assistance at venues that could potentially be a risk.

(8)   Ensure that your first aid skills are kept up to date.

(9)   If you need to extract a client using a first aid method (fireman's lift etc.) then the correct method must be adopted.

(10)   Don't cross the road with your client unless safe to do so. Use a zebra crossing, traffic light crossing or an open space on a road that is unobstructed. *Remember, you're responsible for their safety as well as their security.* Consider orthodox at all times if possible.

(11)   Protect all classified documents you hold as part of your duties in order to avoid the loss of confidential information that may put the team and client at Risk.

c.   *Detail Supervisor/Regional Team Leader*

(1)   Ensure that all subordinates are given sufficient training in CP local specific topics that have a Health & Safety slant as set out by management.

(2)   Ensure that all PSD (Security Drivers) are given sufficient time to become familiar with their vehicles operational and performance capabilities.

(3)   Ensure that all staff are aware of any evacuation procedures at your specific client properties.

(4)   Ensure that you oversee the list above for Security Drivers and CP personnel alike.

4.   **Responsibilities**

It is a fundamental responsibility that all Team Leaders and supervisors conduct an evaluation of risks associated with each PSD on specific assignments otherwise you may be brought to account in the event something goes wrong. If it means teaching your operatives to suck eggs' then so be it. You have a duty and an obligation to inform and uphold all Health & Safety matters upon your subordinates. You will be expected to sign off the fact that all personnel under your command have been advised about associated risks.

a.   The above does not take away the personal responsibility of all PSD personnel in meeting their own obligations and taking due care and attention when carrying out operational needs and tasks.

b.   If possible, avoid wearing jewelry that may be ripped from your skin if caught in a tussle with a hostile or which may become snagged.

c.   If you have long hair or wear a headscarf, make sure it is tucked out of the way or put in a bun or pony tail.

d.   Take reasonable care not to put other people – fellow PSD personnel and members of the public – at risk by what you do or don't do in the course of your work.

e.   To co-operate with your employer, make sure that you have adequate training for something you are expected to do and to follow your employer's health and safety policies. If in doubt then it needs to be raised.

f.   **Do not** interfere with or misuse anything that's been provided for your health, safety or welfare.

g.   Report any injuries, strains or illnesses you suffer as a result of doing your job. H&S need to know from a statistical aspect and to see if this is a recurring risk.

h.   Tell your employer if something happens that might affect your ability to work (e.g. becoming pregnant or suffering an injury). Your employer will have a legal responsibility for your health and safety and may need to address your working conditions.

i.   If you are deployed as a PSD (Security Driver) and you take medications that may make you drowsy, you need to tell your company or its representatives so that a re-evaluation of your employment can be made.

j.   Every member of staff must take reasonable care to look after their own health & safety and that of others affected by their actions and abide by any H&S guidelines and provisions in place.

5. **Who Should Do Risk Assessments**

Risk Assessments should always be carried out by a person who is experienced and competent to do so. Competence can be expressed as a combination of knowledge, awareness, training and experience.

Remember, competence does not mean you know everything about everything, competence also means knowing when you know enough or when you should seek advice from others.

Each supervisor is to compile an audit of Risks associated and relevant to their own assignments. This audit is to be handed to and discussed with your Operational Manager two days prior to the arrival of their respective clients. There is a necessity and need to conduct such an audit and indeed to document what you have identified so that in the event of an incident, then the Risk Assessment summary can be looked at to see what hasn't been considered. All eventualities must be considered that a PSD are likely to come across in the execution of their duties. *It is impossible however to cater for all eventualities.*

It's essential that each supervisor record the signature of their PSDs to confirm their understanding and willingness and personal responsibility to comply with the Risk Assessments identified by each Supervisor or Team Leader as set out by the Ops Manager.

6. **When Should a Risk Assessment be Done**

A separate risk assessment should be carried out for all tasks or processes undertaken by the PSD. They should be carried out before the mission starts or in any case as soon as is reasonably practicable – the earlier the better.

PSD operations are unique in what we do but we should never do anything that is reckless or puts others in harm's way. The correct amount of planning and gathered information that we do and have should allow a correct assessment to be made. This includes assessments for high threat areas that require just as much of a vigorous assessment in order to prevent members of the PSD being fatally injured.

Shown at Table 3.1 below is a 5*5 matrix designed for the benefit of PSD (CP) Operations Only. As a caveat, this document may not be suitable for all CP Operational Posts. The design may appear complex, but after closer scrutiny you should be able to see in which direction it's going.

Following on from the matrix, a Risk Assessment Summary is included at Table 3.2 that outlines some of the activities and potential hazards associated with certain activities in relation to PSD mission deployments. Use this as a benchmark for compiling your own sectional Risk Assessments. The list is not exhaustive, but as you can see, CP personnel are expected to do a lot of things that has a direct client involvement. Equally of course, you may be unlucky and be allocated to a client who hardly ventures out except to shop. The completed document must be shown and explained to each section team member so that they are aware of the relevant and inherent risks associated with the role and location specific requirements. It may be prudent to ask each Detail Supervisor within the company deployment grid to contribute ideas for their own particular allocation that can then be added.

A blank Risk Assessment Summary sheet, for completion by all Detail Supervisor's or Regional Commanders in relation to personnel under their command, is added at the end of this Chapter.

To ensure that you have fully briefed your staff they will need to sign their understanding and compliance. Towards the end of this chapter is a blank signature document (template) to be signed by each PSD personnel to reflect on their understanding of Health & Safety Risk Assessments at their specific location. Revise this for your own needs.

7.   **<u>Non Compliance</u>**

The penalties for failing to carry out risk assessments can be high. Health and Safety Executive can issue improvement or prohibition orders and this is likely to happen where an inspector finds a situation with the potential to cause harm. Equally, if it's a recurring issue then they invariably won't let go and will go through everything with a fine toothcomb. This in itself will inhibit and may curtail your operational deployments.

8.   **<u>Conclusion</u>**

Health & Safety are important issues that cannot be ignored. It's imperative that each individual deployed on a PSD assignment takes reasonable care in whatever duty he or she has been tasked to perform in order to minimise the risk of injury. This must be emphasized and supported by all Supervisors and Regional Commanders to the staff who work beneath them. They must also set an example in the first place as complacency will only bread contempt and before you know it short cuts are becoming the norm.

Health & Safety works both ways from a corporate and personal involvement and no staff should be asked to do anything that contravenes legislation or puts them or others in harm's way outside of their normal scope of job description. Each and every CP operative is trained to provide both security and safety to a client, but unless you are confident in whatever task you are about to undertake, this becomes a risk and requires an evaluation period before executing.

Much of the above is of course common sense, but it is often these simple things which people will neglect since we do a lot of things routinely and without thinking. Some people will play the chicken run when crossing a road rather than wait for the green light to allow them to cross safely. Here, crossing the road was a risk however simply waiting a few moments longer could quite easily have reduced it to within an acceptable tolerance.

Those in positions of responsibilities must ensure that the CP skills the team have are applied under control relevant to their own qualities, abilities and confidence and must be tempered to thwart any hostile intervention within the bounds of current legislation.

***Don't Put Yourself into a Risk Situation Where the Outcome Remains Uncertain
Be Aware***

Table 3.1

RISK ASSESSMENT 5 * 5 MATRIX

Determining the Level of Risk for a PSD (CP) Mission Profile & Associated Events

This document can be used to identify the level of risk and help to prioritise any control measures.
Consider the **consequences** and **likelihood** for each of the identified hazards and use the table to obtain the risk level.

Likelihood	Consequences/Severity				
	1 – Insignificant Dealt with by in-house first aid, etc. No effect on PSD operations	2 – Minor Medical help needed. Treatment by medical professional/hospital/outpatient, etc	3 – Moderate Significant non-permanent injury. Overnight hospitalisation PSD Mission Interrupted	4 – Major Extensive permanent injury Extended hospitilisation Seriously Affects the Mission Profile	5 – Catastrophic Death. Permanent disabling injury Alters PSD Mission Outcome
5 - Almost certain to occur in most circumstances	High (H) 5	High (H) 10	Extreme (X) 15	Extreme (X) 20	Extreme (X) 25
4 - Likely to occur frequently	Moderate (M) 4	High (H) 8	High (H) 12	Extreme (X) 16	Extreme (X) 20
3 - Possible and likely to occur at some time.	Low (L) 3	Moderate (M) 6	High (H) 9	Extreme (X) 12	Extreme (X) 15
2 - Unlikely to occur but could happen.	Low (L) 2	Low (L) 4	Moderate (M) 6	High (H) 8	Extreme (X) 10
1 - May occur but only in rare and exceptional circumstances	Low (L) 1	Low (L) 2	Moderate (M) 3	High (H) 4	High (H) 5

How to Prioritise the Risk Rating
Once the level of risk has been determined, the following table may be of use in determining when to act to institute the control measures.

Extreme	Act immediately to mitigate the risk. Eliminate, substitute, or implement engineering control measures.	Remove the hazard at the source. An identified extreme risk does not allow scope for the use of administrative controls...
High	Act immediately to mitigate the risk. Eliminate, substitute or implement engineering control measures. If these control measures are not immediately accessible, set a time frame for their implementation and establish interim risk reduction strategies for the period of the set time frame.	An Achievable time frame must be established to ensure that elimination, substitution or engineering controls are implemented. **NOTE:** Risk (and not cost) must be the primary consideration in determining the time frame. A time frame of greater than 6 months would generally not be acceptable for any hazard identified as high risk.
Moderate	Take reasonable steps to mitigate the risk. Until elimination, substitution or engineering controls can be implemented, institute administrative or personal protective equipment controls. The time for which they are established must be based on risk. At the end of the time, if the risk has not been addressed by elimination, substitution or engineering controls a further risk assessment must be undertaken.	**Interim measures until permanent solutions can be implemented:** • Develop administrative controls to limit the use, access or activity • Provide supervision and specific training related to the issue of concern. (See admin controls below)
Low	Take reasonable steps to mitigate and monitor the risk. Institute permanent controls in the long term. Permanent controls may be administrative in nature if the hazard has a low frequency, rare likelihood and insignificant consequence.	

Hierarchy of Control – Controls identified may be a mixture of the hierarchy in order to provide minimum PSD exposure.

Elimination	Eliminate the hazard
Substitution	Provide an alternative that is capable of performing the same task and is safer to use
Engineering Controls	Provide or construct a physical barrier or guard
Administrative Controls	Develop policies, procedures and guidelines, in consultation with members of the PSD to mitigate the risk. Provide training, instruction and supervision about the hazard.
Personal Protective Equipment (PPE)	Personal equipment designed to protect the individual from the hazard.

How to Place Risks in the Matrix

A risk assessment matrix is easy to make, since most of the information needed can easily be extracted from the risk assessment forms. The table 3.1 above is the basis from which to evaluate the consequences/severity of the risk on a 5 * 5 scale where the likelihood and extent of any event or the kind of severity that the risks can result in.

A risk assessment form should be the first step in determining the potential risks which requires gathering risk data, determining the probability and the impact levels of the risks, understanding consequences, assigning priorities and developing risk prevention strategies. The risk assessment matrix, just gives the CP Ops Manager and PSD personnel a quick view of the risks and the priority with which each of these risks needs to be handled.

The risks are placed on the matrix based on two criteria;

- Likelihood: probability of the risk
- Consequences: the severity of the impact or the extent of damage/injury caused by the risk to PSD members, 3rd parties or property.

Likelihood of Occurrence – Left Hand Side of Matrix

Based on the likelihood of the occurrence of a risk, the risks can be classified under one of the five (5) categories:

1. **Unlikely**   Rare and exceptional risks which have less than 10% chance of occurrence.
2. **Seldom**   Risks that have a low probability of occurrence but still cannot be ruled out completely.
3. **Occasional** Risks which have a near 50/50 % probability of occurrence.
4. **Likely**   Risks that have 60 – 80% chance of occurrence can be grouped under this category.
5. **Definite**   A risk that is almost certain to show up during a PSD mission. A risk of more than 80% is likely to cause operational problems under this category.

Consequences/Severity – Across the Top of the Matrix

The consequences of a risk can again be ranked and classified into one of the five categories, based on severity of damage to client property (including vehicles) or injury to PSD personnel as follows:

1. **Insignificant**   Risks that will cause a near negligible amount of damage to the overall progress of the PSD mission.
2. **Minor**   If the risk will result in some damage but the extent of the damage is not too significant and is not likely to make much difference to the overall PSD mission outcome.
3. **Moderate**   Risks which do not impose a great threat, but yet a sizeable damage/injury can be classified as moderate.
4. **Critical**   Risks with significantly large consequences that can lead to a great amount of loss are classified as critical.
5. **Catastrophic**   These are the risks which can alter the outcome of a PSD mission and must be the top priority of all PSD personnel including management to minimize this outcome through better planning.

To carry out a risk ranking, simply multiply the likelihood by the severity. Based on a 5 * 5 matrix the max score would be 25, therefore the priorities would be established as follows:

Urgent Action   (Scope 15 – 25)
High Priority   (Scope 10 – 12)
Medium Priority (Scope 5 – 9)
Low Priority   (Scope 2 – 4)
V. Low Priority (Scope 1 – NO ACTION REQUIRED)

Table 3.2

RISK ASSESSMENT SUMMARY

Determining the Level of Risk for a PSD (CP) Operation & Associated Events (UK & Europe)

Activity	Hazard	Those at Risk	Risk Rating L	Risk Rating S	Risk Rating RR	Existing Risk Controls	Additional Risk Controls	Residual Risk L	Residual Risk S	Residual Risk RR	Remarks
Exposure to Violence, Verbal's & Aggression	Physical Assault. Psychological trauma.	PSD personnel. Clients.	3	3	9	Conflict management taught as part of SIA requirements. Surveillance techniques	First Aid taught to all PSDs. MMA trained PSDs	1	3	3	
Driving the vehicle in a PES profile.	RTC leading to personal injury	PSD, Client, other road users, pedestrians	3	4	12	Comply with all current driving laws, company car policy, SOPs	Training in convoy procedures and pursuit driving. Driving Assessment	1	4	4	
Lone Working	Lack of assistance following incident or illness.	PSD Night Response.	2	5	10	Increased Comms. Periodic site visit. End of shift contact First Aid Trained	Flash light issued	1	5	5	
Loss of Confidential Information	Compromise of a PSD Mission. OPSEC	PSD personnel. Client(s)	2	5	10	Control issues of information. Extirpation of all redundant documents		1	5	5	Loss includes SOPs
Loss of Issued Mobile Phone	Degradation of PSD fulfilling mission objectives	PSD personnel. Client(s)	2	2	4	Secondary comms used for back-up	Instant network block once reported	2	2	2	
PSD Occupied Building Fire	Persons trapped Evacuation	PSD personnel. Contractors	3	5	15	Fire extinguishers in place. Regular practices	Identifying and eliminate any fire hazards.	1	5	5	
Re-fuelling of PSD Vehicle	Incorrect fuel: Diesel/Petrol		1	2	2	Narrow re-fuel nozzle for diesel pipes. Fuel cap labeled	Education	1	1	1	
PSD Driving	Tyre Blow Out	PSD Driver, Passengers, Other Road Users	2	4	8	Pressures checked on a regular basis	Checklist to be completed	1	4	4	

Horse Riding	Falling	User, other riders	2	4	8	Horse familiarisation Competent user with qualifications	Type of horse chosen by stable hands based on experience of rider	2	4	8	Unpredictability risk
Hill Walking	Tripping, falling	Walker (either client or PSD)	2	2	4	Scouts with local knowledge. First aid kit carried. Comms available	Helicopter on standby for EVAC	1	2	2	
Roller Blading/In-line skating	Falling, hitting something/someone else	User, other persons/vehicles	2	2	4	Competent user ONLY.	Only used in safe environments	1	2	2	
Skiing	Falling, hitting other users	User, other skiers	2	3	6	Competent skiers only for types of runs being used. Black/Red etc.	Correct equipment used. Dry ski run practice slopes	2	2	4	
Pedalos	Slips, falling overboard. Drowning	PSD & Clients	3	2	6	Competent swimmers only. Briefing by staff. Safety control by PSD	Life jackets worn by all Strict use of pedalo	2	2	4	
Airsoft/BB Guns	Direct hit by BB, Ricochet, Eye wound, Contusions	PSD Client Others	3	3	9	Safety brief by instructors.	Protective gear, eye protection, Safe distance, strict controls enforced by PSD	1	2	2	
Paintball	Flesh wounds, Contusions, Slips and trips, Eye injuries	PSD Client Others	3	3	9	Protective clothing, Safety briefing by Instructors. Eye wear	Shoot from greater distances, follow range rules, keep eye wear on	2	2	4	
Helicopter Lessons	Engine Failure Bad weather Pilot error	PSD Client Crew Others	2	3	6	Reputable company used No lessons in poor weather	Nothing further to be implemented	2	3	6	
Self Defence Lessons	Contact during lessons, Slips, trips, falls. Minor cuts and contusions.	PSD Client Instructor	2	2	4	Reputable & qualified Instructors. Use protective gear when required. Briefings	Instructions to be followed	1	2	2	
Pets & Animals	Bites, stings etc,. Infections & diseases	PSD Client	2	2	4	Books purchased. Instructions followed as given when animal bought	Only experienced and qualified people to feed and handle animals	1	2	2	
Scooters & Bikes	Falling off, accidents with other scooter, people in park	PSD Client Others	3	2	6	Briefing by PSD	Protective gear and helmets worn. Keep safe distance, slow speeds	2	2	4	

Activity	Hazard	Persons at Risk	L	S	R	Control Measures	Further Control Measures	L	S	R
Tree Climbing	Fall Slip	PSD Client Others	2	2	4	PSD not encouraged to climb trees. Only in emergency	Follow staff instructions and use any safety equipment issued.	1	2	2
Jogging with Client	Sprains, trips, tears, type injuries	PSD Client	2	2	4	Are physically fit Passed the PSD fitness test	Maintain fitness levels, correct footwear, conduct warm up and cool down	1	1	1
Running with horses	Sprains, trips, tears, type injury	PSD Client	2	2	4	PSD fitness test. Horse familiarization	Maintain personal fitness levels, correct footwear, conduct warm up and cool down. Safe distance from horse	1	1	1
Laser Tag	Walking/running into walls and other users. Eye damage from laser beams	PSD Client Others	2	2	4	Adhere to instructions, do not run, exercise extreme caution	Never point laser beams into people's eyes. Wear protective equipment. Remain static and defend the base.	1	1	1
Rifle Shooting/Clay Pigeon Shooting	Gunshot wound, Ear Damage, Superficial damage to shoulder/cheek	User and those in proximity	2	5	10	Adhere to instructions Use ear defenders. Wear a shooting jacket with padded shoulder. Appropriate weapons for size of operator. Maintain NSP's at all times	First Aid facilities/personnel on site. Possible use of tripods. Consider smaller caliber weapons. Maintain correct eye relief	1	5	5
Ice Skating	Falling/hitting something or someone. Fingers and hand lacerations	PSD Client Others	2	2	4	Competent user only. Consider exclusive use of rink. Utilise instructor	Use full safety equipment	1	2	2
Theme Parks/Fun Rides etc.	Mechanical Breakdown Psychological trauma Whiplash injury Limb/extremity injury	PSD Client Others	1	4	4	Only use reputable venues. Listen to instructions. Do not take part if suffering from any pre-conditions. Adhere to height restrictions	Conduct dynamic risk assessment prior to taking part. Research venue beforehand	1	4	4
Swimming/Water Parks	Dry & Wet drowning. Collisions on slides Fungal Infections	PSD Client Others	2	2	4	Suitable footwear in showers and other areas. PSD proficient swimmer. Goggles and other aids	Keep greater distances on the water slides. Swim in less deep water	1	2	2

Activity	Hazard	Who at risk	L	S	Risk	Control Measures	Additional Controls	L	S	Risk
Snowmobile	Accidents with other mobiles, trees, roll over, over cliffs. Cold weather injuries	PSD Client Others	3	4	12	Briefing by hire company. Use instructors and guides. Wear correct clothing	No user under 16. PSD to drive. Low speeds. Greater following distance	2	4	8
Dog Sledge	Bitten by dogs Rolling off sledge Accident with 3rd party. Cold weather	PSD Client Other users	2	2	4	Full briefing by hire company. Distance from dogs. Correct clothing to be worn	No multiple users on a sledge	1	2	2
Horse & cart	Horse startled Bucking horse Slipping on Ice (International only) Cold weather	PSD Client	2	2	4	Use reputable company. Keep distance from horse. Wear suitable safety clothing including helmets	Activity done in suitable weather.	1	2	2
Snow walking off piste	Deep snow & unseen hazards, tree stumps, avalanche risks Cold weather	PSD Clients	2	3	6	Suitable clothing worn. Emergency equipment carried. Use guides	Walk on treated snow surfaces and not in deep snow. Capable of doing the walk in 1st instance.	1	2	2
Wall Climbing	Falling from wall Rope burn	PSD Client	1	3	3	Suitable shoes, chalk and safety lines and harness, briefing	PSD to stay off wall and observe/supervise client	1	2	2
Desert 4x4 off road driving	Vehicle rolling, impact injury, whiplash	PSD Client Others	2	3	6	Wear seat belts. Use qualified driving instructor, 1st aid trained PSD on-board. Safety equipment carried	Do not speed, stay on approved routes. Receive correct training and supervision. First aid kit carried	1	2	2
Skate Park	Falling Off, Collisions with fixed points or other users	Client Other Users	3	1	3	First Aid on Site Safety Briefing Given	Helmet & Pads to be worn Stay on ramps suited to own ability	1	1	1
Indoor Sky Diving	Bruises & sprains, head injuries	Client Instructor	2	2	4	Qualified Instructor Tested Equipment First Aiders	CPO to carry out final check of client Safety briefing given	1	2	2
Outdoor Sky Diving	Parachute Failure Health Problems with Instructor Collision with other users Collision with moving aircraft on the ground	Client Instructor	2	5	10	2nd Parachute with automatic activation device fitted to parachute Safety briefing given	Only use qualified seasoned instructors. CPO to be present when harness fitted to client	1	5	5
Wing Walking	Aviation fuel leak Moving aircraft Aircraft stunts	Pilot Client Spectators	2	5	10	Aircraft refueled away from client Client not to approach	CP present when harness fitted Only use reputable	1	5	5

Activity	Hazard	Persons at Risk				Control Measures	Further Action			
						aircraft unless cleared by pilot	company			
						5 point harness attached to rig	Check pilots quals and experience			
						Safety briefing given	Safety briefing given			
Shark Diving	Equipment Problem Shark Attack	Client Assigned divers	2	4	8	Kit inspected before dive Client trained in use of kit Sharks only fed when lights are switched off Sharks fed before arrival Safety briefing given	Assign/pay for 2 divers to shadow client. (Both to be instructor grade) Safety briefing given	1	4	4
Bungee Jumping	Problem with harness Problem with rope (Over extension)	Client Friends CPO	2	5	10	Harness checked by 5 staff members Rope made for 800 jumps then cut up after 500 Safety briefing given	Only use a reputable company Check safety records	1	5	5
Zip Lines	Falling from harness Falling from zipline	Client Friends CPO	2	4	8	Only qualified staff to fit harness Safety brief given to client Harness has 2 point contact with wire. The trolley has 2 point contact with 4 wheels (2 as back up)	Spread team across line in start, middle and end positions. Safety briefing given	1	3	3
Aerobatics	Engine failure Aircraft collision	Client Pilot Ground Personnel	2	5	10	Well-maintained aircraft Pilot has up to date medical checks Pilot is qualified for aircraft being used Air worthiness of aircraft Safety briefing given	Only use a reputable company Enquire into experience of pilot and maintenance of aircraft	1	5	5
Surf Simulator	Falling from surf board	Client	3	1	3	Water cut off switch controlled by 2nd instructor. Safety briefing and equipment usage brief and demonstration	Up dated F/A kit to be present including ice packs. MOI prior to starting along with safety instructions	2	1	2
Go Karting	Crash Impact injury	User Other Driver	3	3	9	Seatbelts if fitted to be worn	Conform to track speed limits.	3	2	6

Activity	Hazards	Persons at Risk	L	S	Risk	Control Measures	Further Control Measures	L	S	Risk
Rib Tours	Whiplash; Crash; Person overboard; Cold injuries; Drowning	PSD; Spectator; Client; PSD; Others	2	3	6	Instructor advice, safety brief, helmets worn, PSD first aid trained; Life Jackets worn by all; On board safety brief; Warm clothing	Travel in a single direction; Safety brief by qualified staff; F/A kit carried	2	2	4
Air Soft Guns	Eye Damage; Trips/Falls; Minor Cuts	Client; PSD; Staff	3	3	9	PPE; Safety Brief; Safety staff on site	F/A kit to hand	2	3	6
High Altitude / Snow Walking	Snow blindness; Breathing Difficulties; Frost bite; Caverness Falling; Avalanche	Client; Friends; PSD	3	4	12	Correct PPE; Stick to mapped routes; Safety brief; ERV; Comms	Portable Oxygen Canister & mask carried by PSD; Water carried; Sickness tablets	2	3	6
Spec Ops / Cash Escort	Armed and aggressive Attack using: Firearms, Vehicles, Wooden or metal bars, Knives, Explosives, Acid; Death; Serious Injury	Client; PSD; Bystanders	5	3	15	Body Armour; 4x4 Heavy Vehicle; Constant Rehearsals; Comms; Code Words; Trauma Med Pack; Advance Teams	Full briefing prior to task; Carry out surveillance; Ability to abort if risk too high; Continuation Training	3	4	12
Krav Maga (Training)	Broken Bones; Sprained Ankles; Dislocation; Bruising	PSD; Bystanders	2	3	6	Use of a Dojo; Use of mats on floor; Use of head guards; Use of boxing gloves; Use of crutch guards; Use of gum shields; Risk assessment	Qualified instructor; Full insurance cover; Instructor F/A trained; Medical kit available	2	2	4
Physical Training	Sprained Ankles; Shin splints; Cardiac Arrest	PSD	3	2	6	Task planning; Use of a recognised course/area for training; Use of suitable equipment; Risk assessment	Qualified Instructor; Full insurance cover; Med kit available; Instructor F/A trained	2	2	4

RISK ASSESSMENT

Document of Understanding & Compliance

Station: _____

Date	Name	Signature	Date	Name	Signature

Notes:

1. This document, once signed by all relevant persons is to be handed back to the CP Ops Manager/Team Leader for retention.
2. By signing this document, you agree to understanding the risks associated with being a member of a PSD and that you will take all reasonable care to mitigate such risks associated with a particular activity in order to prevent harm to yourself or damage to client or 3rd part property.

RISK ASSESSMENT SUMMARY (Live Working Sheet)

Determining the Level of Risk for a PSD (CP) Operation & Associated Ta

Hazard	Those at Risk	Risk Rating			Existing Risk Controls	Additional Risk Controls	Residual Ri		
		L	S	RR			L	S	F

cument is to be completed during the Op Planning stage and included as part of the OpO

vent that an operational incident occurs which has an H&S issue connected to it, then this document must be retained

n concluded

ay be expected to produce your risk assessments so it is important to store them safely along with any relevant OpO f

Chapter 4

PSD (CP) Selection & Recruitment Programme (Advanced)
Non-Hostile Areas

1. **Introduction**

The method of some companies in recruiting their PSD personnel is merely a numbers on seats selection and the exercise of gathering CV's without any real guarantee of employment thereafter has always been a bone of contention of some. This method is based purely on the fact that an individual has successfully acquired his SIA CP licence and therefore what else do you need. This should merely be the beginning of selection and not the only criteria. In corporate industries there tends to be a longer period between selecting and hiring, which will allow for a more in-depth process to choose the right candidate. There are also several job opportunities that require you to start the next day and these are generally through an agency. The circuit is small and often is the case that someone will know someone else. They may make recommendations or simply slate their performance, but whatever is said there is a real need to ensure that selection is set at the right balance and to the highest possible standards given the nature of responsibility that CP has. It is also essential that whilst someone may have a particular viewpoint on a potential candidate because they have worked with them elsewhere, the hiring staff should judge the person on their own merit. Listen to what they say of course however decide for yourself.

Detail Supervisors are in essence leaders and they will at some point in their career be in a position to actually hire and fire people or have influence with their managers and therefore, they do need to understand the process in making it happen.

Several high profile and Gucci appointments on the 'circuit' are what are termed as the 'Closed Circuit'. These are often difficult to get into and often by word of mouth only. Nevertheless, it is essential that the teams are well prepared no matter what appointment they actually end up doing. Even the best of the best can get it wrong and you can only go so far in the selection. You will never really understand the candidate until his personality comes out during the live phase of any mission.

There has to be a level of basic fitness for both new candidates and those already employed within your company/teams. The latter however is an on-going fitness programme that is through self-discipline and motivation. The former will be part of the recruitment process. The object of the fitness assessment should be to gauge levels of endurance, core strength, upper body strength, agility and motivation as well as team support and spirit.

2. **Job Demand List for a PSD (CPO)**

Table 4.1

Dominance	Influence	Stability	Compliance
Moderation	Confidence	Composure	Self-Discipline
Non-aggression	Communication	Re-Active	Compliance

Conservative Approach	Influential	Self-Control	Adaptability
Diplomacy	Positiveness	Patience	Conformity
Carefulness	Participation	Calmness	Rule-Orientation
Unobtrusive	Persuasiveness	Listening	Perfectionism
Mild Mannered	Verbalisation	Steadiness	Meticulousness
Unassuming	Optimism	Consistency	Precision
Accommodating		Dependable	Orthodoxy
Approachability		Stability	

The above list represents the ideal personable qualities that each PSD (CPO) should have (in addition to the PSD Core Competencies as discussed in an earlier chapter) if they are to be effective in their role. These should not be confused with the skill set that each CPO will have both legally and professionally and has no correlation with Graphology either.

3. **Selection Process**

Many people will frown upon having to take part in a fitness assessment, but the industry is saturated with two types - the professional and the wanabees. Those seeking employment may be conservative with the truth on their CV and not have the skill set they describe and ergo, it would be unfair and unjust to have those individuals working alongside those personnel who seek to be the best of the best. Whilst a CV may state that an applicant had served in the military for several years, it would likely be assumed that they would be fit individuals, but unfortunately this is not the case for every ex-military person. Fitness is part of who we are and those who kid themselves are ill prepared for the demands of the industry considering the threats we all face.

Those of you who are fortunate to have CP staff employed full-time will need to consider the fact that any fitness assessment should ideally be carried out twice yearly for those who you employ on a full-time basis. Any fitness program should concentrate on the practicalities of CP and not something that would mirror selection for SF.

Recruitment should ideally be done over two phases since the content of both are considerably different and perhaps timings may not always be favourable to you or the candidate. Phase one will be selection [fitness] and phase two [tasks] will be the confirmation stage. How you put these together will depend on many factors and an example is set out below:

a. *Phase One*. This should include:

   o *Blood Pressure Check*
   o *Isometric Strength Measurement*
   o *Multi-Stage Fitness Assessment (MSFT)*
   o *Mini Assault Course*
   o *Individual Personal Exercises*
   o *Farmers Carry*
   o *Written Assessment for competency values. (Approx. 1 hour – Multi-Choice)*

b. **Phase Two**.   This should include:

- o *Technical Written Assessment Papers (Approx. 1 ½ hrs.)*
- o *Interview (Approx. 1 ½ hrs.)*
- o *Graphology (Approx. 15 min)*

4. **Phase One**

a. <u>Blood Pressure Check</u>   It is essential that each and every candidate are assessed for their blood pressure prior to any physical exercise being undertaken. If there are any doubts or concerns either by the candidate or the assessor then it must be referred to the candidate's own doctor to have confirmation whether or not they are able to proceed. Each candidate should sign a disclaimer once the blood pressure check has been carried out and a medical questionnaire will need to be sent to the candidate prior to the assessment day that they will need to complete and bring with them on the day of the activities. Borderline results should be discussed at the time and the disclaimer signed if any concerns are raised. The final say as to whether or not the candidate is allowed to take part will be the Manager's along with the fitness assessor. Bear in mind there will be anxiety amongst the candidates which will raise their levels

b. <u>Isometric Strength Measurement</u>   The purpose of this assessment is to determine the candidate's hand and forearm muscle strength. As a PSD (CPO) you are likely to use your hands in various ways and as such, strength will be vital if you are to take control of a physical situation where intervention is required. The guide below is the ideal benchmark for which a candidate should aspire to achieve. Very Good and Excellent should be their target. There are several hand held machines on the market and will either be mechanical or digital.

Table 4.2

Isometric Strength Measurement Guide		
Rating	**Males (kg)**	**Females (kg)**
Excellent	> 128	>100
Very Good	>112 - <=128	>84 - <=100
Above Average	>104 - <=112	>76 - <=84
Average	>96 - <=104	>68 - <=76
Below Average	>88 - <=96	>60 - <=68
Poor	>80 - <=88	>52 - <=60
Very Poor	<=80	<=52

The results in both the male and female columns are the combined scores of both the left hand (a) and right handed (b) efforts. There needs to be 3 attempts using both hands to gain an average. (a+b)/3 = c where c ranges between the above values as per the example below:

Table 4.3

Left Hand			Right Hand			TOTAL /3	Result (See Above Guide)
42	40	38	44	46	45	255/3 = 80	80 = Very Poor (Male) 80 = Above Average (Female)

c. Multi-Stage Fitness Assessment. This stage is included as part of the assessment to gauge the overall fitness level of a potential candidate. This assessment is sub-divided as follows:

(1) Multi-Stage Fitness (Beep Test (CV)) – 20 metre
(2) Press Ups (Upper Body Strength)
(3) Sit Ups (General Core Movement)
(4) Farmers Lift (CV & Upper Body Strength)
(5) Individual Ex (CV, Endurance, Agility)

Table 4.4

Criteria For Multi-Stage Beep Test		
Rating	Male & Female	Remarks
Excellent	>Level 8.1 - <= Level 8.11	8.11 = Minimum Standard
Very Good	>Level 7.1 - <= Level 7.10	
Good	>Level 6.1 - <= Level 6.10	
Average	>Level 5.1 - <= Level 5.9	
Poor	>Level 4.1 - <= Level 4.9	
Very Poor	<= Level 3.8	

Completing level 8.11 should be the minimum standard achieved for a CPO.

Table 4.5

Measuring Criteria with Minimum Achievements			
Event	Criteria in 2 Minutes		Remarks
	Male	Females	
Press Ups	50	50	Both events should be demonstrated before attempting
Sit Ups	50	50	

Very good and excellent should be the ideal target for the candidates.

d. Mini-Assault Course. Flexibility and durability are key assets to a CPO's working conditions and this part of the assessment should be to gauge not only the endurance over and under several obstacles, but also to see how quickly and easily they can make adjustments in terms of coordination and dynamic approach in the best way to complete the course. This needs to be a timed event and scored accordingly.

e. Written Assessment. A set of multi-choice questions (at least 50) should be prepared for this part. It should cover a variety of both CP questions and general questions but linked to the security sector. Ideally a time of one hour should be set aside to complete. There should be no need for any prior preparation that the candidates need to research before taking the written assessment. These assessments should not be to trick anyone but merely to asses their basic knowledge prior to being selected for phase two.

5. **Phase Two**

a. The Interview. This should be broken down into 2 parts as follows:

(1) *Bio-Graphical Questions*

The interview is a vital and integral part of any selection and recruitment process and will generally be carried out by a member of the HR team. This process gives an opportunity for the selection panel to verbally communicate with the candidate in a two-way dialogue. It's essential that the manager, team leader or detail supervisor an HR understand the candidate's background, qualities, experience and what they are looking to achieve. The biographical questions are not unusual and the answers you will already have, as they will be from your own life experiences. The panel will just need to extract them.

(2) CP Related Questions

These questions should be asked by the CP expert on the panel, whether it is the Regional Team Leader or CP Manager. As this is phase two, the questions will be more intricate and advanced than those at Phase one. There should be no trick questions here but should be more technically designed to test the candidate.

(3) Technical Assessment

This part will encompass the more advanced aspects of the industry and what is expected of a PSD member. The assessment is intended to challenge the minds of candidates and for them to think outside the box. Several papers should be designed with varying topics as their theme. Only one paper should be given to the candidate. There should be no right or wrong answers to the papers as every candidate will have their own way of tackling the problem but they must give answers that are CP relevant in completing the task. There may be some answers that the candidate has given and may be conceivable and therefore should be considered as a valid argument.

The papers that may be of interest could cover areas such as:

(a) Surveillance & Counter Surveillance
(b) Duties of an overseas PSD (SAP) team in answer to a given scenario. This is where the SAP will be on their own and they will need to make decisions from start to finish.
(c) Consultancy – Provide a full PSD based on the given scenario and will cover aspects from zero to completion and what information and assets are required to make the mission a success.

(4) Graphology.

This area is covered in more detail in Chapter 2. In order to analyse the sample of handwriting, the candidate should provide a written passage from a thought-provoked script they receive.

(a) It should take no more than 15 minutes to write.

(b)   It should be written with a second page underneath the top page. This is so that pressure readings can be taken.

(c)   The name of the candidate should be written at the top of the page.

(d)   Whether left or right handed should be annotated underneath the candidate's name.

(e)   Candidate's should ideally use a pen of their own choosing and one which they are comfortable in using. This would typically bring out their personal writing style. If they don't have their own pen then one should be provided.

(f)   They should end the script by signing off with their usual cheque book signature directly beneath the last line of writing.

(g)   At least half a page of script will be sufficient to interpret.

(h)   Permission should be asked of the candidate if they are happy to have their handwriting analysed and to receive feedback.

6.   **Scoring**

Once you have established what you intend to include into your selection program, you will know what results you seek from the individuals. At that point, the way you score or mark the assessments will become evident and you will know the benchmark (PM) to be achieved. An example of how to set up a scoring matrix is shown towards the end of this chapter. Also included are examples of scoring sheets.

7.   **Terrorist Groups**

There is an underlying deficiency in the knowledge base of CP operatives as to the kind of terrorist groups currently prevalent the world over. This lack of knowledge may under mind their overall ability to provide the level of service clients today expect. The threat, whilst the event may occur in the UK, the strings will be pulled by leaders overseas. Whilst it is accepted that most individuals will research some activity of the country they are being deployed in it is essential that teams understand that criminal and terror groups are the fundamental reason why security is provided in the first instance and their relevant threat level is graded accordingly. Fame and fortune are secondary but the latter has a correlation to criminals and terrorists due in part to K&R. Naivety as to where a threat will come from will be the ultimate downfall of a team and its client. Just because a terror group occupies one country, it doesn't mean they can't target another. The Kenya shopping mall bombings in 2013 are a prime example. This terror group; Al-Shabaab led by Abubaker Shariff Ahmed had stated that his group would spill over to Britain. Equally the Muslim Brotherhood responsible for the Arab uprisings in the Middle East can pose a threat to a majority of the Arab clients most CP teams are allocated to in the UK. Threats are real but unseen until they happen which may be a contradiction in terms but a CP team have to have eyes in the back of their heads and be mindful of surveillance being carried out in the first instance. An understanding of capabilities and MO of a terrorist group would provide a team with active information to respond to. It is therefore essential that teams are well educated in terms of groups who make up the list of international terror groups to keep them at the top end of their game.

Some groups, which may pose a threat to the UK in one-way or another, include:

- Boko Haram
- Al Shabaab
- RIRA
- CIRA
- Al-Nusra Front
- Al-Qaeda
- LET
- TTP
- Liberation Tiger of Tamil Eelam
- ISIL

Carrying out research is a great opportunity for CP personnel to be more astutely aware of things happening around them and the direct consequences of being naïve could at worst mean that the team or individuals lose their lives. Those who pay lip service to the demands of what a CPO should be familiar with are ill prepared to meet head on the challenges, which a client will expect and one which holding a SIA licensed badge should also demand

PSD (CP) Blue Team Selection

Phase One Fitness Assessment

Flow Chart

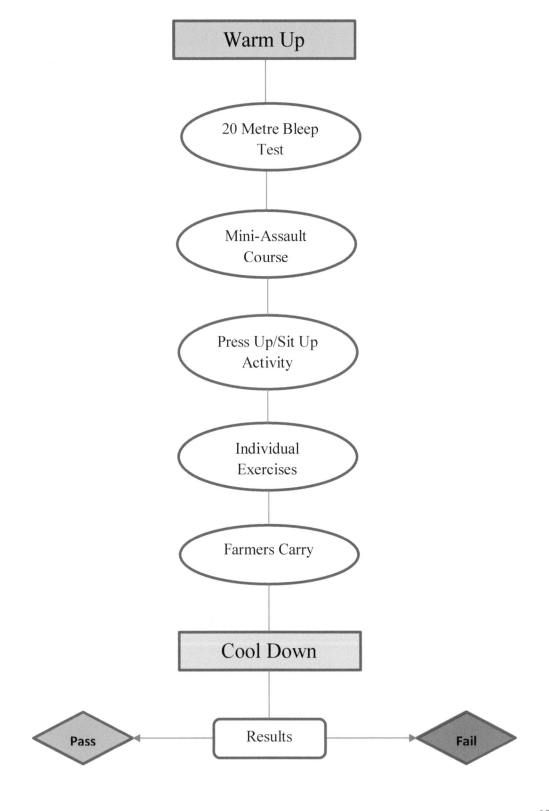

PSD (CP) Selection Programme
Events Scheduling Example – DD/MM/YYYY

Ser	Timings	Event	Location	Target to be Achieved	Remarks
01	1330 - 1345	Opening Remarks Introduction to afternoon events	Classroom	Awareness/Understanding of requirements	
02	1350 - 1450	Written Assessment	Classroom	Knowledge	Multi-choice questions All completed papers handed to HR Rep
03	1450 - 1500	Change in to sports kit	Changing Rooms		
04	1500 - 1545	Blood Pressure Check + Dynometric test	Classroom	Health & Well-Being	Check all candidate medical documents (PTI)
05	1545 - 1555	Set-up activities	Sports Hall		
06	1555 - 1600	Brief Introduction	Sports Hall	Understanding what is expected	
07	1600 - 1605	Warm-Up	Sports Hall		
08		Shuttle Run (20 metres) (Timed and graded effort)	Sports Hall	Endurance and CV	
09		Sit ups & Press ups (Timed effort)	Sports Hall	Upper body & core strength	
10		Assault Course (Timed Effort)	Sports Hall	Agility/Flexibility	
11	1605 - 1705	Individual Exercises (Timed and graded effort)	Sports Hall	Endurance/Strength/ Agility	
12		Farmers Carry (Individual, timed & graded Effort)	Sports Hall	Strength/Endurance/ Determination	
13		Return sports equipment to store room	Sports Hall		
14	1705 - 1710	Closing remarks	Classroom	Closure of Phase One	

SCORING MATRIX EXAMPLE

Table 4.6

The Beep Test (20 metre) [Both Genders]			
Ser	Lower Level	Upper Level	Graded Points
01	$\geq$ Level 8.11	Infinity	20
02	$\geq$ Level 8	$\leq$ Level 8.10	15
03	> Level 7	$\leq$ Level 7.10	12
04	> Level 6	$\leq$ Level 6.10	10
05	> Level 5	$\leq$ Level 5.9	5
06	$\leq$ Level 4.9		2
A minimum standard of level 8.11 to be achieved.			

Table 4.7

Press Ups – Upper Body Strength [Both Genders]			
Ser	Lower Level	Upper Level	Graded Points
01	> 40	$\geq$ 50	10
02	> 30	$\leq$ 40	6
03	> 20	$\leq$ 30	4
04	> 10	$\leq$ 20	2
05	> 0	$\leq$ 10	1

Table 4.8

Sit Ups – Core Strength [Both Genders]			
Ser	Lower Level	Upper Level	Graded Points
01	> 40	$\geq$ 50	10
02	> 30	$\leq$ 40	6
03	> 20	$\leq$ 30	4
04	> 10	$\leq$ 20	2
05	> 0	$\leq$ 10	1

Table 4.9

Farmers Carry [Both Genders]		
Ser	Time	Graded Points
01	<= 15 seconds	10
02	>= 16 - <= 20	8
03	>=21 - <=25	6
04	>=26 - <=30	4
05	>= 31	2
This is a individual event covered twice [40 metres]		

Table 4.10

Isometric Strength		Males		Females		Graded Points
Ser	Rating	Lower Level	Upper Level	Lower Level	Upper Level	
01	Excellent	> 128		> 100		10
02	Very Good	> 112	$\leq$ 128	> 84	$\leq$ 100	8
03	Above Average	> 104	$\leq$ 112	> 76	$\leq$ 84	6
04	Average	> 96	$\leq$ 104	> 68	$\leq$ 76	4
05	Below Average	> 88	$\leq$ 96	> 60	$\leq$ 68	3
06	Poor	> 80	$\leq$ 88	> 52	$\leq$ 60	2
07	Very Poor	$\leq$ 80		$\leq$ 52		1

Individual Performance Calculation & Data Capture Sheet

Table 4.11

Level	Shuttles Completed	Speed		Time Per Shuttle	Cumulative Timings p Level	Distance Covered		Time Taken	
		kph	mph			metres	miles	seconds	min:secs
1	1.1	8.5	5.28	9.00	9.00	20	0.012	9	00:09
	1.2	8.5	5.28	9.00	18.00	40	0.025	18	00:18
	1.3	8.5	5.28	9.00	27.00	60	0.037	27	00:27
	1.4	8.5	5.28	9.00	36.00	80	0.050	36	00:36
	1.5	8.5	5.28	9.00	45.00	100	0.062	45	00:45
	1.6	8.5	5.28	9.00	54.00	120	0.075	54	00:54
	1.7	8.5	5.28	9.00	63.00	140	0.087	63	01:03
2	2.1	9	5.59	8.00	8.00	160	0.099	71	01:11
	2.2	9	5.59	8.00	16.00	180	0.112	78	01:18
	2.3	9	5.59	8.00	24.00	200	0.124	86	01:26
	2.4	9	5.59	8.00	32.00	220	0.137	94	01:34
	2.5	9	5.59	8.00	40.00	240	0.149	102	01:42
	2.6	9	5.59	8.00	48.00	260	0.162	110	01:50
	2.7	9	5.59	8.00	56.00	280	0.174	118	01:58
	2.8	9	5.59	8.00	64.00	300	0.186	126	02:06
3	3.1	9.5	5.90	7.58	7.58	320	0.199	133.58	02:14
	3.2	9.5	5.90	7.58	15.16	340	0.211	141.16	02:21
	3.3	9.5	5.90	7.58	22.74	360	0.224	148.74	02:29
	3.4	9.5	5.90	7.58	30.32	380	0.236	156.32	02:36
	3.5	9.5	5.90	7.58	37.90	400	0.249	163.90	02:44
	3.6	9.5	5.90	7.58	45.48	420	0.261	171.48	02:51
	3.7	9.5	5.90	7.58	53.06	440	0.273	179.06	02:59
	3.8	9.5	5.90	7.58	60.64	460	0.286	186.64	03:07
4	4.1	10	6.21	7.20	7.20	480	0.298	193.84	03:14
	4.2	10	6.21	7.20	14.40	500	0.311	201.04	03:21
	4.3	10	6.21	7.20	21.60	520	0.323	208.24	03:28
	4.4	10	6.21	7.20	28.80	540	0.336	215.44	03:35
	4.5	10	6.21	7.20	36.00	560	0.348	222.64	03:43
	4.6	10	6.21	7.20	43.20	580	0.360	229.84	03:50
	4.7	10	6.21	7.20	50.40	600	0.373	237.04	03:57
	4.8	10	6.21	7.20	57.60	620	0.385	244.24	04:04
	4.9	10	6.21	7.20	64.80	640	0.398	251.44	04:11
5	5.1	10.5	6.52	6.86	13.72	660	0.410	258.30	04:18
	5.2	10.5	6.52	6.86	20.58	680	0.423	265.16	04:25
	5.3	10.5	6.52	6.86	27.44	700	0.435	272.02	04:32
	5.4	10.5	6.52	6.86	34.30	720	0.447	278.88	04:39
	5.5	10.5	6.52	6.86	41.16	740	0.460	285.74	04:46
	5.6	10.5	6.52	6.86	48.02	760	0.472	292.60	04:53
	5.7	10.5	6.52	6.86	54.88	780	0.485	299.46	04:59
	5.8	10.5	6.52	6.86	61.74	800	0.497	306.32	05:06
	5.9	10.5	6.52	6.86	68.60	820	0.510	313.18	05:13

Level	Shuttles Completed	Speed		Time Per Shuttle	Cumulative Timings p Level	Distance Covered		Time Taken	
		kph	mph			metres	miles	seconds	min:secs
6	6.1	11	6.84	6.55	6.55	840	0.522	319.73	05:20
	6.2	11	6.84	6.55	13.10	860	0.534	326.28	05:26
	6.3	11	6.84	6.55	19.65	880	0.547	332.83	05:33
	6.4	11	6.84	6.55	26.20	900	0.559	339.38	05:39
	6.5	11	6.84	6.55	32.75	920	0.572	345.93	05:46
	6.6	11	6.84	6.55	39.30	940	0.584	352.48	05:52
	6.7	11	6.84	6.55	45.85	960	0.597	359.03	05:59
	6.8	11	6.84	6.55	52.40	980	0.609	365.58	06:06
	6.9	11	6.84	6.55	58.95	1000	0.621	372.13	06:12
	6.10	11	6.84	6.55	65.50	1020	0.634	378.68	06:19
7	7.1	11.5	7.15	6.26	6.26	1040	0.646	384.94	06:25
	7.2	11.5	7.15	6.26	12.52	1060	0.659	391.20	06:31
	7.3	11.5	7.15	6.26	18.78	1080	0.671	397.46	06:37
	7.4	11.5	7.15	6.26	25.04	1100	0.684	403.72	06:44
	7.5	11.5	7.15	6.26	31.30	1120	0.696	409.98	06:50
	7.6	11.5	7.15	6.26	37.56	1140	0.708	416.24	06:56
	7.7	11.5	7.15	6.26	43.82	1160	0.721	422.50	07:03
	7.8	11.5	7.15	6.26	50.08	1180	0.733	428.76	07:09
	7.9	11.5	7.15	6.26	56.34	1200	0.746	435.02	07:15
	7.10	11.5	7.15	6.26	62.60	1220	0.758	441.28	07:21
8	8.1	12	7.46	6.00	6.00	1240	0.770	447.28	07:27
	8.2	12	7.46	6.00	12.00	1260	0.783	453.28	07:33
	8.3	12	7.46	6.00	18.00	1280	0.795	459.28	07:39
	8.4	12	7.46	6.00	24.00	1300	0.808	465.28	07:45
	8.5	12	7.46	6.00	30.00	1320	0.820	471.28	07:51
	8.6	12	7.46	6.00	36.00	1340	0.833	477.28	07:57
	8.7	12	7.46	6.00	42.00	1360	0.845	483.28	08:03
	8.8	12	7.46	6.00	48.00	1380	0.857	489.28	08:09
	8.9	12	7.46	6.00	54.00	1400	0.870	495.28	08:15
	8.10	12	7.46	6.00	60.00	1420	0.882	501.28	08:21
	8.11	**12**	**7.46**	**6.00**	**66.00**	**1440**	**0.895**	**507.28**	**08:27**
9	9.1	12.5	7.77	5.76	5.76	1460	0.907	513.04	08:33

Table Showing Distance verses Time against Level

.12

Shuttles Per Level	Cumulative Shuttles	Speed		Time Per Shuttle	Time Whole Level		Distance Per Level	Cumulative Distance Metres			Cumu Tir
		kph	mph		seconds	min:secs		Metres	Miles	Km	min:
7	7	8.5	5.28	9.00	63.00	01:03	140	140	0.09	0.14	01:
8	15	9.0	5.59	8.00	64.00	01:04	160	300	0.19	0.30	02:
8	23	9.5	5.90	7.58	60.64	01:01	160	460	0.29	0.46	03:
9	32	10.0	6.21	7.20	64.80	01:05	180	640	0.40	0.64	04:
9	41	10.5	6.52	6.86	61.74	01:02	180	820	0.51	0.82	05:
10	51	11.0	6.84	6.55	65.50	01:06	200	1020	0.63	1.02	06:
10	61	11.5	7.15	6.26	62.60	01:03	200	1220	0.76	1.22	07:
11	72	12.0	7.46	6.00	66.00	01:06	220	1440	0.89	1.44	08:
11	83	12.5	7.77	5.76	63.36	01:03	220	1660	1.03	1.66	09:
11	94	13.0	8.08	5.54	60.94	01:01	220	1880	1.17	1.88	10:
12	106	13.5	8.39	5.33	63.96	01:04	240	2120	1.32	2.12	11:
12	118	14.0	8.70	5.14	61.68	01:02	240	2360	1.47	2.36	12:
13	131	14.5	9.01	4.97	64.61	01:05	260	2620	1.63	2.62	13:
13	144	15.0	9.32	4.80	62.40	01:02	260	2880	1.79	2.88	14:
13	157	15.5	9.63	4.65	60.45	01:00	260	3140	1.95	3.14	15:
14	171	16.0	9.94	4.50	63.00	01:03	280	3420	2.13	3.42	16:
14	185	16.5	10.25	4.36	61.04	01:01	280	3700	2.30	3.70	17:
15	200	17.0	10.56	4.24	63.60	01:04	300	4000	2.49	4.00	18:
15	215	17.5	10.87	4.11	61.65	01:02	300	4300	2.67	4.30	19:
16	231	18.0	11.18	4.00	64.00	01:04	320	4620	2.87	4.62	20:
16	247	18.5	11.50	3.89	62.24	01:02	320	4940	3.07	4.94	22:

Chapter 5

Protocol

1. <u>**Introduction**</u>

So many people get this wrong almost by ignorance alone. Working with Middle-Eastern clients for example demands a change in mind set which must be instilled from the outset. What you see as being innocent may seem offensive to others. They are culturally different and unless you are willing to adapt your working environment then the survival rate of the team can be measured in days rather than months. It is essential that all PSD (CPO) Detail Supervisors/Team Leaders understand the importance of this very subject so that you can educate those members of staff under your command. Get this wrong and you may have to keep replacing people or at worst, you lose your contract. The nature of the work carried out by those involved in Close Protection will inevitably bring them in close contact with some very senior people; be it Russian billionaires, foreign royal families or international celebrities. The behaviour, manners and demeanour of the team are naturally very important if an individual or team are to remain acceptable to the client and not damage his/her image nor cause offence by failing to understand your client's culture. Protocol is therefore about the conventions of correct behaviour within a large number of areas. Most CP work in the UK is generally with Middle-Eastern clients and Protocol is the cornerstone for survivability and success. Not all CP training Academies teaches this topic and if you're lucky, the ones who do will only scratch the surface. This chapter is mainly focused towards Middle-Eastern clients but may be used for other nationalities where a structure needs to be in place. Every client will have a set of rules that the team must be able to accommodate fully if they are to be accepted. You will only ever be allowed to make one mistake.

Protocol (or lack of it) is the single most common reason why a CPO is removed from an assignment. There is a probability that as many as 80% will be dismissed through a lack of understanding of this basic fundamental requirement alone and this is something that needs to be addressed from the outset and balanced accordingly. Offending your clients by your actions or habits will shorten your time on the assignment.

The definition of Protocol can be interpreted as:

'Conducting yourself in a manner synonymous with the Principal and the situations that you may find yourself in'

Protocol has to be mastered. It's not given to you and nor is it hereditary. Some people can grasp the concept of what is required in the early stages but others will struggle to make any headway at all. The finer points of protocol however can be picked up as teams go through their assignments and they will hopefully be able to gauge what is right and what is wrong as early as possible. It's essential that everyone understands Protocol from the outset and that it forms part of a Supervisor's and Regional Commanders brief. It is one of the basic fundamental activities of a PSD that can make or break the whole team. Most mistakes will fall under one or all of the following categories:

- Dress
- Hygiene
- Habits
- Behaviour

Some of the above are explained further in this chapter.

2. **Protocol (Diplomacy)** Protocol is commonly described as a set of international courtesy rules. These well-established and time-honoured rules have made it easier for nations and people to live and work together. Part of Protocol is the acknowledgement of the hierarchical standing of all present and is based on the principles of civility. It is important that what follows is instilled into each and every team member but it's also important that Protocol is embraced from the Supervisors in the first place for it to have any real success in being implemented and enforced.

3. **Principles**

    a. **Dress**

        (1) **Female Operatives**

             (a) Attire must be appropriate for the task and be respectable.
             (b) All tattoos must be covered. If necessary, wear longer than normal sleeves.
             (c) *No* strap tops to be worn that show bear shoulders.
             (d) *No* low cut tops to be worn that become revealing.
             (e) *No* skirts to be worn whilst on duty.
             (f) Suits to be worn if travelling into London, to any airport worldwide, or any event that requires a dress code 1.
             (g) *No* sunglasses to be worn by operatives unless driving.
             (h) Blouses are to be worn with suits. T-shirts are not acceptable.
             (i) Stud earrings are acceptable, long dangly and eccentric ones are not.
             (j) For practical reasons, jewellery should be kept to a basic minimum.
             (k) Training shoes/boots are not to be worn with a suit nor with casual attire. Flat shoes should be something to consider.
             (l) No facial piercing to be worn
             (m) *Do not* wear tight fitted clothing. Lose fitting is the goal which allows you to move around more easily. If there is extra poundage then you'll need to change your wardrobe.

        (2) **Male Operatives**

             (a) Jeans may be worn when working provided they are not torn and they must be clean.
             (b) Combat pants may be worn provided they are clean and sensible but only in certain given situations.

    (c)   *No* shorts to be worn whilst on duty unless on the beach in the Maldives etc.

    (d)   *No* t-shirts to be worn that have slogans on that may be offensive.

    (e)   All tattoos must be covered.

    (f)   Suits to be worn when either travelling in to London or to the airport or for any other event that requires a suit to be worn. This includes if travelling on a private flight. Suit jackets are to be worn by the security driver at all times during this part of a move.

    (g)   Dinner jackets to be worn when required at certain events.

    (h)   *No* sunglasses to be worn by field operatives unless driving.

    (i)   Ear rings or any piercing is not to be worn.

    (i)   Be aware of bling and over doing it.

    (k)   Sensible and practical shoes.

b. **Dress Code (s)**

To avoid any confusion as to what to wear for a particular event then it may be useful to have a coded system in place. An example could be:

(1) Code 1 Formal Attire (eg. DJ's, morning suits)
(2) Code 2 Suits, rain jacket if required.
(2) Code 3 Smart Casual that includes Chinos, Cords, suit trousers, slacks but no jeans. Open neck shirts, polo shirts but no T-shirts.
(3) Code 4 Smart clean jeans, appropriate footwear, T-shirts, jackets.

c. **General Points**

(1) Do not overdress. Be practical and sensible.
(2) Top coats should be waterproof or shower resistant
(3) Dress conservatively. No loud colours and avoid coloured or patterned shirts. Stay with white or blue if wearing a suit.
(4) Shoes to be both practicable and sensible and cleaned regularly.
(5) Do not over spray with perfume or after-shave as to others it may be over powering.
(6) ID cards to be carried at all times (including the SIA badge) and presented when required. Passports should also be considered as a means of ID. Your SIA badge does not need to be overt on CP ops.
(7) No member of the CP team is to fraternise with each other. It is a guarantee that you will be removed if found in breach of this.
(8) Passports are to be carried by all field operatives as part of their individual personal equipment. These may be requested at airports to support your ID and equally may be requested if you happen to be staying at a London Hotel.
(9) Ensure that your time keeping is kept in check. When a time is given to you for reporting, this should be **5** minutes before the stated time.
(10) Be a team player and support your colleagues. There is no room for isolation in a team environment.
(11) *No* children from any of the operatives are to be brought on to any site at home or overseas or conveyed in any Op vehicle. This also includes relatives, spouses and partners.

(12)   *No* children of any of the operatives are to be taken on any client planned trips.   If requested, politely refuse on the grounds of professionalism and inform the CP Ops Manager (TL).

(13)   *Do not* post photographs of clients or their mode of transport (aircraft or vehicles) on Facebook/Internet Forums (any other social mediums) or any of the properties that they or the CP team reside in.

(14)   *Do not* wear training or sports shoes in any dress code, nor sandals, flip flops or high-heeled shoes.

(15)   *Don't* make attempts to become the best friend of your client or any entourage. It won't work and you are likely to be stood down in a heartbeat.

d.   **Behaviour**

(1)   Ensure your staff are aware of:

(a)   Expressing personal feelings unless asked. Let them be honest but brief.

(b)   Bad and offensive language will never be tolerated.

(c)   *Do not* get distracted by flirting with members of staff whilst on duty.

(d)   Disturbing actions (flatulation, picking nose etc.).

(e)   Over familiarity with clients or household members.

(f)   Incorrect salutations

(g)   Smoking in the presence of the client or family.

(h)   *No* drinking alcohol whilst on duty. Soft drinks are acceptable as is water.

(i)   ***Consider banning alcohol for the live op or out of respect of your clients if Muslim.***

(j)   *Do not* arrive for work with breath smelling of alcohol.

(k)   *Do not* smoke whilst on duty in Company vehicles or property. It's Illegal.

(l)   Courtesy at all times is to be extended to household members. Politeness goes along way. However, don't grovel; it's a sign of weakness.

(m)   *Do not* be frivolous or overly serious.

(n)   *Do not* take on additional tasks that are outside of your remit that would distract you from your main purpose. In certain locations the family may ask you to find out certain things for them or make arrangements for some maintenance work to be carried out. You must politely refuse as if you do it the once they will continue to ask.

(o)   Ensure that your own personal admin is taken care of in your own time so as not to distract you from your working routines.

(p)   Any short fuses you may have ensure that they remain under disciplined control with conflict management.

(q)   If you are under contract with a company, do ***not*** give out any ***<u>personal business cards</u>*** or those of others to any client, household member or member of staff. This is unethical and may not do your career any good.

e. **Personal Hygiene**

This is a must and key area for all CP Operatives to address in the early stages. CP personnel come into contact with some high-powered people throughout their careers whether it be celebrities, business people or royalty and you should be prepared to make some changes to your dress and hygiene if you are to be accepted into these circles. Ensure that:

(1) Clothes should be regularly cleaned. Either washed or dry-cleaned.
(2) Keep a check on body odour
(3) Shave regularly and before duty.
(4) Clean hands and manicured fingernails
(5) Do not use strong smelling deodorants.
(6) Have a change of clothing readily available so as to remain smart and presentable at all times.

f. **Discretion**

(1) Client confidentiality. ***Do not*** repeat information or items of conversation that has been overheard. Respect their privacy. The more information that is shared with others will only make your job more difficult. Keep it on a need to know basis and only amongst those team members who work with and support you.
(2) Do not impose on the client or household. It may come across that you are being nosey as to what is going on outside of what you need to know.
(3) Use common sense.
(4) Know the distance you need to keep away from your client. Also be prepared to step in if necessary.
(5) Be sensible as to who you know the client will be happy to meet when out and about. Step in when facial expressions or body language seems uncomfortable, you sense an incident is about to go down or you're asked to step in closer.
(6) Be familiar with dining etiquette. Don't be a slob; have some manners.
(7) Attempt to learn the cultural ways of your client's own country. Ignorance will not be tolerated as an excuse.
(8) Preserve the client's image.

g. **Salutations**

Addressing a client can be fraught with many pit falls. On meeting the client for the first time, it would be wise to ask how they would like to be addressed. As a guide, the following should ideally be considered for those working with Middle Eastern clients:

(1) Female Clients. Whether it's a teenager or a reasonably aged child then address as 'Princess', 'Sheikha' or possibly Ma'am for the mature clients. A younger client may request you to use their first name when out of sight of other members of the family but allow them to tell you that – Don't assume.

        (2)   <u>Male Clients.</u> Address as 'Sir' or again for the young ones, you may be able to address them by their first name. Again start off with a professional approach with a more formal greeting.

3.   **<u>Photographs (At any residential or Holiday site)</u>**

Many Middle-Eastern clients don't like to have their photograph taken whilst out in public areas without permission being granted in the first instance. The taking of photographs of any client using your own (including cameras on mobile phones) or another's camera will no doubt be ***STRICTLY PROHIBITED.*** (This does not include being asked to use the client's own or one of their friend's cameras to take photographs of them). The storage, retrieval, circulation and distribution of such photographs on a CPO's personal camera is against the very protocols that a team are there to uphold. No person should knowingly allow himself or herself to be photographed amongst the client's crowd. It is almost certain that those who see the picture will misinterpret this.

4.   **<u>Eating & Drinking</u>**

To be polite, accept any food or drink that is offered. If unsure or a bit apprehensive, try a small portion. If for health or religious reasons you cannot try a small portion of a particular food or drink, it is acceptable to refuse with a short explanation. When dining out with the clients, Protocol here would be:

a.   Wait until invited in. Don't take it for granted.

b.   Miss a course so that you are able to leave the building before the clients have finished.

c.   Male CPOs are ***not*** to be in line of direct visual sight of the female clients when choosing or sitting at a table.

d.   The tables chosen will be separate to those used by clients.

e.   Make sure that a thank you has been offered to the client or an influential member of the group at the end.

f.   Do ***not*** stay at the table when finished as this may be interpreted that you are still hungry.

g.   If you are unsure as to which piece of cutlery to use for what piece of food, then ask others in the team who may know.

h.   Remain alert during eating and don't get distracted. It might seem a cosy atmosphere but you are still working.

i.   Do ***not*** shake hands with your left hand. The left hand is used for bodily hygiene and considered unclean.

j.   Do ***not*** hand anything across to another person using your left hand, as this would be an insult.

k.   ***Do not*** order any alcohol. Stay with water or carbonated drinks.

5.   **<u>Etiquette</u>**

As a PSD Supervisor or Regional Commander you need to understand what etiquette is and how it is transferred into yours and the teams working environment. It is important that your teams understand this. Etiquette encompasses the body of manners and these are prescribed by customs, usage and authority. It is accepted as the correct behaviour when people deal with each other. It preserves respect for the rights and dignities of others. As with any rule of the road, a charted course will get you to a specific place at a given time for a certain occasion. Proper etiquette is not artificial; it is a practical set of rules. When learned, these rules save time that would be wasted in deciding what is proper. Etiquette helps people proceed with the more important phases of social interaction. Etiquette is dependent on culture; what is excellent etiquette in one society may shock another. Etiquette evolves with culture. It is therefore a code that governs the expectations of social behaviour according to the contemporary conventional norm within society, social class or group. Etiquette may reflect an underlying ethical code or it may grow more as a fashion.

6. **Etiquette with Middle Eastern Groups**

As expectations regarding good manners differ from person to person and vary according to each situation, no treatise on the rules of etiquette or any list of faux pas can ever be complete. As perceptions of behaviour and actions vary, intercultural competence is essential. However, a lack of knowledge about customs and expectations of people from the Middle East can make even the best-intentioned person seem rude, foolish or worse. In order to be accepted into these circles, it is often the case that we need to change some of our ways of doing things. These things we often do without thinking especially when we are in the UK, but whilst in the company and employ of our clients it is necessary that some changes take place. Some points to consider are:

a. Feet. Never sit or lounge in a way that will cause the soles of your feet to point directly at someone else. Pointing your feet, even by accident is considered extremely offensive in the Arab culture.

b. Hand Shakes. Arabic handshakes are different from the Western power shakes in that each is often followed by the touching of the heart by the palm of the right hand as a gesture of sincerity. Not always the case but be mindful of what it means.

c. Losing Face. Never criticise or correct a client, colleague or friend of the client in front of someone else. This public loss of face will be deeply resented by the individual. Keep all sensitive matters until later and away from the clients.

d. Sense of Humour. Don't assume your sense of humour is accepted across the four corners of the globe. What might be classed as funny, puerile, ironic, satirical or anarchic in Britain might very well be considered deeply offensive in the Arabic culture.

e. Don't Photograph without Thinking. Whilst the Arabic women who travel to our country are often very decorative, it is offensive to photograph women unless given permission to do so. Equally, photographing the men is only to be done with their express permission.

f. Communications. The person who generally asks the most questions or talks for the world is often the least important in the group. The decision maker is often the silent observer.

g.   <u>Behaviour.</u>   Avoid admiring an item to excess, as the client may feel obliged to give it to you or buy it for you. When offered a gift however, it is impolite to refuse.

h.   <u>Shoes.</u> If your team are invited into a client property (not one used by the CPT) then it is custom to remove your shoes before entering the building. You will generally see lots of shoes by the door way in some of the properties, which is an indication that you must do the same. Make sure you don't have holes in your socks either. If in doubt, ***Ask***

i.   <u>Food.</u> Whilst working with Muslim families, anything from a pig is to be avoided (pork, ham, sausages etc.). If you are eating separately and money is provided for you to buy food, then you must be mindful of what you eat as it will be itemised on any bill submitted for re-imbursement and questions will certainly be asked if questionable items are listed.

j.   <u>Gestures.</u>   Some can interpret the 'Thumbs Up' gesture as being offensive. It is best to avoid doing this so as not to embarrass.

7.   **<u>Social Norms</u>**

These are defined as the rules that a group or individuals use for appropriate and inappropriate values, beliefs, attitudes and behaviours. Social norms indicate the established and approved ways of doing things, of dress, of speech and of appearance. Deference to the Social Norms maintains your acceptance and popularity within a particular group, but ignoring the Social Norms you risk becoming unacceptable, unpopular or even outcast from the group. Social Norms can best be described as:

a.   <u>A Descriptive Norm</u> refers to people's perceptions of what is commonly done in a specific situation.

b.   <u>An Injunctive Norm</u> refers to people's perceptions of what is commonly approved or disapproved of within a specific culture.

Social norms can also be viewed as statements that regulate behaviour and act as informal social controls. They are usually based on some degree of consensus and are maintained through social sanctions.

8   **<u>Habits</u>**

a.   <u>Smoking.</u>   Do ***not*** smoke when on duty or nip away for a sneaky cigarette. The smell clings to your hair and clothes and makes your breath smell foul. It can be offensive and dirty to others and looks unprofessional.

b.   <u>Chewing Gum.</u>   Don't do it whilst working. It looks bad, sounds terrible and certainly unprofessional.

c.   <u>Bad Language.</u>   This kind of language will not be tolerated when working. It's not necessary as there are other words in the Lexicon to use. Swearing is a sign of aggression and if your client hears it or their children, then you are likely to be dismissed from your assignment and contract. CPO's should act in an intelligent manner at all times.

d. Looking Bored. Nothing looks worse to a Principal than a bored looking CPO. If you're doing your job properly then you can't ever be bored. Look animated and show them that you are doing your job.

e. Personal Opinions. Keep these to yourself especially on subjects such as politics and religion. If you are asked directly to comment and you feel the need to answer, do so but not showing any strong views on any subject and this will stand you in good stead. Try the opposite and you may have a confrontation on your hands.

f. Familiarity. Even if your Principal is relaxed or insists that you call them by their first name, you should still strive not to become over familiar. Getting too close to the Client or any member of the family or house staff, will almost certainly lead you to dismissal. You may be treated in a friendly manner but take a periodic reality check. You have been recruited as a CPO. You are not a member of the family and you are there to do a job and it's quite easy to get drawn into this false sense.

g. Drugs. Today's culture makes it easy for people to try/use substances of varying kinds. There are many side effects to taking Class A – C drugs and as a professional individual, you need to remain focused at all times. Random tests will be carried out to ensure that this habit is not common amongst individuals. Failure will mean automatic dismissal and the individual will lose credibility within the industry and it is likely that the SIA licence will be revoked as a result.

h. Alcohol. It is necessary that operatives conform to the needs of the assignment and to hold the client's wishes and culture in high regard. This means that *NO* alcohol is to be brought into any client property (including vehicles) or consumed therein. Equally, *NO* operative should report for duty in an intoxicated state or smelling of alcohol. This is likely to lead to instant dismissal. It's offensive to the client(s) and may also lead to low morale within the team as others conform to the expectation of their role (s). The company you work for may have their own policy on this subject but make sure all team members are aware of it.

9. **Travelling on a Private Royal Flight**

It is possible that members of a CP team assigned to high valued clients may at some point in their career travel with their client's on board their private aircraft. The kind and size of aircraft will most certainly depend on the country your client is from and also where they intend to travel. The Middle-Eastern client's tend to travel in large aircraft against others who may travel in business jets. If any members of your team do travel, then some simple codes must be adhered to:

a. Do *not* board the aircraft before the client (s). Remain by your vehicle (s) or at the foot of the steps until all clients, their friends and other influential people are on board. This is not only a security requirement (whilst your client is out in the open then you need to be there) but it also allows you the opportunity to ensure that all personnel are accounted for.

b. If there are boarding stairs at the front and rear of the aircraft, then board using the **rear steps** unless otherwise instructed.

c. If using the front stairs of the aircraft then on entering turn right and move towards the rear tail section. Do *not* loiter in the forward areas and do *not* be drawn to the comfy seats in other parts of the aircraft. *Security* will travel in the rear section *only* along with any other security personnel and staff.

d. On leaving the aircraft at your arrival destination, Security will be the first off. Once the aircraft has come to a standstill at its gate then;

  (1) Make your way towards the front of the aircraft. Make sure that you have all your personal cabin baggage with you. Do *not* make any eye contact with any of the client's or their friends whilst moving through the aircraft.

  (2) Leave the aircraft once the door has fully opened and head down the staircase towards the waiting vehicles.

  (3) Identify the security vehicle (s) and those of the clients. You don't want to be following the wrong vehicle.

  (4) Wait until all clients are secure in their respective vehicles and then get into yours and follow on as usual.

10. **Confidentiality**

Being a professional CPO at times puts you in a situation whereby you become privy to information, actions by the very client's to whom you have been assigned to and occasionally you gain an incline into their private lives. CPOs must have a duty of loyalty, integrity, diplomacy and confidentiality. ***NO INFORMATION*** of any kind regarding the lives of the client's will be promoted in book format and subsequently published unless authority is given in the first instance. Any information leaked in whatever format to any outside source inevitably becomes damaging to the client (s) and is unethical. CPO's must be mindful that legal proceedings *may* be taken against any CPO who infringes these basic fundamental privacy rights of clients. Confidentiality needs to be a 'Need to Know Basis' that forms the cornerstone of information security in today's environment.

It is essential that *no CPO engage himself or herself in conversation with any person concerning any operational matters that they do not need to know as part of their immediate duties. This includes CP personnel assigned to other locations whether they are friends of yours or not.* Each family work and relax in their own and private ways and other locations and families do not need to be apprised. Passage of operational/personal information concerning teams and clients alike should be restricted to that team only and not discussed with drivers, gardeners or house keepers, hotel staff and other people who may be included within a group etc. All departments have their own responsibilities and working conditions and they may test your resilience by asking pertinent but obscure questions. Whilst all departments work together for the common goal there are certain things that they don't need to know. Resist the temptation and just politely say that you know nothing otherwise you will affect the whole CP team structure. If you give anyone a whiff of anything you'll end up digging a hole for yourself. Think of OPSEC, which follows later.

11. **Non-Disclosure (Confidentiality) Agreement (NDA)**

In order to fulfil the requirements of para 10 above (confidentiality) it is necessary for all CPOs to sign a NDA. An NDA is in effect a legal binding document between your employee and an employee deployed on such duties as a CPO or Security Driver. It outlines confidential material, knowledge or information that may be gleaned prior to, during or on cessation of the assignment. The NDA shall protect the non-public business and private information of the company and client's alike. This will protect any type of confidential or proprietary information being passed to a 3rd party. The NDA is restricted to a single CPO who will be named on the appropriate document for signing.

There are several examples of NDA's that you could use but each must be tailored to your own specific requirements to ensure that all eventualities are covered and that you are not left you or your company wide open. The basic requirement of course is confidentiality.

NDAs perform several functions, not least the following:

a.   Firstly, they protect sensitive information concerning the company and client alike from disclosure to others. The CPO named in the agreement may promise not to disclose information received from the company, clients or other figures directly or indirectly associated with the business of the company or clients. If any information is revealed to another individual or company, the company you work for or its client's reserve the right to have just cause to claim *'Breach of Contract'* and to seek injunctive and monetary damages from the individual or parties concerned.

b.   Secondly, NDA's define exactly what information can and cannot be disclosed. This will be accomplished by specifically classifying the non-disclosed information as confidential or proprietary. The definition of this of course is subject to negotiation and interpretation. What types of information that can be included under the umbrella of *'Confidential Information'* are limitless but areas that are relevant to both the company and client must be included as a fail-safe mechanism.

Ensure that you have a NDA document signed by all operatives at the time of assembly of all asset personnel. It is not unusual for an NDA to be included within the terms of a contract of services but make sure that it covers all aspects of employment. The design of an NDA is very much at the companies or manager's discretion and what is relevant at the time. It may be worth having one looked over by a lawyer to ensure that it is legal binding.

12. **Conclusion**

The application of the principles of Protocol appropriate to Close Protection is largely a matter of common sense. It is important, however that all members of a CPT conduct themselves at all times in such a manner that befits their profession and does not cause undue offence or embarrassment to the client. It is also important that as a Detail Supervisor you remain above reproach at all times and you set the standard that others are expected to follow. Close Protection personnel are often chosen for their intelligence and judgement, their initiative and attitude, physical health, strength and agility, appearance and demeanour and lastly, their experience and background. Not only will you and your team be judged on how you perform your duties but also you will be expected to adhere to the Principle's above to ensure full compliance in the execution of your duties.

Chapter 6

Using Helicopter Assets on PSD Deployments

1. **Introduction**

The helicopter is a fast and efficient method of travel for a client. It is also relatively safe in that a helicopter transits at altitudes between locations so is not as vulnerable in the normal way as a convoy on the ground would be.

Many current CPO's have never been in the position of travelling by helicopter in the UK and therefore this will be quite new in their planning phase. All eventualities will need to be covered when flying to ensure that nothing is overlooked and safety will be paramount for both client and CPO alike. All CPO's will be expected to be comfortable in travelling by helicopter so this chapter is included as a reminder of what to look out for and what to consider. It is also worthy of note that you will have to be in contact with the PiC (Pilot in Command) before travel so that he can relay to you any updates or last minute details relevant to that particular flight. He will also let you know if the flight is a 'No Go' possibly due to weather or mechanical issues so that you can consider any other contingencies factored into your movement orders.

As an active duty CPO you may at times be required to travel in this form of transport throughout your career second to hostile environments. There are many variants to the types used by Clients but no matter which type you are travelling in, there are a number of principles that must be applied when working with or near these machines. Whilst they may seem common sense it is worth revisiting as a reminder for you to pass onto your staff.

With the considerations and safety issues listed below, it will be necessary to advise clients on some of the safety aspects. We are after all there to look after their safety as well as security. Team leaders/supervisors should ensure the following:

2. **Principles**

The following must be applied:

a.   If time allows, get to know the aircraft (not the aspects of flying) but how many doors for loading/un-loading passengers. Do they open both sides? Are they sliding doors or do they open outwards? Seat configuration, baggage stowage facilities etc.

b.   Seat belts – how to fasten them competently and correctly. The clients may look to you for guidance.

c.   How to secure doors and how to open them from the inside.

d.   Operation of the headphones for comms with the Navigator or Pilot as well as your client (if travelling on the same aircraft). Know where the jack plugs are and what to connect them to and where the presell switch is located on the headphones coax.

e.   Know the emergency procedures for the specific aircraft being flown in. If in doubt, ask the pilot if he doesn't brief you prior to take off.

f.   Know where and how to operate the life jackets if available.

3.   <u>Considerations</u>

Consider the following:

a.   Embus and debus drills and protocol

b.   Use of eyes in flight

c.   Know your location and expected flight time duration

d.   Follow route whilst in the air

e.   Use of aircraft intercom

f.   Arrival procedures

g.   Emergency procedures

h.   Location and usage of safety and survival equipment

4.   <u>Safety Rules</u>

The following safety rules must be applied:

a.   Do **not** approach the aircraft unless you receive '*thumbs up*' from the pilot or navigator regardless of whether rotors are turning or not.

b.   Approach from the front elevation only.

c.   No smoking in or around the helicopter

d.   No small or free flowing articles.

e.   Do not undue seat belts until told to do so.

f.   Don't leave the aircraft until the engines have been switched off or the pilot has given you the ok.

g.   On leaving the aircraft, move away in a crouched position whilst the blades are rotating.

h.   Do not approach or depart a helicopter while the rotors are being engaged or disengaged, as the blades will be in a drooped configuration until fully rotated.

i.   Approach a helicopter walking up hill or crouching if on the level.

j.   *Never* approach a helicopter from above (Main Rotor)

k.   Do *Not* approach a helicopter from the rear.

l.   Hold onto all lightweight items as they could be blown away on approach to the aircraft. Equally, hold onto all items whilst in the aircraft as they could be thrown around the passenger compartments.

m.   Do *Not* raise your hands above your head whilst approaching the aircraft with blades engaged or disengaged.

n.   Stay well to the side of the HLS when the helicopter is arriving or departing

o.   Protect your eyes against blown dust and particles.

p.   Secure clothing and any head gear against rotor winds

q.   Keep any bags at your side, never over your shoulder or above your head.

r.   Never throw items towards or out of helicopters.

s.   Load cargo carefully and secure it against movement

t.   Do not distract the pilot during take-off, manoeuvring or landing

u.   Read any instructions on the operation of the doors, emergency exits and the location of the ELT (Emergency Locator Transmitter) and emergency equipment

5.   **During an Emergency**

a.   Follow instructions given to you by the crew

b.   Do not distract the pilot

c.   Check that any loose gear in the cabin is secured

d.   Wear the helmet if provided

e.   Remove any eye glasses and put in your pocket (You might need them later)

f.   Assume the brace position:

      (1)   Tighten seat belt
      (2)   With shoulder straps, tighten and sit upright, knees together, arms folded across chest.
      (3)   With shoulder straps, bend forward so chest is on your lap, head on your knees, arms folded under thighs

g.   The pilot will make a May Day call giving location, POB and the situation.

6.   **After an Emergency Landing**

a.   Wait for instructions to exit unless obvious

b.   Assist others to evacuate well clear of the helicopter

c.   Remove first aid kit and any other emergency equipment after no threat of fire

d.   Administer first aid if required.

e.   Remove the ELT if the pilot is unable to

f.   Do not wander from the crash site, as the sites near coordinates would have been given to ATC.

7.   **When Flying Over water**

In addition to the above:

a.   Listen carefully to the pilots overwater pre-flight briefing

b.   Wear a lifejacket and/or immersion suit

c.   Know how to operate the ELT

d.   During an emergency:

      (1)   Obey the pilot's ditching instructions
      (2)   Remove tie, loosen collar
      (3)   Assume brace position when advised by the pilot

e.   Wait for instructions to exit, or until rotors stop turning

f.   After ditching:

  (1)   Establish a reference point
  (2)   Release seat belt
  (3)   Inflate lifejacket and life craft when clear of aircraft

NEVER MOVE TOWARDS THE REAR OF THE AIRCRAFT

CHAPTER 7

Advanced Vehicle Searches

1. **Introduction.**

It is common knowledge by all that the main choice of transport used by a client will invariably be the car. This is at the point in which you are placed at your most vulnerable especially at the beginning and end of a journey. A client may often be defined by their use of a car and sometimes the more ostentatious the vehicle then the more open they are about its use. The more wealthy clients may like to arrive in style and use a helicopter as their means of travel especially for those time sensitive meetings but there may still be a need to use a vehicle at some point. This chapter covers the searches of vehicles where there has been a credible threat against your client and therefore heightened the security status. As a supervisor, team leader or manager you will need to be assertive in how a vehicle search is conducted. There is no margin for error and no second chances against a determined terrorist.

The spate of terrorism that struck the heart of London in Jul 2005 was randomised and unpredictable. They could strike anywhere and at anytime and their objective is simply to cause **Disruption, Chaos, Mayhem or a Financial Hit.**

Time is the critical factor for those terrorists wishing to plant devices. They certainly don't want to get caught and if time has been on their side then a cursory search of the vehicle isn't going to find a great deal.

If there is a heightened level of security that needs to be put in place for the clients then vehicle security is just as equally important as the other measures that CP personnel apply.

There are many books on the market that explain vehicle searches and all have different guidance instructions. As a supervisor, team leader or prospective manager, you will need to develop your own method of searching vehicles in a high threat scenario. Whilst the information that follows will hopefully help and guide you to some extent, each search that you do will be on its own merit and with its own set of rules.

Searching a vehicle has to be carried out in a similar fashion to that of searching a room. It has to be methodical, concise and commensurate with the current threat level. There also has to be a purpose. The normal assigned driver plus one other should carry out the search between them. It should take as long as is necessary to be fully satisfied that the vehicle is 'Clean' and ready to be used. If in any doubt, seek a replacement vehicle from the motor pool.

What follows is an overview of the correct conduct of a vehicle search should there be a need to implement such a measure. A concluding part to this chapter reflects on the Short Check that should be done daily in a perfunctory manner when the threat level is low. Like anything else in life there is no rigid ideal as each search will be dependent on the circumstances and what is required at the time and also the type of vehicle being used. The team must remain flexible to the ever-changing needs of the role. However;

Complacency = Danger. Don't be caught out and use the time to your advantage and not the terrorist.

2.   **How Devices May Be Activated**

The comprehensive arsenal that the modern terrorists have at their disposal has allowed them to make a device of any kind to fit into any situation.   Micro technology available today has also come out in favour of these people by allowing them to create smaller devices able to fit into crevices that were impossible before. These small devices can pack a mean punch that will most certainly ruin your day. The following is a short list of possible ways in which a device may be triggered and it is something you need to be mindful of each time you carry out a search. Not fully understanding how devices can be triggered merely means you won't know where to look in the first place and therefore miss the opportunity to identify a specific device.:

- o   Pressure Pads
- o   Mercury Tilt Switch
- o   Movement
- o   Electrical
- o   Thermal
- o   Chemical
- o   Barometric

3.   **The Main Problem Areas**

Terrorists have the ability to buy, hire or steal a vehicle of whatever type they wish to target and on which to practice (means of entry and planting a device). The 'Die Hard' enthusiastic terrorist of today will take time in identifying his target so as to make sure that he has a confirmed kill. Failure for them is not an option.

The 3 areas for consideration by the terrorist are:

1.   The device which is planted quickly by either, lent on, balanced against or attached to the vehicle. This could happen by pedestrians when the vehicle is stationary or from a passing motorcycle whilst mobile.
2.   A well-hidden device that may have been planted some time ago. The device may be timer activated or remotely detonated.
3.   The Car Bomb – a device that has required a large amount of time to plant since the device may either be excessive in size or intricate in its construction.

4.   **The Vehicle Search**

The team that have been tasked to search a vehicle must conduct it in a clinical manner similar to that of searching a building or room. It must be methodical, controlled and planned thoroughly. The TL should give a briefing prior to the search commencing. It will not be a complete vehicle strip like CSI but must be thorough enough given the potential threat that has been issued. You will need to be conclusive and convincing during and after the search, as you will be giving the 'All Clear' and the green light for that vehicle to be used later that day. The risks are most certainly at the high end. It's like being in charge of the maintenance crew of an aircraft, the onus will come down to the personnel involved if anything goes badly wrong.

Once the search has finished and everyone is satisfied that it is 'Clean' and it is not expected to be used until later that day then it is important that it is not left unattended at any time from hereon. If you are able to move the vehicle to some kind of lock up or secure car park which is being monitored then this may be a good option.

Depending on how much manpower you have available, the search should be carried out by two CPO's, preferably one of those should be the driver who will be familiar with the vehicle. The other should also be a CPO and not just a spare person from another department. The two CPO's will mutually support each other throughout. A third person, usually the TL would act as the recorder to ensure that nothing is overlooked. The TL will not be involved in the search but will confirm the presence of a device if one is found. The care and degree of the search are all linked to the circumstances pertinent to the threat and a **Cat 1** search may take an hour or the **Short Check** may take two minutes. Do not be pressured by the allocation of time. The more time you have then the more confident you'll be when you eventually move the vehicle.

Ideally, a vehicle needs to be searched:

- o Daily before use.
- o After service or repair if no CPO has been present during this event.
- o After being left unattended in an unguarded compound for a period of time no matter whether either a long or short duration.

To carry out the search effectively, the following equipment should be made available:

- Pliers
- Vehicle tools if available
- Screwdrivers (cross and flat heads)
- Torches
- Mirrors
- Coveralls
- Flexible plastic strips (banding strips are sufficient)
- Specialised search detection equipment such as explosive detectors, electronic detectors (especially for trackers)
- Any other equipment necessary or relevant to the vehicle being searched.

Before the search commences, the search area should be divided consciously into sectors and marked on the TL grid accordingly. The TL should have with him:

- A current map overlay of the surrounding area with sufficient detail embedded.
- A comprehensive checklist covering the vehicle being searched. If searching a BMW X5 then have that checklist available and not a Mercedes ML one.

Whilst it is crucial to look for explosive devices, the searcher should also take advantage and consider the following, which may give you a bad day if unchecked:

- o Brake cables cut
- o Wheel nuts loose
- o Sugar in the petrol tank
- o Is the clutch/brake and engine oil ok. (Has anything been drained off)
- o Damaged tyres. Check spare if you have one. Most high-end cars today will use run flats
- o Radiator leaking
- o Trackers. (Use commercial Electronic Tech Sweeps)

The vehicle and surrounding area should be sub divided in a conscious manner and areas of responsibility allocated to search members. Ideally, there should be a minimum of two people for the search and anyone not involved should be kept at a safe distance in order to minimise collateral damage. ***Remember: - NO RADIO OR TELEPHONE EQUIPMENT TO BE USED DURING THE SEARCH OPERATION due in part to possible similar frequencies which may trigger the device.***

All pagers and watches with alarms must be removed from the search personnel prior to the search commencing and this should be checked off on the sheet as being completed.

Before commencing the search, it is important to establish a reason for doing it.
- o Is it a search that is simply routine?
- o Has the vehicle been left unattended, which in light of whatever threat Cat is in place would give cause for concern?
- o Is there a specific reason to suspect a problem?
- o Is the proposed next journey an indication of the type of device (i.e.; mountains or hilly terrain – barometric)?
- o Details of the last search and details of when the car was last serviced if applicable

5.   **Stages of the Vehicle Search**

Developing a systematic way of searching a vehicle will be beneficial in the long run. It is important that you don't get bogged down by following search routines as written in books, be open minded and flexible but never cut corners. Doing it this way you are less likely to miss something or trigger a device by jumping the search too far ahead. With H&S being involved in anything we do, working in a safe environment will be your immediate concern. It is necessary therefore to ensure that the area around the vehicle is as safe as it can be before you begin the search. This is therefore where we start. Ideally, you would have a third person as note-taker (ideally the TL) to ensure that all areas have been checked and should the vehicle detonate, you know at which point you reached before the lights went out and recruitment begins again.

Diagram 1

a.   <u>Surrounding Area.</u>

Bombs and devices are not always where you would expect them to be. They can be nearby or close to the vehicle. The terrorist will probably be familiar with the way a search is conducted and if they can cause death or injury by whatever means then they have partially succeeded in their agenda. It is essential that each CPO works diagonally on opposite sides of the vehicle and make a complete circuit.

- Remember that a device may be away from the vehicle but triggered by it such as by a command wire, electronic etc.
- Look for disturbances in the ground; i.e. footprints/tyre prints and marks where a jack may have been used recently.
- Car park, garage doors, and the immediate surrounding area to the vehicle, drains, freshly cultivated areas, hedges and culverts.
- Look for oil /fluid patches on the floor and look for pieces of broken glass, fresh paper, tape, string and pieces of wire.
- Check for spillage or tyre imprints where the vehicle may have been rocked backwards and forwards to insert pressure switches under the wheels.
- Keep the TL up to date of where you are during each part of this search. He will need to tick off this particular square on the grid.

b.   <u>Vehicle Exterior</u>

Cars today are mostly shiny especially the ones used by CP teams and clients alike as there is an expectation to keep the vehicle clean at all times. This can provide us with an advantage especially looking at:

- Pay close attention to the paintwork, chrome, mirrors, bumpers, Alloys & hubcaps, windows, fuel filler caps and light clusters both back and front.

All these areas can provide a wealth of information and can reveal:

- Tampering
- Forced entry
- Smudges and oil marks
- Fingerprints

Whilst looking over the exterior, it is important that you advice your team that they must not touch the vehicle during this inspection.

Also check:

- Half open doors
- Take advantage at this point to look through the windows. Don't just look on the seats, check also the floors.
- Look for any strands of wires coming from the seat belts.
- Any switches in the on position.
- Keep the TL up to date as to what has been searched at each point.

c.   Wheels and Arches

- Again without touching the vehicle, check for cuts in the tyres and brake pipes.
- Check that there are no sharp objects that have been inserted into the tyres.
- Check that the wheel nuts have not been loosened.
- Without using your hands to feel, check carefully inside the wheel housing, on top and behind the wheels.
- To prevent a magnetic device from being secreted in the wheel arch, grease this area or use under seal.
- Keep the TL up to date of where you are at during each part of this search

d.   Underneath

This will be a lengthy process and must be thorough in its execution. It's important that the driver has a serious bond with his vehicle and that he knows where all the nooks and crannies are. We live in a digital age and it may be useful to take a picture of the underside of the vehicle when you have the opportunity once the car is 'clean' to use as future reference. Try not to use mirrors, as they are not 100% accurate especially if there is a secreted spot underneath that the mirror can't get into. Use the coveralls to get underneath.

- The entire chassis must be checked from front to back.
- Check the engine compartment and the whole length of the exhaust pipe. If twin exhausts then check both.
- Check inside the wheel areas that you were unable to see from the outside.
- Check the base of the fuel tank.
- Check the area beneath the passenger and drivers seats.
- Look for oil leaks and heat sensitive devices near the fuel tank.
- Check the shock absorbers and transmission parts for fine wires such as fishing line attached between a moving part and a device.
- Keep the TL up to date of where you are at during each part of this search.

Moving forward from this point, the sequence of search may differ as dictated by a number of factors. At some stage you will need to disconnect the battery and a school of thought reasons that whichever area the battery is in you should move onto that area next. The battery of course will usually be housed in the engine compartment for a majority of vehicles. Equally as important is the means to open the bonnet; this may only be an option from the interior so this may come higher up the sequence of searching rather than the boot.

As mentioned previously, don't fall foul or victim to a pre-set sequence that you have previously read elsewhere outside of this book – apply a common sense approach here. In this instance however, the procedure will assume the need to access the interior to open the bonnet. This is something that will need to be considered deeply as going through the boot next there is a need to lift out the spare wheel and this may cause a disturbance to the balance of the vehicle triggering possibly a mercury tilt switch mechanism. *Only the search team at the time will know the correct sequence of events.*

e. Boot

The top end cars, which EP and clients tend to use mostly, have electronic keys with some using biometrics. If a key is available then try to use this method rather than from inside the vehicle.

- Open the boot under control as most will have a hydraulic system and the 2nd CPO should look around the mechanism for any tell-tale signs of any wires attached before allowing the boot lid to fully extend open.
- Remove all items from the boot and check the whole boot area.
- If the vehicle has a spare then check its condition. Most heavy-duty vehicles today however use run flat tyres.
- Carefully remove the spare tyre if present as this may cause an imbalance of the vehicle and trigger a tilt or movement device.
- Check carefully around the fuel tank.
- Check the tread of the tyre, pressure and ensure that there are no cuts in the tyre wall.
- Keep the TL up to date of where you are at during each part of this search

f. Interior

- Don't jump straight into this part. First, before moving in to the vehicle, inspect the whole compartment through the windows from both sides for anything suspicious. The driver should be present, as he will know what the condition was like when he shut it down the last time.
- Open each door slowly checking for wires whilst the other CPO looks through the opposite windows to assist in the observation as you open the door. This is one of the greatest dangers you will face so take your time.
- Use a plastic strip if necessary as well as your sight.
- As the door opens further, check the hinge area.

- Repeat the same procedure for all four doors.
- Ensure initially that there are no wires leading from the inside light.
- ***DO NOT OPERATE ANY SWITCHES AT THIS STAGE.***
- There is no hard and fast rule to open the front doors first. Consider opening the rear doors first if you are not happy about opening the front ones.
- Most high-end cars today use an electronic means to unlock vehicles. If there is a key available for when the remote fails then use the key in, knee in method to help control the door.
- Leave the doors opened until the whole search is completed.
- One person searches the front and one searches the rear systematically from the floor upwards.
- Check under the floor mats.
- Check under and inside the seat, armrests, ash trays, door pockets and panels, pedals, air ducts, CD players, speakers, glove compartment, sun visors, parcel shelf, head restraints and any other area peculiar to the make and model of vehicle being searched.
- ***DO NOT LEAN ON THE SEATS WHILST YOU INSPECT ELSEWHERE UNTIL YOU ARE SATISFIED THAT THERE IS NO PRESSURE SWITCH IN PLACE.***
- Keep the TL up to date of where you are at during each part of this search.

g.   Bonnet

Engine compartments today are so tight with engine parts that it can impossible to notice anything secreted in the lower parts. If the driver is not acquainted with his vehicle then any device may be missed. An electrical device can have just the same devastating consequences as all the others.

- Similar to the boot, the bonnet will be pressurised. Release the bonnet under controlled pressure, i.e. one-person holds whilst the other releases the catch from inside the vehicle.
- Check visually for attached wires whilst the other searcher slowly raises the bonnet on command, after releasing the safety catch under the bonnet.
- Use a plastic strip to feel for wires/resistance. Raise the bonnet when satisfied.
- If you disconnect the battery at this stage then you need to be mindful that by doing so you may trigger a device caused by a collapsed circuit. Ensure that there are no other wires attached.
- Search the whole engine compartment slowly.
- Look for places where power can be drawn e.g. battery, ignition and also places created by the car body.
- Look carefully at the windscreen washer reservoir for any contaminants.
- Leave the bonnet open until the whole search has been concluded.
- Check the clutch, brake, accelerator linkages and steering column.
- Check the carb, air filters, access panels, fuses boxes, lamps and wiring.

- Check the radiator and in particular the fan – remember some fans are activated electronically when the coolant reaches a certain temperature.
- You can then test the vehicle with a long tow to rotate the wheels and drive shaft.
- If you are still not sure about the condition of the vehicle, then tow it up a ramp and you are sure to find a tilt switch then.
- Keep the TL up to date of where you are at during each part of this search

7. **Zonal Searching**

Searching vehicles when you may or may not know that a device has been planted creates a different mind-set to just looking over a vehicle on a day-to-day basis. In order to maximise the time and effort put into vehicle searching, it may be useful to create zones to search in. Some kind of coded check whether colours, numbers or letters could be arranged and introduced and established as the agreed format. A checklist should equally be considered so that all areas searched are marked as complete. These zones for example could be as follows:

- Zone 1   Full left side of vehicle
- Zone 2   Full rear of vehicle (not inside the boot)
- Zone 3   Full right side of the vehicle
- Zone 4   Full frontal (not under the bonnet)
- Zone 5   Complete underside of vehicle
- Zone 6   Wheels/arches (Left side)
- Zone 7   Wheels/arches (right side)
- Zone 8   Inside of the vehicle (Drivers side first)
- Zone 9   Inside the vehicle (Front seat passenger compartment)
- Zone 10   Inside the vehicle (Rear nearside passenger compartment)
- Zone 11   Inside the vehicle (Rear offside passenger compartment)
- Zone 12   Inside boot compartment
- Zone 13   Under the bonnet

All radios, pagers, mobile phones must be switched off before the search commences in case there is a similarity to the frequencies of any device.

8. **Final Checks**

It is important to realise at this point that although the team have completed their search of the vehicle, there is no guarantee that when it moves it's not going to ruin your day. Having completed all the checks, leave the doors open and start the engine. Check all electrical equipment – indicators, lights, wipers, horn, heater, AC and radio. Take a short test drive and go through all the gears including reverse. Check the brakes and also listen to the sound of the engine. **Do these checks with as few people in the area as possible.**

9.   **The Short Check**

It should become a matter of routine to do the Short Check as this will satisfy many areas of concern. With Low Threat assignments and if you find yourself short of time, particularly where the vehicle has only been left for a short time, then a short search can be carried out looking at the following areas:

a.   Surrounding Area
b.   Exterior of the car (Coachwork)
c.   Wheels and Arches
d.   Underneath

If you become concerned about anything during the short search then 'STOP' and go through the search as mentioned earlier.

10.   **Finding a Device**

Use the 5 C's – Confirm, Clear, Cordon, Control and then Confirm that everything has been done.

11.   **Conclusion**

Books on this subject are indeed useful and information should become shared information for the benefit of all who put their lives at risk by doing what we have chosen to do – Executive Protection. If you know a different way of doing the same thing then share it with the CP community. It is likely that most of the assignments that your teams are engaged on may be low risk, but it must be remembered that the stakes can change in a heartbeat. Some groups only need a split second to accomplish their objective. The preceding checklist should be born in mind for just such an occasion but in the low threat category, it is only necessary to apply the **Short Check.** It's important to remember that any device may be planted in such a way as to deceive by means of the obvious. A cereal box or a similar innocuous package in the vicinity may easily contain a device but may look innocent in its appearance but deadly in its content.

Your company may use reputable car rental agencies for the provision of their vehicles and therefore the sending of the vehicle to an unknown garage should not cause an issue. When one of the fleet of cars is taken away for a service it is not practical to send a CPO with that vehicle every time to ensure its sterility throughout. Once the vehicle is returned it is necessary to go through a thorough check especially if a replacement has been provided whether temporarily or otherwise.

A vehicle left un-garaged overnight in the grounds of the residence, even where the residence is guarded with a RST, there will be a need for that vehicle to be searched each morning by the driver. Such a search is likely to be measured in minutes, as the threat must be low enough to have allowed the vehicle to be left in the open and in an unguarded area in the first place. The driver should never fall out of the habit or routine of a daily search.

It takes a terrorist only a matter of seconds to fix a device on a vehicle as he walks past and stops to ostensibly tie his shoelaces. A device, secured magnetically, measuring only 6" x 2" will be sufficient to demolish the car and its occupants.

Remember:- Just because you don't see anything during your search should not be construed as evidence of absence

Chapter 8

Surveillance & Operational Awareness

"The clever combatant imposes his will on the enemy, but does not allow the enemy's will to be imposed on him"

Sun Tzu

1.   Introduction

There is a misconception by some in the industry as to the value that surveillance can give to CP officers and the correlation between the two. This is one of the most important topics you will have to deal with during a CP operation and whilst it is lengthy the aim will be to try and prepare you and your team and give a better understanding of how helpful it will be to you with given examples of the many pitfalls if you don't consider it as a functional necessity. For those on your team who have never been exposed to surveillance this will only lower the standard set by others who have and this will be reflected on the whole team. It is essential therefore that the topic of surveillance is addressed in the early stages of any CP deployment. History has shown that before any attack takes place there is always a period of surveillance that is undertaken to ensure a successful outcome and whether or not the target is worth the expense of all the resources deployed.   From the more complex events (kidnappings, assassinations etc.) to a basic handbag snatch in the high street there will be an element of surveillance that will take place. Surveillance is a massive subject that has to be understood by all if you are to be able to apply every aspect of your training to your role as a CPO/Supervisor. Surveillance should be like a forensic examination, nothing should be overlooked or left to chance. Surveillance has been included in this book so that you are in a better position as leaders whether supervisors or managers to ensure that this subject is very much at the forefront of any deployment or CP planning you undertake.   This is a major subject and one that you as a leader will need to fully grasp its benefits from the outset if you're going to have any chance of a successful mission outcome. It's the easiest thing in the world not to do anything to instil and impart knowledge and to rely on the trust and instincts of your team but you wont be fulfilling your obligations to your client unless every team member are fully trained in tactics necessary to protect their client.

It's vitally important to stress to teams under your command the role which surveillance has in any deployment.   Surveillance plays a key role in Close Protection and there is an obvious correlation between CP and surveillance and it's impossible to do your job correctly without these two elements running side by side and at times inter linked. Those who think otherwise are not only putting their own lives in danger but those of their clients also and equally you will not be fulfilling the obligations of your contract. Surveillance is misguided amongst CP personnel and its true importance is not expressed deeply enough. Without this knowledge how can you truly protect your client?   Just by looking around and observing people's movements by people watching is surveillance in its simplest form. Your team needs to be both mentally and physically prepared to meet any threat and it can only be done if the team remain alert to counter any challenges against the team or clients alike. Spatial awareness is paramount and any distractions that your teams have will be seen as a vulnerability in the eyes of those watching you and will be seen as leave everyone open to all sorts of surveillance tactics hence the need to remain focused to the ever changing picture that appears in front of you. Complacency will be one of your teams' weakest points and one that you will need to guard against and to enforce. It is essential therefore that all team personnel have attended a reputable surveillance course to give them this foundation of knowledge. Equally, if there is any lead time before your op goes into its live phase then use this time wisely and practice surveillance with given scenarios if necessary including the benefits of counter surveillance.

By countering surveillance with proven tactics your team and clients will win the day and be ready to meet any eventuality. But you have to take the upper hand. It is essential therefore that you don't give the initiative to those carrying out surveillance on you. You need to take back this initiative and some of the control from the surveillants so that you can dictate the terms and they have to respond to you but you can't do this unless you've identified surveillance on you in the first place. The threat we all face is real and everyone needs to be prepared to meet these challenges. These challenges are unprecedented and a weak member of the team will put the overall mission at risk.

No matter whether you are in hostile territory overseas or on a low threat tasking in the UK it is important that your training in tactical awareness as a CP operative continues. This chapter is included to make you aware that there are people on the streets who are observing your every move – innocently or otherwise. Whatever your actions these will dictate whether or not they continue to observe both the team and client. If you are seen to perform professionally through drills and observation, then there is a likelihood that any continued surveillance par say would be discouraged and disrupted and they will either move on to another target or continue surveillance in the hope that you'll make a mistake at some point. In which case you were never aware that you were under surveillance in the first place. This may then lead to a fatal mistake.

The security of the world we live in is so unpredictable and people sometimes do things for the strangest of reasons. Their tactics are continually evolving and it's imperative that everyone understands the severe consequences of failure. I discussed in earlier chapters about knowing who the global terrorist groups are and this becomes relevant in surveillance. Terrorism today will strike without warning but no modern group will mount an incident without first carrying out intensive surveillance of the potential targets or dummy runs to confirm that there will be an element of success and it is the job of your Close Protection Teams to identify this surveillance and to prevent or at best, limit the ability of the terrorists/criminals in carrying out their mission in the first instance. Several examples are included at the end of this chapter to highlight the importance of carrying out surveillance but before you can carry out drills to identify whether or not others have interest in you or your client, you need to understand what surveillance actually is in the first place. If you don't have the luxury of time or financial resources to allow your teams to attend a surveillance course, then it may be prudent to put together an in-house course to cover all the relevant points associated with surveillance. It is vitally important to ensure that each team member is fully aware of the potential of what surveillance can do and the damage it can eventually cause if the team are ignorant of its benefits. Knowing how to defend against this will ensure that your team (s) will be better equipped to carry out their duties. This chapter is not intended to replace an invaluable training course but merely to get you to understand where it fits into your CP role and that of your team.

2.   **Terminology**

All supervisors and team leaders need to have a knowledge and understanding of surveillance themselves in order to maximise its value to CP and it's application to the mission. As a reminder, there are three terms involving the word 'Surveillance' in Close Protection. The first one is generally carried out by groups who have an agenda intent on gathering as much intelligence as they possibly can on a particular target. This target could be the CP Team, clients, family members etc. The second two are more concerned with the role of a CPO.

1. Surveillance. This is generally defined as:

    'The covert observation of places, persons or objects for the purposes of obtaining information or actionable intelligence concerning the identities or activities of subjects'

    In other words, it is the observation of a potential target by a group and legitimate members of that group. That is to say, persons who are not directly involved in acts of terrorism/criminality or the final act and have cover stories that will withstand examination by the security services or police.

2. Anti – Surveillance. This is defined as:

    '...the technique of detecting surveillance by the object or target of surveillance, without surveillance being aware of its detection. This may also include evading surveillance'

    The measures taken here are intended to **LOCATE, IDENTIFY, DISRUPT**, and **REPORT** surveillance of all types and would be the actions carried out by the deployed CPT. Good anti-surveillance drills begin, not with techniques but with an attitude of mind. This attitude firmly states that you are at all times being watched by someone (whether innocently or not) and that the perceived threat or risk should have no bearing on that simple truth pervading your thinking at all times.

3. Counter – Surveillance.   Can be defined as:

    '...the technique of identifying surveillance with the assistance of a third party, without surveillance being aware of its detection.'

    Counter-Surveillance tends to be designed and implemented to deceive, degrade, evade and attack active and passive sensors used in detection and surveillance. This kind of operation can only be mounted when information from other sources enables one or more of the terrorists/criminals to be identified.

These last two techniques (Anti & Counter) are necessary if a CP team is to be both professional and successful in the application of its duties. To miss just one part will mean the difference between success and failure. It should be an on-going thought process no matter what level the threat or how small the team. The only difference is how you apply that process.

3.   **Threats & Risks**

Threats – Intentions + Capabilities (of the attacker) = Threat
Risk – Assessed Threat + Vulnerability = Risk [Risk is not constant but ever fluid]

4.   **Purpose of Surveillance**

Surveillance is carried out for a particular reason and may include:

- Gathering background information
- Profiling (likes/dislikes, hobbies, relationships)
- Establishing a pattern of life (routines, activities, vulnerabilities)
- Disruption (surveillance can be overt)
- Harassment ('Hard' surveillance to intimidate)
- Containment (priority is to see where the subject goes)

5.   **Surveillance & Threat Spectrum**

Diagram 8.1

Diagram 8.1 above depicts the varying stages from target acquisition through to the end result. It encompasses the fluidity of selection of both target and attack site.

6.   **Principles of Surveillance**

a.   *Cover* - A surveillance team generally do not want to be seen so will work hard to fit into their operating environment and not stand out. Clothing will usually be non-descriptive, suitable for both task and environment. They will either try to conceal themselves from view or use props to give themselves and apparently benign persona. They will also try to appear confident and purposeful when in close proximity to the subject.

b.   *Distance* – Surveillance is like a bungee cord, contracting or closing up on a subject in busy areas close to transport options, and then stretching out in quiet or open areas where escape routes and cover for surveillance is limited.

c.   *Timing* – Surveillance must adjust their timing in the follow (i.e. decide when to go around corners or enter premises) in order to maintain control of the subject and maximise any information gain without being compromised.

d.   *Anticipation* – Surveillance will constantly analyse what they know of the subject and what is happening on the ground in order to predict what the subject might do next. This can enable them to regain control in the event of a loss, or give them the ability to place someone ahead.

e.   *Behaviour* – Surveillance will try to display a natural demeanour consistent with the people around them. They will try to avoid surveillance traits (talking to themselves, hands in pockets, reacting to the subject etc.) and will try to act as naturally as possible.

f.   *Local Knowledge* – Surveillance may use their knowledge of the ground to plan ahead and take cover. They will invariably feel more comfortable in a familiar environment.

Remember – the aim of surveillance is to maximise the chances of information gain whilst minimising the chances of loss or compromise. An error in timing, distance or anticipation can result in a loss. An error in cover or behaviour can result in a compromise. Compromises are usually down to:

- Multiple Sightings (of the same person but far enough apart to negate the circumstantial)
- Unnatural behaviour (consistent with surveillance activity)

A combination of these two is the clearest sign that surveillance is present. The most sensible course of action is always to extract to a place of safety whilst further consideration is given to whether this attention poses an immediate threat to safety and security.

7.   **Stages of a Surveillance Operation**

a.   *Pick Up/ Lift* – A 'trigger' observing the subject premises alerts the rest of the team to movement of the subject.

b.   *Follow* – The team monitor movement of the subject (e.g. using the ABC method).

c.   *Stop/Housing* – Identification of the subject premises and formation of a surveillance 'box'. A 'trigger' is deployed to observe the subject premises and the rest of the team cover escape routes.

Example:- Subject departs the office (Pick Up/Lift) and travels (follow) to a coffee shop (stop/housing).

Surveillance must be able to judge whether there is anything to be gained from sending an operator into the premises behind the subject, or simply triggering movement at the exits in departure.

8. **Loss and Compromise**

Surveillance carried out covertly is a series of controlled losses. This means that surveillance purposely allows a subject to go unsighted at certain times, whilst still maintaining overall control. This technique of not having to retain sight of the subject at all times means that surveillance can better manage their own exposure levels. Surveillance is at its most vulnerable during a total loss – one that has happened by accident, rather than design – and the subject's whereabouts are completely unknown. There is a danger the subject might be in a position to observe surveillance trying to regain control. Signature search behaviour includes:

a. Quickening of pace
b. Looking all around
c. Darting in and out of premises
d. Lack of purpose
e. Agitated demeanour
f. Raised alertness
g. Overt reaction to regain control

9. **Surveillance and Targeting by Terrorists/Criminals**

If your team is under surveillance from potential criminals, stalkers, media or terrorists, your anti-surveillance measures will detect, and in some cases defeat criminal surveillance or intrusive observation; hence the importance of understanding surveillance in the first instance.

These groups will generally select their targets from publicly available information such as articles in the news media. Targets may be selected for their financial, religious, political or symbolic position or merely be a random target. Ideology can be a powerful statement. If any of your clients are High Valued Targets (HVT) then due consideration must be given to the fact that surveillance will at some point be carried out against them and those around them.

The first step in any surveillance will always be to obtain positive identification of the target, probably by photography of:

o The target themselves.

o The residence

o Members of the family.

o Locations where large groups of people gather – theme parks etc.

o Members of the current PSD

Once confirmation has been established then it must be borne in mind that if your client has been identified as a HVT, they will become the subject of all forms of surveillance to ascertain:

o Their routine

o Existing security measures both residential and the PSD

o   Vulnerable points

o   Weaknesses or failures in existing security (RST/PSD)

o   Family routines and weaknesses

If the target is seen as a HVT then it is likely that the budget for surveillance will be high and at this point you are likely to be under surveillance by multiple teams who are well versed in their particular trade craft.

The CPT alone can also be subjected to surveillance both on and off duty, as it is not always centred purely on a potential HVT. Eliminating a CP team would be a prime consideration of the terrorists/criminals since the team ring fence the client and the team will be seen as a hindrance/obstacle to the final act. The team therefore have a duty to protect themselves also which can be a double-edged weapon by killing two birds with one stone. In other words, if your surveillance skills are sharp enough then you will be able to identify a surveillance team and thereby protect both parties. The best way for the terrorists and criminals to have current HVT information is to infiltrate the operation itself. It is not unknown for them to be a member of the security detail for instance or a member of the house staff. He may also be a driver with the task of driving main family members. It is important therefore that each and every person within the operation, security, client's family and staff are vetted to the highest degree if you are to eliminate a threat from within. Security will never be 100% guaranteed but your actions alone will go a long way in hindering any possible attack. Being aware is the key to a successful day for your client and the CP team alike.

10.   **Potential Indicators and Reactions**

The determination of terrorists should never be over looked or under estimated, as their will to succeed is their motivation to do what is necessary to achieve the end result. There is no rulebook. Diagram 8.2 below shows the eight signs of terrorism that brings together other elements of surveillance:

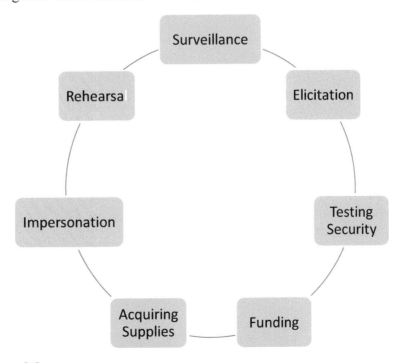

Diagram 8.2

1. *Surveillance.* Taking into account what has been said earlier in this chapter, they may test security response times to incidents that may occur at the residence. They may also ask questions in an innocuous way to gain the answers they need to fit the jigsaw.

2. *Elicitation* Terrorists and criminals may try to gain information about your operations and the PSD or RST with the HVT. It may include asking questions at the school where the client's children attend, the local shop, by telephone, email, in person or even by gaining employment at the house or to find a way into the team should one operative suddenly become sick for example.

3. *Testing Security* Be aware that someone may use different methods to test security, such as trespassing into a restricted area at the RST or office complex, leaving a bag unattended in a place which may cause damage or injury for them to see how long it takes for security to respond and what action they take.

4. *Funding* Terrorists need to raise money for their operations; equipment, manpower, vehicles etc. and they would need to spend it in a way that wouldn't draw attention. Be mindful of someone soliciting for a charity you've never heard of, or large amounts of money being syphoned from the clients account over time.

5. *Acquiring supplies.* To conduct an attack, terrorists will need a variety of supplies, such as weapons, transportation and comms kit. Suspicious activities could be vehicles left in an unusual place or people dressed in official uniforms with false ID.

6. *Impersonation* It's not unheard of that terrorists may impersonate police officers or traffic wardens, paramedics etc. Someone who doesn't ooze confidence in their role could be a red flag. You will also see this from their body language.

7. *Rehearsal* Terrorists more often than not will rehearse a planned attack, possibly several times to make sure nothing has been over looked. An ambush for instance could be staged to gauge the response times for the emergency services. This will be factored into their planning to confirm the window of opportunity open to them and to identify any limitations.

8. *Deployment* This is the stage when the terrorist will be putting their plans into position and executing the attack.

11. **Passive Anti-Surveillance**

You must emphasise to your teams that this is carried out at all times, even when the likelihood of being monitored is not suspected. This kind of surveillance makes you aware of your observers and able to detect the pattern of surveillance around you so that you can be 'seen' when you want to. Whatever your position in life, passive anti-surveillance should be part of your day-to-day routine even when off-duty.

o All personnel concerned with the Principal's security must consciously observe what is going on around them.
o The CPT must report their suspicions in detail so that counter measures can be taken.
o There should be no deliberate deviation from normal everyday activities; however drills and changes to procedures will be necessary to provide increased protection to the Principal.
o There should be no indication that you have observed being monitored. Eye to eye contact must be avoided.

12.   **Active Anti-Surveillance**

If any of your teams suspect that they are under surveillance of any kind then they must instinctively use active anti-surveillance measures which if applied correctly will leave the potential perpetrator, and others in no doubt that their surveillance operation has been detected or disrupted. In other words, blow their operation before it gains any impetus. Good anti-surveillance is a good deterrent and consideration by your teams should be given to the following:

o If necessary, vary departure and arrival times as well as routes. Bearing in mind though that delaying by 10 minutes or several hours may not be enough for the surveillance team to pack up and go. It may be wise to have your client cancel his diary for the day.
o Make deliberate movements such as sudden stops, starts or changes in direction.
o Make more than one circuit of a roundabout.
o Stare openly at suspect vehicles or persons.
o Use illogical routes.
o Attempt to throw the suspected surveillance team 'Close Shaves' at traffic lights or when overtaking. Due care must be exercised so as not to put the client at risk.
o Consider the use of decoys.
o If required, use a layback vehicle to carry out further observations of suspects or to effect delays in traffic.
o Consider driving off a motorway and then back on again.
o False use of indicators.
o Pull into a rest area and let the traffic go past.
o Accelerate away quickly or on occasions slow down markedly.
o Do not advertise your presence by inconsiderate or dangerous driving which would attract the attention of others. You may also be pulled over by the police.

Look out for:

o Erratic driving
o Multiple sightings
o Early morning appearances – remember everyone has a reason for being where they are
o The vehicle that does not overtake when the opportunity presents itself
o Motorcycles holding back
o Passengers giving directions
o Vehicle occupants with heads down

- o   Erratic behaviour
- o   Over exposure
- o   Fluctuating, excessive speeds
- o   Pedestrians in odd locations
- o   Reacting to a subject vehicle
- o   Overt comms
- o   Poor cover
- o   Use of maps
- o   Queue jumping
- o   Run red lights

13.   **How to Detect Surveillance and Shadowing.**

Surveillance is without doubt a specialist subject and personnel under your command should pursue this as an alternative qualification. All CPOs should at least have an inkling of the importance that the threat of surveillance has on people's lives.
Prior to any commission of a major crime, surveillance is an important part in ensuring that the outcome is favourable to those taking part in the execution to ensure its success and an exit strategy has been considered and is viable.

In order to gather information concerning a particular target, those carrying out surveillance will use all manner of methods. In the end though, surveillance is a major part of this information gathering process without which, the picture just wouldn't be complete. Detecting surveillance deprives the criminalist of vital information in order for the event to be executed. The more complex the planned crime, then the more effort is spent on surveillance and the preparatory phase of collecting information lasts longer. Professional surveillance is expensive and not every criminal client can afford it.

The major problem for surveillance teams is being spotted (burnt), therefore a professional team will use all manner of guises and equipment in order to maintain a degree of anonymity. Shadowing is seldom done by individuals since there is an increased likelihood that the surveillance team will be spotted on numerous occasions and there will be a need for some level of comms to be exchanged between those on foot or mobile. It is essential that if a surveillance team is spotted that you do not highlight their presence in the early stages otherwise they will abort and may use additional resources or more elaborate methods of shadowing the target provided that he is still deemed a valuable asset and worthy of continued interest. This will undoubtedly make your job that much more difficult since you suspect there is undue interest.

The simplest form of surveillance is *Static Surveillance* as it is conducted from a fixed observation point in a place where its presence would be acceptable and where there is an opportunity to control all approaches to the subject/target. It is difficult to reveal this kind of surveillance. To do this, the CPT should carry out regular checks of the surrounding area where these kinds of static observations can be mounted. You should emphasise upon your teams that the following should arouse some kind of suspicion:

- o   A parked vehicle with people sat inside which has been stationary for long periods and is in a place which would provide optimum observation.

- o Strangers staying in a controlled area for long periods. Unlike shadowing, stationary surveillance does not impose restrictions on an observer's appearance and the circle of involved people can be that much larger. It can be a café visitor sitting at a table near the window; a man pretending to read a newspaper; a woman ostensibly speaking on her mobile phone but is in fact watching the entrance to some property; a person in a shop who buys nothing but is standing by the window and looking out on to the street; a driver 'repairing' his car; a couple of young lovers; a young mum with a child; an elderly woman stirring on a bench. Special attention should be paid to places which facilitate surveillance – shade in hot days; places protected from the cold and wind in cold days; places under a roof on rainy days.
- o An imperceptible car driving off or people running about or using mobile phones once a target has moved off.
- o Official activity of uniformed workmen whose appearance and conduct generates suspicion especially if no work of any substance is being carried out.
- o Using binoculars, high magnification lenses or night-vision or thermal-imaging devices to observe the HVT, building or security.
- o Someone sketching notes, drawing maps or diagrams, photographing, videotaping or otherwise monitoring a building or people.
- o Collecting details of building entrances, exits, driveways, parking spaces etc.
- o A street traffic warden in a false uniform with false badge pretending to be busy issuing tickets.

a. **Mobile Surveillance** (Shadowing). This can either be carried out by mobile or foot. Professional shadowing is usually carried out with between three and eight persons, including at least 1 woman, using several cars (with not more than two up in each vehicle).

To detect shadowing it is necessary to spot vehicles and passengers and try to identify them as they pass by. The main distinctive feature of a shadow vehicle is its multiple appearances in several places. When you spot such a vehicle, keep in mind its VRN, model, colour, and direction of travel and any descriptions of those on board. Bear in mind though that the driver can leave his vehicle around the next corner for someone else to take over so whilst the driver description is valuable, the details of the vehicle will be more important at this stage.

To detect foot shadowing:

- o Pay attention to multiple encounters with the same people at different points on the route.
- o Look out for inadequate behaviour of those carrying out surveillance. It can be explained by their contradiction between their desire not to lose the target and the need to conduct surveillance secretly.
- o Surveillance teams have to use some comms so focus your attention on people using mobile phones, radio microphones or those with hands near their mouths. Some teams will use open microphones, which are more difficult to detect/observe as the connection is always active and all they do is speak into a microphone fixed about their person.
- o Eye contact

- o Peeking
- o Agitated
- o Nervous
- o Cross Contamination
- o Blinkered
- o Fighting for control
- o Reacting to a subject
- o Poor cover story
- o Lack of purpose
- o The surveillance teams over anxious fear of being photographed. Try under a plausible pretext to take photos of the street and you will see those who hurry away from the screen shot.
- o Whilst passing along shop windows, stop and look in them. Use any reflections to your advantage to observe people passing by.
- o You can look back to see those people behind you but it must be done in a natural way so as not to alarm your surveillants.
- o Slow down your pace and pretend to speak on your phone and then thoughtfully look back.
- o Drop something and then turn quickly to head back and bend down to pick it up and at the same time look down the street as you do so.
- o Cross a street. It is perfectly natural to move your head from side to side to make sure it is safe to cross. Use this motion to observe people on either side of you and in front also.

It's critically important that surveillants don't 2nd guess your movement intentions. Remain calm and notice everything that goes on around you. As professional CPOs any fumbling, stumbles or irrational behaviour will alert the surveillants that they have been 'burnt'.

Be mindful that just because you haven't seen any surveillants it is not to say that you haven't been observed in one form or another.

The following is an aide-memoir for MEMORISING/DESCRIBING people or vehicles. A pneumonic is an invaluable way to remember information. There are 2 tables that follow and approach the information gathering in a slightly different way. Either can be used and it would be ideal to produce and laminate copies for your team members.

Table 8.1

DESCRIPTIONS - PEOPLE			
Serial	Option 1	Serial	Option 2
01	Age	01	Age
02	Build/Size	02	Build/Size
03	Clothing incl footwear	03	Colour (IC Code)
04	Distinguishing marks (Tatoos, scars etc.)	04	Distinguishing features (Tattos, scars, bald)
05	Elevation (Height)	05	Eyes (colour, shape, spectacles)
06	Face (Shape, complexion, eyes, nose, eyebrows, ears etc.)	06	Face (Thin, oval, round)
07	Gait	06	Gender (Male/female)

08	Hair (Colour, short/long, bald)	07	Height

Table 8.2

DESCRIPTIONS - VEHICLES			
Serial	Option 1 [SCREAM]	Serial	Option 2 [SCRIM]
01	Size	01	Size/Shape (Compact, hatchback, saloon)
02	Colour	02	Colour
03	Reg No.	03	Reg No.
04	Extras (Roof rack, spots, towbar etc)	04	Identifying features (Scratches, dents, bumper, stickers)
05	Age (Condition)	05	Make/Model
06	Make/Model		

b. **Counter – Surveillance.** For effective and covert detection of shadowing, counter-surveillance techniques are often used. A CPT who has the luxury of a separate detail can afford to detach personnel to carry out this specific duty. They would be deployed as 'On-Lookers' to notice the innocuous details of people who do things out the ordinary and may be perceived as surveillants. If a member of the CPT was able to look back from where the detail had come from, then any movement discrepancies would be picked up by the 'on lookers'.

Counter-surveillance begins by drawing up a plan. It can't be done efficiently with an ad-hoc method or attitude. A proposed route has to be mapped out or at least knowledgeable to the 'on looker' team(s) and areas listed where it would be plausible to conduct a counter-surveillance operation. Consider:

- o All manoeuvres should be motivated and justified. The route should not be an obscure one to the extent that any surveillants would immediately register as being compromised.
- o There should be several places within the agenda for the 'on-lookers' to be positioned to observe their Field of View.
- o By the 'on-lookers' knowing an itinerary or agenda would allow them time to move to other locations and settle down before the party arrives. This would provide the 'on lookers' the opportunity to observe if any surveillants have themselves moved into the area prior to the target arriving.
- o Any proposed route to detect shadowing should be long enough and with complex situations. A route of between 1-2 hours is the preferred optimum.

Counter-surveillance is generally carried out from pre-selected points and may be:
- o Passages between two streets, short and narrow lanes, streets and pavements.
- o Double exit courtyards with offices, cafes.

- o Shops or buildings with large windows through which the street is well visible from the inside.
- o Car parks
- o Tube stations
- o Stairs/escalators leading to the side from where the target is coming from.
- o Tourists sights where one can turn around and take photos.

In the process of counter-surveillance, all discrepancies in appearance and behaviour of people and vehicles in the area of visual control, the facts below should cause suspicion:

- o Vehicles in parking areas with people inside them
- o Vehicles which start to move simultaneously as the target moves, especially those who follow behind or pass the target then park nearby.
- o Any vehicle with an antenna that differs from a normal one.
- o A vehicle that indicated to turn but didn't carry out the manoeuvre.
- o Any vehicle which makes a turn after the target vehicle
- o Too fast or too slow vehicles
- o Any vehicle, which goes around the block before or after the target stops.
- o Vehicles signalling to each other by use of headlights
- o A vehicle keeping the same distance between itself and the CP vehicle
- o Vehicles going along parallel streets with little traffic and the same speed
- o Vehicles which slow down then try to hide behind other vehicles when the target brakes
- o Any vehicle that has been noted two or more times and in different periods of the counter-surveillance operation
- o Any vehicle which follows the target after a U-turn has been made or a junction turn completed.
- o A vehicle tailing the CP vehicle through a roundabout
- o A vehicle driving across a red light and then holding back.

For shadowing on foot, some additional points to those already mentioned above:

- o Any person communicating by radio
- o Everyone who turns away to avoid face-to-face contact with the team or target
- o Anyone who shows hesitation and/looks around before entering a building after the target
- o Everyone who leaves a vehicle at the time the target leaves his.

14.   **Purpose of Counter Surveillance**

To identify surveillance – not evade it.

Counter Surveillance (CS) should not be confused with 'Protective Surveillance' that may be deployed as a form of physical protection. CS is discreet and pre-planned, and requires the full cooperation of the client/principal to act as 'Hare'. CS done correctly is very difficult for even the most sophisticated surveillance teams to avoid. CS should always be conducted covertly (i.e. without alerting any surveillance presence to the use of sophisticated surveillance detection techniques.)

15.   **Counter Surveillance Considerations**

Consider the following:

a.   Who is the hare (subject)
b.   What is the threat
c.   Who is the CS team
d.   What is the CS communication plan
e.   What is the planned CS method (static, foot, mobile, combined)
f.   How long is available
g.   How can you minimise impact on the client /principal

16.   **Principles of Counter Surveillance**

a.   *Duration* – Decide how much time you have available to carry out a CS op. Bear in mind that a route that is too short may not deliver a positive result.
b.   *Start Point* – Choose a start point. This is usually somewhere where surveillance may use as a start point such as a home or business address.
c.   *Choke Points* – Identify several points where surveillance will be drawn through and forced to make a positive reaction.
d.   *Stops* – Identify natural locations along the route for the hare to make a brief stop. This will enable CS to observe movement in and around surveillance box positions and, if necessary, it will allow time to leapfrog between CS positions.
e.   *Route* – Throughout the route remain static and in position long enough to observe any hostile threat. If leap-frogging between CS positions, avoid travelling the same route as the hare, or passing through areas that might be occupied by surveillance. Test the route (from the hare's perspective) and resolve any identified problems.
f.   *All Clear* – An all clear will be reassuring to the hare. Conversely, if surveillance is detected, the hare can be evacuated quickly to a place of safety.
g.   *End Point* – The end point is usually a destination pre-determined by the client/principal and might be somewhere the client visits regularly.

17.   **What to Look Out For**

If you suspect that you are under surveillance and it is likely that a CS team have been deployed, then consider the following:

a.   There may be activity in and around identified surveillance positions.
b.   There could be an issue with cross contamination
c.   Hesitation
d.   Unnatural/illogical movement
e.   Overt communications
f.   The 'box' setting up and collapsing.
g.   Repeated sightings

18. **Psychology of the (Average) Criminal or Attacker**

Any attempt by a criminal or terrorist to carry out an act of violence or aggression requires a specific mind-set. Some examples are set out below:
- He will be nervous and tense at the point of initiating his intention
- He will be fearful of being caught
- He wants to get the whole process over with as quickly as possible but with a successful outcome
- He will not want to attract attention so will use all his skill to meet this.

19. **Techniques and Modus Operandi**

Over time surveillants have evolved to be cunning operators.

- He may or may not have a plan – Opportunist or professional
- He may have a cover story; such as 'Conducting a Safety Survey'
- If tailgating, he is likely to choose busy times like lunch and shift changes.
- He may loiter near entrance doors and may use smoking as cover.
- He may wear clothing, such as a suit or High-visibility jacket to fit in.
- He may use props, such as a clipboard or hardhat.
- Likely to cover or hide his face, especially in areas where CCTV are visible.
- He may also wear a baseball cap, glasses or hoodie, where appropriate.
- His behaviour might be shifty.

They will take on guises in order to deceive you and to get closer. It'll be your awareness of this that will make things stand out for you to react accordingly.

20. **Vehicle Attacks**

Unless you are spatially aware of what is around you, you may never see an attack about to go down and an attack would only be implemented after a lengthy period of detailed surveillance. Whilst mobile, these can come in two (2) forms:

1. Motorcycle
2. Vehicle (car, van, lorry)

To survive an attack from a moving vehicle is similar to an attack by a motorcycle but there are some very important differences. In surviving an attack from a moving vehicle, really your only protection is ramming the car or forcing the car off the road. How you evaluate a situation before it develops can only come with experience but it may be possible that a common sense approach may win the day. The objective here is not to give these hostiles too much freedom in which to command the situation leaving you no way out creating an end game where your options are greatly reduced. Survival has to be an instinct in which to react and at which point adrenalin starts to flow. Provided it is a controlled instinct then all aspects of your survivability should come in to play. Don't allow the hostiles too much freedom of movement; use your own vehicle as a weapon if necessary.

The live case scenario's, which follow at the end of this chapter, are for information only and should be read as such. They have been written by others and made available so that lessons can be learnt. ***They are attached to show the reality of surveillance and the consequences of failure and complacency.*** They are extracted from the public domain.

21. <u>**Developing a Vehicle Ambush Counter Measure Programme**</u>

A protective movement is the process of getting our client from Point A to Point B in a safe and timely manner. To do this safely in a convoy it is essential that a vehicle ambush counter measures programme is developed specifically addressing all aspects of the vehicular movement. Historically, a targets greatest vulnerability is while in transit between work and home and these two points are where an attack can take place. With surveillance they can establish our client's routine and route between these two points. Establishing this expands the potential attack points significantly. Most people will suggest changing routes and whilst this is meaningful advice, it is usually seriously flawed. *'You can change your route to work or travel into London each day, but when you leave the drive way you turn left or right and those watching you know this'.* If you are dealing with an ambush at this point then it is too late.

Since the route any intended target takes is so critical to the targeting process, a counter-measures programme must include thorough route planning and analysis. Unfortunately, expedience, lack of time and sudden changes to our client's schedule all contribute to route planning and analysis being neglected. Proper route planning conducted in conjunction with proactive and alert counter surveillance will provide the ability to adjust routes and timing in a meaningful way to avoid an attack. The essence of the plan is developed by:

- o Planning primary and secondary routes
- o Analysing the routes for choke points, danger zones, safe havens and the zone of total predictability.
- o Documenting the analysis and route development
- o Establish IAD's to be taken in the event of an attack at critical junctures in the route. These actions are counter ambush drills composed of a combination of evasive manoeuvres.
- o Plan routes through map appreciation and Google earth or Street Finder etc.

a. Analyse the route and identify the following:

- o *Zone of Total Predictability*
  Is that part of the route our only choice? e.g. a single road into a cul-de-sac, a single road that must be taken to get to a major road, a dead end street
- o *Check points*
  Something in the terrain that is visible day or night and in any weather. E.g. a tall building, phone mast, railway crossing, a large bridge
- o *Choke Points*
  Areas where vehicle movement is restricted and you are forced to slow down, e.g. a bridge, a tunnel, one-way street, constructions zones, traffic lights (temp & fixed), stop sign, blind bend

o *Observation Points*
This is a location that occupies a dominant terrain feature where covert observation may be conducted over a critical portion of the route. This location may be a building, a hill or even something as overt as a street café

o *Danger Zone*
Similar to a choke point. It is an area where movement is not only restricted but additionally you may have to stop due to circumstances outside of your control and concealment is given to a potential attacker. If obstacles are present (fixed, as in construction, an accident – staged) or (mobile, as in vehicle) this becomes a point of a likely ambush. A choke point can become a danger zone when the above factors are present

o *Safe Havens*
This is a place that is ideally open 24hrs a day or if not it is open when you drive by, there are people around, good comms (telephones, radios) are available and medical assistance is available also. E.g. Police, fire stations, hospitals

b.   Every destination our charges go to should have a primary and secondary route. The results of any route analysis should be documented in a Crisis Management folder that accompanies the driver. On one side are the written directions whilst on the opposite page is a strip map of the route with both danger zones and safe havens marked. Addresses and telephone numbers for the safe havens should be obtained and up dated when required. All team members must be familiar with the content of that document in the event some duties change and others are rotated

a.   Drive the route and determine through observation what normal activity for that area is at the time. This is called '*Surveillance Detection Route (SDR)*'. When performed by the SAP it is called '*Counter Surveillance*'. Take notes whilst travelling the route and record times and distances using the odometer

b.   The SAP is to check the route prior to the client transiting the same route looking for pre-incident indicators, factors out the ordinary that would lead you to believe that something is not quite right here. This will be your early warning capability

c.   If an assignment is protracted, the SAP will be used on a regular basis as a counter-surveillance team

22.   **Surveillance Detection**

We can never say that something will never happen and they would be the words of a foolish man if that were the case. Using this adage it is essential that some protocols are in place in the event that an incident does take place. Whilst it may seem a little extravagant to write such a doctrine for use here in the UK unless you are prepared to act in a manner that should befit your profession then your dedication could be misconstrued and even misplaced. The act of unpredictability should keep us on our toes all of the time without the need to question any ethics.

Detecting surveillance is the best method available for preventing a possible target from being a victim of any type of attack. This doesn't merely have to be a terrorist incident; it could quite easily be a criminal in the street ready for a bag snatch. Your *awareness* would be the key to the failure of the criminal by your actions early on. These could be criminals with an MO of being opportunists but still play a significant part in your surveillance skills as the team need to be able to prevent it before it even begins. Terrorists however require time to meticulously plan a larger event. If the team miss an early opportunity it only makes it more difficult later on.

Detecting terrorist preparation requires that the CP team become familiar with their working environment near to home and places that may become regular haunts. Anything that is the slightest bit unusual must be noticed and acted upon. Whether you cascade a Situation report (Sitrep) as an all-points bulletin for the whole team or just localise the information will depend on the circumstances at the time and also how you came about the information in the first place. The CP team must be as meticulous and organised in their efforts as much as possible to detect a likely incident as the terrorists begin the process of setting up.

Looking for terrorist surveillance should not be left to chance. The CP team must have the ability to accurately describe and record anything they see that is unusual. This can only be done if you increase your powers of observation. As with the Alfred Herrhausen case described later the terrorists were obvious enough when setting up the ambush that it aroused the suspicion of the neighbours but not his PSD.

In most situations involving the CP team, environmental factors around the home dictate security. It is essential that close and constant observation of dangerous roads is necessary. Routes should be re-evaluated over time. The CP team should examine the area around the client's home and develop a danger zone log. The CP team should carry out careful examination of all the possible routes in an attempt to avoid this:

Diagram 8.3 Dealing with the aftermath...

a. ***Understanding Choke Points***

It must be remembered that the type of road that we travel on with our client's has a lot to do with the type of attack any terrorist would mount if the client is finally chosen as the selected target. Special emphasis needs to be placed on locations along the route to and from the house. Typically these are *'Choke Points'*. To be effective and to provide a valuable contribution all CPOs need to know:

- What is a choke point?
- What, if anything can be done about it
- What to do if you are in one

A 'Choke Point' is locations near the home or place of work that due to environmental factors you cannot avoid, e.g.

- Narrow roads with calming measures in place
- Slow driving areas, schools, bus stops, bridges
- Blind spots in roads

At choke points, all CPOs should be looking out for changes to this environment that would signify something out of the ordinary. You should consider:

- What cars should be there? Is it residential, commercial, rural
- What people should be there and at certain times of the day.
- What are the legal reasons that something is there that shouldn't be, e.g., parked on double red lines, double yellow lines, bus stops

The above should not be a guess. A plan should first consist of knowing the location of all possible choke points along any intended route. Each security driver should at any time know exactly where he is. You are given 10 days prior to the client arriving to orientate yourself with areas both locally and away from base. Where necessary and if required, a SAP should travel ahead of the client with a clear understanding of what to look out for. As a rule of thumb, *'We can never say never'!* and remember the problem with ***Herr Herrhausen?***, the CP team were organised, trained and ready for the classic vehicle ambush but they got a roadside bomb instead. An ***advance*** can be a minute in advance to scout the area for signs of some irregularities. It is essential that the SAP knows what their responsibilities are and what constitutes as being ordinary or out of the ordinary otherwise everyone could be paranoid and opportunities are missed. They will look out for not only people but also things. In the Herr Herrhausen incident it was a bicycle. What are the signs of an ambush? It could be anything that makes your car slow down.

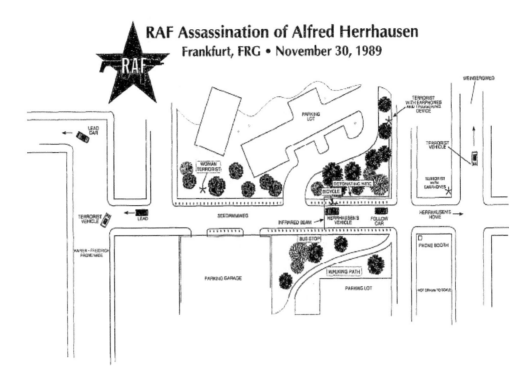

Diagram 8.4

For the Herr Herrhausen ambush, there was a school and a bus stop that forced all vehicles to slow down to 30-35 kph. This was an ideal choke point that was part of the environment and was seemingly natural. If the threat area signifies an assassination then it will be something you drive by. To gather all the actionable intelligence you need to succeed is complicated and time consuming but what are the alternatives? The only chance that *the financier* had was if the CP team had carried out counter-surveillance – the detection of the signs of an ambush in a choke point using a secondary team. For him, there should've been no questions asked if additional resources were needed and something which larger teams should consider as part of the planning process. Equally, it should be the subject of on-going assessments as to whether it is needed or not.

As the CP team and client leave their residence, the options are less. Most incidents will occur near the home or office and it would be the ideal to send out the SAP to check for immediate dangers prior to the client driving out of their gates. This is very much relevant if the client has limited options to his choice of routes. Defensive measures should concentrate on the following:

(1)   If there is limited access in and out of the area then meticulous advance reconnaissance is necessary on all roads that, for whatever reason, the client must unavoidably take.

(2)   All terrorist attacks are preceded by surveillance. These types of surveillance are not necessarily that sophisticated in which the average person with some reasonable training couldn't spot.

(3)   Anything that appears on your route that wasn't there yesterday should be questioned. If you have a high valued asset as a client then you may gain some support from the police in assisting you with verification. These contacts are something you will need to establish early on in your mission.

The key to an effective surveillance awareness programme is ***alertness***.   The philosophy should be adopted that once is happenstance, twice is coincidence and three times is hostile.   It's interesting to read a kidnapped persons perspective before his kidnap.   In this case, Sir Geoffrey Jackson (1915 – 1987) the British Ambassador to Uruguay whose chauffer driven car was ambushed in Montevideo on 08 January, 1971 by Tupamaros terrorists and then kidnapped and held for 8 months described his awareness of their surveillance in this manner:

> *"…when, after a relatively quiet life, nocturnal calls begin to proliferate, when one's hitherto pleasantly solidarity walks along the beaches and sand dunes and in pine forests begin to bristle with horizon-marching silhouettes and sudden encounters with the young in unlikely trio formation, when one's golf game – not only one's own – regularly begins to be interrupted by casual young spectators on remote fairways, where for the third time one's path is crossed by professional violence literally at one's door step – by this time the least perceptive of mortals begins to grasp that, however much the world around him may be changing, his own private world is changing still more…"*

The above is an eloquent description almost code like of surveillance and awareness of a changing environment.   He was released after a deal had been brokered by the Chilean President, Salvador Allende and a payment of £42000 from the UK Government.

Before his ambush and subsequent kidnap, Sir Geoffrey noticed that the couple picnicking across the road from his home were in fact surveillants.   He also noticed the same motor scooter each day as he commuted to the Embassy.   Whilst this scooter had different passengers on board each day, he later recounted that this scooter had in fact cut his driver off and forced him to stop on some occasions or to slow down on others.   Sir Geoffrey in hindsight wished that he had acted on his suspicions at the time and there lies the moral of the story.   If you are suspicious of being under potential surveillance then you probably are and it would be wise to carry out anti-surveillance drills to confirm.

The level of awareness must be raised to a point where:
- o   Strange vehicles park near a residence that appear to be abnormal for the area
- o   People standing, walking or sitting in cars near a residence must be observed by the CP team.
- o   The CP team recognise that they are being followed.

Many people will associate surveillance detection with watching for someone following you on foot.   Although it's a good idea to do that, it is as important to watch for cars and more importantly for signs of an ambush as you near or reach the DoP.   In the Herr Herrhausen incident no driving manoeuvre or armoured car would have prevented the incident.   Choke points need to be watched closely and re-checked for any anomalies if we are to do our job effectively.   Teams are bound by limitations and most ops, less those in hostile areas are low profile/threat assignments which generally mean that the manpower you have to fulfil the clients requests are at the lowest end of the threat grid.   This means little or no surplus manpower to carry out additional safety measures or security tasks.   In other words you may have to make it work with the resources you have.

On Nov 17, 1986, George Besse, president of the Renault car company was assassinated as he walked from his chauffeur driven car to the front door of his apartment building by a couple of women who had been waiting on the pavement until his arrival. The females shot Besse 4 times in the head and chest with a 9mm handgun. The French terrorist group, Action Direct (AD) claimed responsibility for the assassination of the executive.

Later in Mar 1987, French police raided a farmhouse in France. Inside, they found videotapes of Besse, another assassination victim, General Rene Audran plus 60 additional videotapes of other prominent French business people.

The videos were an important discovery certainly in 1987 as very little was known as to the depth to which assassins conduct target selection. They showed the business people going about their daily routines in only two locations; near their homes and offices. The videotapes proved two important points; terrorists rely heavily on surveillance, and their surveillance is concentrated around homes and frequently visited locations.

The tactic of video taping during surveillance is no different what the police forces or security services of the UK conduct. AD used a modern convenience of a video recording device to carry out surveillance. The time and date and place for attack would be selected from this footage. The clarity of the video allowed the terrorists to decide with a degree of confidence the site in which to carry out their acts.

The Besse assassination is one of many where terrorists relied on surveillance. The solution therefore is for clients to avoid routines and change their routes. Whilst this is obviously sound advice and should be adhered to whenever possible, but being CPOs on this assignment we know that to get a client to change routes is not easy. They are creatures of habit and if they travel along a strange route they will become a little anxious.

Ask yourself this question; *does altering a routine make a difference?* If departure and arrival times can be varied significantly, the answer **may** be yes. However, if the timings were varied by 10mins, 20mins or 1 hour then it wouldn't make a blind bit of difference. All it would mean is that the terrorists would have to wait a little bit longer in order to execute their plan. If of course there is an infinite delay then the terrorists would be wary of being compromised if they remain in the area for too long. Once they have decided on an execution date, they either take it, delay or abort; a strategy which is not too dissimilar to the military ideology.

Equally, even if a departure time can be changed, in most instances the route cannot; which are the main reasons why targets are selected in the area around their homes or a place that becomes a regular haunt. Herr Herrhasuen's ambush was a typical scenario.

Statistics also indicate the area around the home, office or places of regularity are the most vulnerable. These are well documented case studies and are touched briefly below:

- o 30 Nov 1989, a German Business man, Herr Herrhausen was assassinated 300yards from his home by terrorists
- o 17 Nov 1986, a French Businessman, George Besse was assassinated on his doorstep by terrorists.

- ○ 29 Jun 1988, a US military Attaché, Capt. William Nordeen (US Navy) was assassinated 300yards from his home in Athens.
- ○ 08 Jun 2000, British Military Attaché, Brigadier Stephen Saunders was assassinated in Athens on his way to work at the British Embassy.
- ○ 28 September 1981, John Butler was assassinated by roadside bomb 300 metres from his home in Bogota, Columbia.

Within a few streets from where someone lives, it is common to see the same people and cars in roughly the same places. If something or someone enters this environment, it should be questioned before eliminating the process. This is often where the system fails resulting in dire consequences. Most of the time when people notice something out the ordinary, they do nothing. Instead it is often rationalised as to why something is there. It has to be an instinct and it is a lot easier when someone has an inquisitive nature to question its reason for being there. Detecting surveillance requires alertness. It must become an unconscious habit. Paranoia should not be encouraged but developing a sense of what is normal and what is unusual around the home, office or any transited routes and any frequented places can be the most important security precautions a CP team can provide to a client. Get this bit right and you reduce the chances significantly of a successful incident-taking place. Get it wrong and you'll have your work cut out. As mentioned earlier, special emphasis should be placed on *choke points* around the home, en-route and any routinely visited locations. Near the home though and often at some of the places frequented by the clients in London, choke points are inevitable. Awareness here needs to be off the scale.

The SAP needs to be regularly deployed along intended routes (primary & secondary) to establish any changes. Records should be kept showing any differences from one period to another. Photographs and video footage could be made to compare one period with the next.

23. **Attack Cycle**

For your CP team to be successful, they will have only four chances in which to identify, locate and disrupt any chance of terrorists carrying out an aggressive act against your client. The following suggests what these four chances are but the team must bear in mind that they will actually only have three. This is graphically represented and explained below in diagram 8.5.

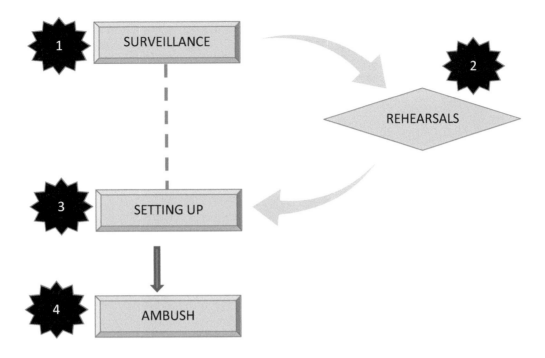

Diagram 8.5

a.   *Surveillance.* This will be the first and best opportunity for the team to identify that they are under surveillance. If the signs are positive, bearing in mind what has been mentioned early on in this chapter then they can react accordingly. If they miss this chance then their opportunities for locating surveillance start to diminish.

b.   *Rehearsals.* Often than not, terrorists generally rehearse their attack ideas off the beaten track and therefore it will be increasingly difficult for the CP team to be able to identify any wrong doing or suspicious activity. Terrorists will generally set up a mock location to be able to go through all the information that has been collected through surveillance. By not taking this opportunity into account, the options for the CP team have now been reduced

c.   *Setting Up.* Once the terrorists are satisfied that the surveillance has gathered enough actionable information and the rehearsals have been successful then they will begin to move all their equipment and resources into position. The CP team will have another opportunity at this point to identify suspicious behaviour. The only problem the CP team face at this point is that they don't know the time line between setting up and the ambush itself. It could be minutes, hours or days. Miss this opportunity however and it's 'Game Over'. This was proven during the assassination of the German Banker. The CP team had 10 days from the moment the terrorists began setting up to the fatal execution in which to identify and disrupt terrorist activity.

Whilst some plots are thwarted at the last second, it cannot be stressed enough that all PSD personnel for the most part must detect and interdict the plan before it gets to the attack stage if they are to have any chance of stopping it. Once the bullets fly or the ambush is initiated there is little that your team can do except go through any SOP IA drills in an effort to mitigate the attack and to prevent any further casualties.

It has been frequently known that those who conduct terrorist surveillance tend to be quite sloppy in their tradecraft. This creates a significant vulnerability in the attack cycle.

Additional surveillance is often conducted at later stages of the attack cycle such as in the planning stage and even sometimes as late as the ambush itself. This is so that all previous surveillance intelligence can be confirmed or adjustments made to the final part of the op. This will provide your teams with an opportunity for the terrorists to be identified and hopefully prevent an attack.

24. **Terrorists Planning Cycle**

Terrorists have an option if operations are planned or underway in that they may be altered, delayed or cancelled due to changes made by the target or changes in local or environmental conditions. Tactical missions combine to compliment operational objectives and strategic goals. The psychological impact on the target is the overarching objective of any terrorist operation where a specific person has been identified. Target selection is covered further in this chapter but if there is to be any degree of success by the terrorist in their actions then their operation needs to be meticulously planned. There are generally seven stages to a terrorists planning cycle as outlined below in diagram 8.6.

Diagram 8.6

a. *Broad Target Selection.* This phase will be used as the collection of information on a number of specific targets. Information will be gathered from several sources including open source and general information. Potential targets will be screened based on intended objective and assesses areas such as symbolic value, critical infrastructure, mass casualties or the potential to generate high profile media attention. It must be stressed that the target numbers will be limited only by the capabilities of the terrorists to

Executive Protection – The Next Level

collect information. Targets which are considered to be vulnerable and which would further the goals of the terrorists are selected for the next phase of intelligence gathering.

b.   *Intelligence Gathering & Surveillance.*   Where there are signs of vulnerability with the target then additional attention may be given and a priority of effort. This effort will aim to establish the requirement to gather additional information on a target's patterns/routines over a given time period. This period could either be short or spread over a few years. Elements typically gathered would include:

   (1)   Practices/Procedures/Routines. This could include scheduled deliveries, shift changes, identification procedures and other actionable observations. For individuals, it could include car parking locations, laundry pickup points, scheduled errands etc.

   (2)   Transportation/Routes of Travel. Where the target is an individual this will relate to the mode of transport and common routes to any regular destination such as house, work, gym and school. Also egress and ingress points, and the types of vehicles allowed into the target area.

   (3)   Security Measures. This will cover many points but will include the complexity of the security around the target, presence of a CP detail, the reaction time of any QRF, any hardening of structures, barriers or sensors, personnel, package and vehicle screening procedures and the type and frequency of any emergency reaction drills are examples of key collection objectives. For an attack due to take place at a location, this is one of the most important areas of information since an intent is to bypass and avoid any security measures and be able to strike the target during any period.

c.   *Specific Target Selection.*   Once the target has been confirmed, then the actual operational planning will consider some of the following:

   (1)   Will a successful outcome affect a larger audience than the immediate target(s)?

   (2)   Will the target attract high profile media attention?

   (3)   Does a successful outcome make the desired statement to the correct audience?

   (4)   Is the effect consistent with the objectives of the group or random in its execution?

   (5)   Does the target provide an advantage to the group by demonstrating its capabilities?

   (6)   What are the overall costs versus benefits of carrying out the operation?

119

Whilst there is a lot of information gathered the decision to proceed will require continued surveillance and intelligence against the chosen target. Any target not receiving immediate consideration may still be collected against for future opportunities and consideration.

d. *Pre-attack Surveillance and Planning.* It is at this point that members of the actual operational cell begin to show their faces amongst the group. The attack team will confirm information gathered from previous surveillance and recee activities. Any areas of concern will essentially be the same as in the intelligence-gathering phase but with greater focus based on known or perceived vulnerabilities. The type of surveillance employed depends on the target's activities and if the target is seen as a 'Hard Target' then the planners will simply move onto the next target on the list. Any information gained could then be used to:

(1) Conduct security studies

(2) Conduct detailed preparatory operations.

(3) Recruit specialised operatives.

(4) Obtain a base of operations in the target area (safe houses, arms caches etc.)

(5) Design and test escape routes.

(6) Decide on type of weapon and attack location.

d. *Rehearsals.* As mentioned earlier on in this chapter, terrorists tend to plan an operation similar to that of any military operation. Rehearsals are conducted to improve the odds of success, confirming planning assumptions, and to develop contingencies. It is not unusual for terrorists to use both their own people and unsuspecting people to test target reactions. A typical rehearsal will include:

(1) Equipment and weapon training and performance.

(2) Staging for the final preparatory checks.

(3) Deployment into target area.

(4) Actions on the target

(5) Escape routes.

Terrorists will also carry out tests within the target area to confirm:

(1) The validity of the target information gathered to date.

(2) The validity of the targets pattern of activities/routines.

(3) Physical layout of the target site or operational area.

(4)   Security force reactions for RST or CP detail such as state of alert, response timing, equipment and routes.

e.   *Actions and Objectives.*   At this point it should be noted that the odds favour a successful attack against the target and that the terrorists possess important tactical advantages. As the attacker they possess all the advantages of initiative and provide:

(1)   Element of surprise

(2)   Choosing of time, place and conditions of the attack.

(4)   The implementation of any diversions and secondary or follow-up attacks.

(4)   Deployment of secondary security and support positions to neutralise any QRF response and security measures.

It is highly likely that because of the extensive preparation through both surveillance and reconnaissance that any responsive security measures would be factored into the terrorists planning with a view to neutralising at the outset of the ambush.

f.   *Escape and Exploitation.*   The terrorists will ensure that any escape plans they intend to introduce will be both well executed and rehearsed. The exception to this of course will be the suicide bomber. An escape plan will still be part of the planning since each suicide bomber will usually have a handler or support personnel and they will require to escape or evade any attack by a a QRF or PSD.

The primary objective of the operation will be exploitation. It will be important for the terrorists that the operation must be properly publicised to achieve the intended effect. This of course in return will assist in funding, bring favourable attention, notoriety and support.

Unsuccessful operations are disavowed as soon as possible. A failed operation creates the perception that the group have failed which may severely damage the organisations prestige, ineffective conduct or shows vulnerabilities.

Regardless of whether the attack is a suicide attack against a church in Siberia or a timed incendiary attack in Athens then the attack cycle will be exactly the same. With a view to thwarting future attacks, the PSD can use the attack model to understand how an attack will be planned and executed.

25.   **CP Perspective in Reducing the Leverage to the Terrorists**

If you receive no warning that an attack is about to take place or you are unable to identify the attacker, the PSD will have very little leverage available to the team in order to defend the attack. This was researched and documented by Atif Ahmad from the University of Melbourne who gave me kind permission to reproduce some of his work. Your PSD will not know with any degree of certainty the timing of the attack in which case they are likely to be caught off-guard and unprepared and in a location to their disadvantage. In most situations, the attack is deliberately chosen to exploit the vulnerabilities of the target or PSD. This tactic will work in the favour of the terrorist and will reduce the likelihood of an effective defensive strategy by the PSD. All route reconnaissance reports will show various routes that are deemed vulnerable for the many reasons set out earlier. It will be up to you as supervisors or team leaders to decide the best course given the nature of any vulnerabilities identified. You will also need to decide how best to mitigate the chances of an event-taking place.

Fig 8.1 below shows that the situation puts control well and truly in the hands of the terrorist.

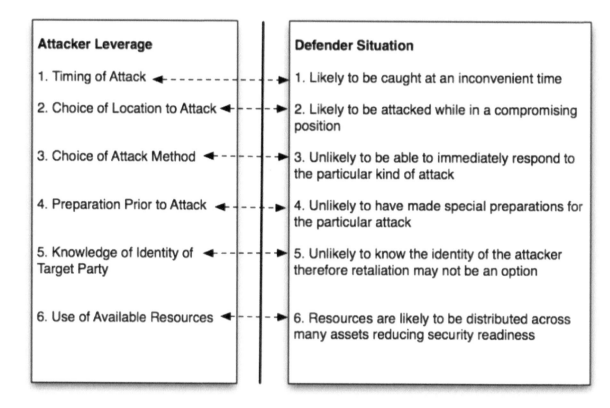

Attacker Leverage

1. Timing of Attack

2. Choice of Location to Attack

3. Choice of Attack Method

4. Preparation Prior to Attack

5. Knowledge of Identity of Target Party

6. Use of Available Resources

Defender Situation

1. Likely to be caught at an inconvenient time

2. Likely to be attacked while in a compromising position

3. Unlikely to be able to immediately respond to the particular kind of attack

4. Unlikely to have made special preparations for the particular attack

5. Unlikely to know the identity of the attacker therefore retaliation may not be an option

6. Resources are likely to be distributed across many assets reducing security readiness

Fig. 8.1

Fig. 8.2 goes someway in addressing this in balance and to try and swing some of it back into the hands of the PSD. By applying simple procedures, which all CP personnel should already know will go a long way to moving the odds away from the terrorist.

The professionalism of your team on the ground is a major obstacle to any terror group who may see the hardened ring fence of security you have around the client as being problematic. They may decide at this point to move to their secondary target or they may be stubborn enough to think that the high value of your client is worth the risks.

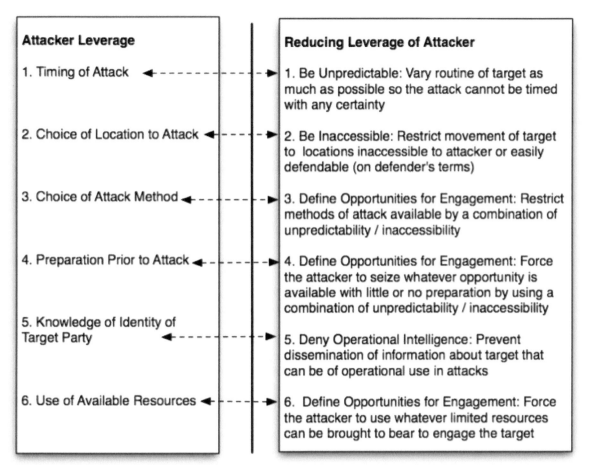

Fig. 8.2

The graph shown at fig. 8.3 below describes the leverage to the terrorist after the event has taken place. Whilst anonymity is often the case, there is a growing trend to admit an atrocity especially if it has an overwhelming impact. At the point where t=<0 then the PSD have no warning and very few advantages to thwart the attack if nothing has been identified through anti-surveillance. The terrorist will be in control at this point and as the diagram at para 24 above (attack Cycle) shows that you only have three possible chances to stop an attack from taking place in the first instance.

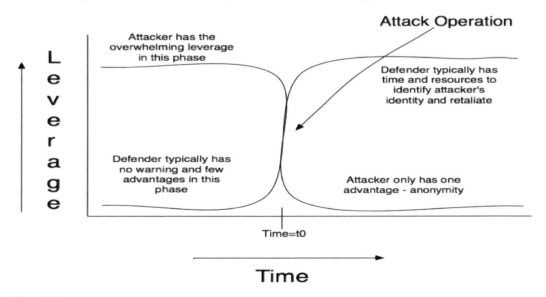

Fig. 8.3

Fig. 8.3 above shows that in times of conflict, the choice of timing, location, method of attack, best use of resources and time to prepare, all allows the terrorist leverage against an adversary. After an event takes place however, these advantages fall squarely on the defenders shoulders as a follow up investigation takes place.

Whilst there is considerable leverage in the terrorist favour, there is much the PSD can do to restrict and minimise the leverage the terrorists have. It will be necessary for the PSD to create a carefully designed defensive system that will maximise the PSD's advantages; it could be the case that you may feel it necessary to place obstacles or challenges in the way of terrorists to inhibit their planning. This could be by the use of dummy vehicles, changing the client vehicle to be at the front instead of the standard configuration or additional SAP vehicles to scout the route and many more. Some clients are understanding of the risks against them and others won't change their ways and they expect you to provide security regardless. It has to be said though that there is no 100% guarantee that security will be 100% effective all of the time.

26.   **Target Selection**

This chapter has covered a substantial amount of surveillance as both background information and how best to apply surveillance to your teams' everyday operation. It is a major logistical event for terrorists and without surveillance they wouldn't be able to strike with efficiency and confidence. Terrorists will plan their operation in a similar manner to how the military would conduct such an operation. It's both tried and tested and it is often said that '*Any plan will often fail when it first comes into contact with the enemy*'. This is merely due to the unpredictability of the target or security team. It's worth understanding the stages of a terrorist operation and target selection is part of the bigger picture of the attack cycle. Table 8.4 below outlines such an operation.

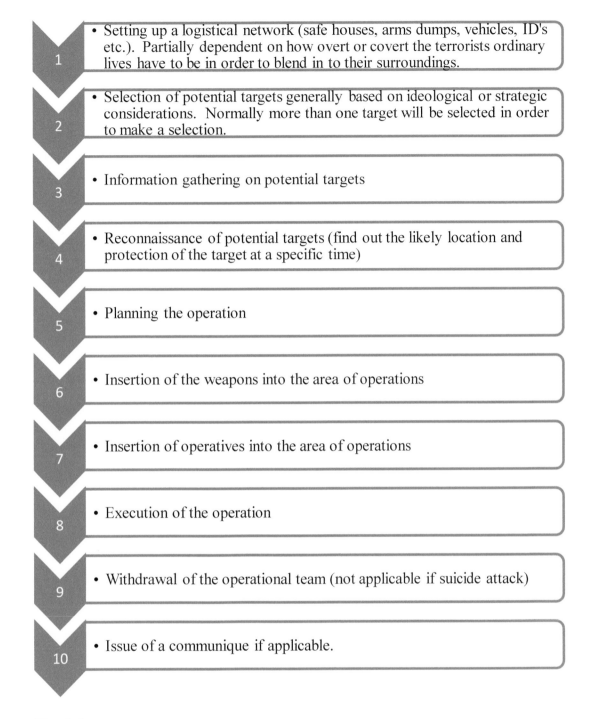

1 • Setting up a logistical network (safe houses, arms dumps, vehicles, ID's etc.). Partially dependent on how overt or covert the terrorists ordinary lives have to be in order to blend in to their surroundings.

2 • Selection of potential targets generally based on ideological or strategic considerations. Normally more than one target will be selected in order to make a selection.

3 • Information gathering on potential targets

4 • Reconnaissance of potential targets (find out the likely location and protection of the target at a specific time)

5 • Planning the operation

6 • Insertion of the weapons into the area of operations

7 • Insertion of operatives into the area of operations

8 • Execution of the operation

9 • Withdrawal of the operational team (not applicable if suicide attack)

10 • Issue of a communique if applicable.

Fig. 8.4

27. **Conclusion**

Surveillance cannot be emphasised enough and it is vitally important that all those under your command are well versed in the aspects of this topic. As was mentioned at the start of this chapter, the measures introduced here are to be applied in some instances especially ***Passive*** surveillance that should be used at all times. If the goal posts change and information has been received that the situation has escalated, then the CP Team will move up a gear and become ***Active***. Detection early on by the CP Team will not only give the team the knowledge that their client is of interest but it may also dissuade those watching from making any move. If you're complacent you'll have problems identifying any real threat until it's too late.

This is just one part of your duties as a CPO. You should have a good working knowledge of surveillance methodology which should include:

- o Know the purpose of surveillance
- o Know the techniques used
- o Know the tell-tale signs
- o Know how to spot surveillants without them knowing
- o Know the general capabilities of surveillance

Consider the following acronym T E D D [i] that is expanded upon below at Fig. 8.5:

T *Time*
E *Environment*
D *Distance*
D *Demeanour*

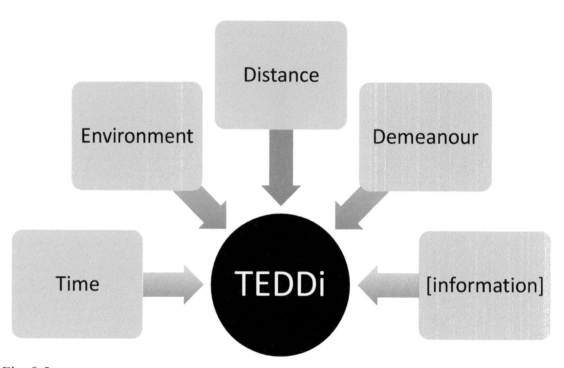

Fig. 8.5

Time – If you see the same individual at disparate times, it will become obvious to you that you have seen the same person not once, not twice but three times. You will begin to wonder what are the chances of this recurrence of either vehicle or individual(s)? If you see them again after a period of time you should start to begin thinking surveillance.

Environment – This is another characteristic that you should pick up on subconsciously. If you're out shopping and you see a female with purple hair window-shopping for high heels one minute and then you travel to another store and you see the same female checking out at the counter next to you then this should provoke suspicion. If you then see her again at the fish counter in Harrods then you will begin to look at everyone around you – the worst nightmare of a surveillance team.

Distance – If you see an individual in one place, travel a long distance to another and see that person again you will soon realise that the statistical probability of two people travelling the same long distance and ending up at exactly the same spot is pretty low. This will be particularly apparent with distinguishable vehicles. If a bright coloured neon yellow Jeep Cherokee with a tailgate and oversized tyres is driving in front of you in one place and then you travel a hundred miles and you see it parked across the street the you should start to connect the dots and think surveillance. Real surveillance may not be that obvious but just general vehicle attributes such as stickers or damage can be useful in this regard.

Demeanour – This is the last element of the TEDD acronym. This is what surveillants train most to avoid triggering, so you will probably not notice as much with trained surveillance. However, you may still catch surveillants in the midst of a burn syndrome attack. When noticed they may look shocked or surprised and then ashamed or even horrified (primarily at the thought that they just burned the whole surveillance operation), and then turn suddenly to get away from you. With untrained surveillance this burn syndrome can be common. When noticed, however minor it may be, this is a strong indicator of surveillance activity.

Putting all this together, if you observe someone repeatedly over a period of time, in different environments and at a distance or someone who displays poor surveillance skills then you can pretty much assume that you, the team or the client are under surveillance.

TEDD is best utilised in surveillance awareness by paying attention to the details of everyone around you. Notice people, faces, postures, scars, gaits, movements and anything that is distinguishable. An inherent part of surveillance trade craft is to change the surveillants 'silhouette', by donning different wigs, fat suits, hats, clothing styles, fake tattoos, nose rings, jewellery, gaits, movement styles and baseline facial expressions.

A last latter which could be added to TEDD is 'i', for information. Surveillance gathers information on you. When they deal with as much information as they gather, sometimes it can be difficult for them to keep track of what they know about you and what they shouldn't.

One consistent theme in surveillance detection is that detection is rarely dispositive when dealing with early covert phase of surveillance. Indeed, a normal person will be conditioned to consciously dismiss those indices that they do see, to avoid being paranoid. If someone looks at you and then they look away ashamed, it is more tempting to think that they noticed you by accident than thinking you have a highly trained team around you. Whilst you are likely to dismiss this event, it should be something that you could recall at a later date. The key is to accept the uncertainty, or even the improbability inherent to such subtle indications. You can't know what you don't know thus all possibilities must be accepted as possible.

In addition, for the CP teams to continue reviewing their environment, the only other fairly reliable way to detect surveillance is by using surveillance detection techniques and understanding how surveillance operates. This will allow the teams to understand how and what is occurring around them that might make sense in the context of a set of standard procedures and decisions made by a surveillance team.

Understanding how surveillance teams think and operate can allow you the opportunity to notice patterns that are inherent to their operations. As an example, surveillance that is following you will often not follow you. Everyone who thinks they are going to be surveilled will watch their rear view mirror. For that reason, the primary car following you, or in command of you, will often be right in front of you in what is called 'a cheating command'. It will hand off command to another car by allowing that car to turn into your lane, in front of it before turning off itself or allowing you to pass.

In another example, to avoid Distance violations of TEDD, larger surveillance operations will sector surveillance. This is where all specific cars will be located within a sector. These cars will hand you off to each other as you move around so that you won't notice the same BMW has been following you in disparate locations. It is likely that if you see the same vehicle in the same area a few times then you may think that he hangs around here. However, if you notice the same cars around you in one area and then the same cars in another you can probably understand why phased coverage would be beneficial to the surveillance team. This is only possible by the teams being able to understand surveillance procedures and seeing the world through the eyes of the surveillance teams.

If you don't understand any of the above, then you will be unable to carry out your duties effectively and efficiently. Just because nothing happened one day is not the premise that nothing will happen any other day. The only easy day was yesterday. Being prepared will create instinctive reactions from individuals or the team collectively and hopefully will win the day. Training in aspects of these techniques is therefore crucial and clients would expect your professionalism to be at the high end of your employment. Being fully prepared in this industry in both knowledge and skills is key to your success and safety of your client.

Remember, no client means no job and you don't want to be that one CPO who is remembered for the wrong reasons by losing the client on your watch.

Whilst the examples reflected upon in this chapter are aged, there is one constituent part that remains modern throughout all of this and that is Surveillance…

If you don't believe that you are being watched, you will have no motivation to act appropriately – BELIEVE IT

"In making tactical dispositions, the highest pitch you can attain is to conceal them"

Sun Tzu

Carrying out Vehicle Attacks – What is The Target Selection Process (Examples of Real Scenarios) By A. Scotti

Phase One

The selection process is a series of steps taken by terrorists to develop a list of potential targets. The criteria the terrorists use to select targets in this initial phase vary. In some countries, being a foreigner is enough to get you included into this category. In others, they single out either military, members of the business community or wealthy individuals. At this stage, there may be more than one target selected primarily to establish which are soft or hard targets. You will never know at this stage whether or not you have been selected and there is little to avoid at this phase of selection.

The selection of many prominent targets and those working in high-risk environments are on the list. Surveillance will eliminate the hard to get and this should in effect be your CLIENT. The following phases of examples will use more surveillance on the selected targets until they eliminate all and then select the weakest.

Phase Two

Now that the terrorists have selected their targets, they move onto the phase two. They will carefully run the potential victims through a well-designed and thorough selection process. They will, through meticulous surveillance gather information about the lifestyle of their targets. The purpose of the surveillance is to gather as much background and intelligence to successfully complete the operation. This is another part of the process that cannot be avoided and is the most important stage of the process. It is the part of the process where the terrorists decide whether to leave the potential targets name on/off the list. If they are looking for eight people you can rest assured that one of these will stick out that is a person who is not security minded and is much easier to attack than everyone else. If they decide to list a group of individuals who are security conscious, it comes down to a test of 'who has the weakest security' and it's not rocket science to suggest that the one with the weakest security will fail. This places and extra burden on the CP team to ensure they are aware of their surroundings at all times whether in low or high threat situations. Both demand awareness but at different levels and intensity.

The best way to get off a terrorists list is to make the target hard to get. Be professional and alert at all times and don't let your standards drop. Report anything suspicious but without making it obvious that you may have spotted your surveillants. The fact that nothing has happened one-day just means it has been put off until another. We have to plan for the worst and hope for the best.

Phase Three

Once they have selected a group of targets and conducted the surveillance on them, they will initiate phase three and making the final decision on who the actual target will be. Terrorists will make a risk versus success assessment. If they feel one target is easier than another they will focus their efforts on the person that offers the least risk and the highest possible return for a successful outcome. This stage is a good argument against the asinine comment *'if they want me they're going to get me anyway so why have protection or take any precautions.'* This is a self-fulfilling prophecy. The issue here is that in many cases they don't want that particular person they initially selected, it is just that person happens to make himself or herself an easy target. Terrorists must rely on the victim's complete unawareness of what's going on around them. They will narrow down the group to a chosen few.

Phase Four – The Final Piece

They will conduct more surveillance. It may take weeks, possibly months or even years to gather all the information especially if the target is a complex person. The victim's movements will be analysed and patterns of habit scrutinised. The most important piece of information they will produce is any daily routine movements and timings etc. This time schedule will accurately outline the target's every move during the daily routine so that they can guarantee with some degree of certainty that the target will be in a certain place at a certain time. One of the first things they will document is the type of vehicle being used by the victim and his security detail including VRN, colour, make etc. They will also note the number of security personnel and what positions they take up when driving/walking etc. They will take photographs to support their findings and to present to any briefings. Other facts that will be of interest:

- What time does he leave for work/shopping etc
- Does he always play tennis at the same time and on the same day
- What time does he go for lunch and where
- Does he drive himself
- Is anyone armed

They will know the victim's routine better than himself as the victim will tend to do it simply as a routine. A final risk assessment will be taken to ensure that the element of surprise will be in the terrorists favour at all times.

Case Study of Two Surveillance Examples by A. Scotti

Aldo Moro

Aldo Morrow is a classic case. It is very old but nevertheless a valuable piece of reference. The kidnapping of the highly respected elder statesman of Italian politics, Aldo Morrow shocked the world. It would've been similar to the kidnapping of ex-presidents Ford, Nixon, Carter or Reagan at the time. The entire country of Italy came to a standstill. Shortly after 0900 on 9 May '78, having stopped at a nearby church for communion, Moro was en-route to Parliament in his dark blue Fiat 130. He went to the same church and at the same time each morning. He established a pattern that was easy to figure out. Every morning you could count on Moro being in the same place at the same time. In the Fiat were his driver and a CPO. Three CPOs followed in a white Alfa Romeo. As the vehicles moved through a fashionable hotel district and approached an inter-section, a car bearing diplomatic plates pulled ahead of the Fiat and stopped suddenly at the inter-section. Moro's driver applied the brakes sharply and so abruptly that the chase vehicle hit Moro's vehicle hard.

The driver and passenger of the blocking car got out as if to check as to whether any damage had been caused. Approaching Moro's car from both sides they pulled out pistols and shot the driver and CPO who was sat in the front seat of Moro's car. Both were killed instantly.

Prior to the incident being executed, four men dressed in Alitalia uniforms had been standing at the inter-section as though waiting for a bus. As the action commenced, they crossed over to the cars and pulled out automatic weapons from their flight bags. They fired at the CPOs in the chase car killing two of them instantly. The third CPO rolled out of the car onto the street and was able to get three shots off before he was neutralized by a fatal shot from a sniper on a nearby roof.

The obvious planning and attention to detail in this kidnapping was remarkable even when compared to the precision tactics of other kidnappings.

Target selection by terrorists is crucial. If they feel that they have a hard target to carry out surveillance and execution then it is likely they will move on. It has to be said here that Moro was not the initial target. The man the Red Brigade wanted to get was driving in an armoured car and his CPOs followed in another armoured vehicle. He changed his routes all the time and his CPOs were well armed. During the selection process for the final target, the terrorists decided that the original target was too hard to get and would in effect be a costly attack with no certain outcome of a victory for the Brigade. In the end they went for the easier target – Moro.

Sidney Reso – President of Exxon International

On Apr 29, 1992, the president of Exxon International, Sidney Reso left his house for his usual trip to work. He made the decision to drive himself to work and not to have a driver pick him up for his daily morning trip to work. He stopped his car at the end of his 250-foot driveway to retrieve the newspaper. When he got out, a white van pulled in front of his car. A man in a ski mask covering his face stepped in front of Reso and forced him into the van. According to the kidnapper, once Reso was in the van he (Reso) was accidentally shot in the arm.

The kidnappers took Reso to a public storage area where they had rented a garage in February. They had already made a box with ventilation holes in it for Reso to breath. The box was 6'4" long, 3'high and 3'6" wide and the top opened with hinges. During this period, Reso's eyes and mouth were covered with tape and a sleeping bag and blankets had been put into the box to make him comfortable. Twice a day they would give him crushed vitamins and have him make recorded messages but unfortunately he died five days later possibly due to an infection in his wound. However, some three years earlier, Reso had suffered a heart attack which may have contributed to his death also. Once he was dead, they took his body to a secluded area of New Jersey and buried him. 12 hrs after his death, the kidnappers demanded $18.5 million. His death was not discovered until Jun, 1992 when the kidnappers were apprehended and one of them broke down and confessed to the kidnapping.

The main brains behind the kidnap was Arthur Seal, an ex Exxon employee who was an ex police officer who worked in the security department at Exxon. He left the company in 1987 and moved to another state and started his own business that soon began to have financial problems and went broke and Seal left that state owing close to $1,000,000. He conceived the plan to kidnap an Exxon executive with his wife Irene in order to pay off his huge debts. He followed a number of executives until he decided on Reso. He picked Reso because he thought Reso would be easier to get to than other executives and he was also known as 'Mr Exxon' and was probably worth more than the others. He made the decision after reviewing the routine of many other executives. Although Seal wasn't the classic terrorist he nevertheless followed the classic guidelines for selecting and executing the operation.

The decision to kidnap Reso was decided upon in Dec, 1991 and was seen as an easy way to get out of debt. They researched the homes and routines of several Exxon executives and decided to pick the house that offered the most seclusion and that house was Reso's. They watched the house for the next several months and in February they rented a storage facility where they hoped to keep Reso until the ransom money had been paid. They initially wanted to kidnap Reso in the middle of the week and have their money by the week-end and several times they were ready to kidnap Reso but had to abort due to a change in his routine.

Although the kidnappers were not terrorists by normal standards, they used the same procedures for selecting their targets. This could very well have been due to the background of Seal and his role of security at Exxon and at one time or another he was involved with the protection of executives. The first message sent to Exxon from Seal said that the kidnappers were from the '*Fernando Peireira Brigade Warriors, warriors of the Rainbow*'. Fernando Peireira was a Greenpeace activist who was killed in 1985 when French agents sank the Greenpeace ship Rainbow Warrior. Seal had done his homework.

Attacks Whilst Mobile by A. Scotti
(Examples of Real Scenarios)

Orvile Gunduz

Orvile Gunduz was the Turkish Consulate General in Boston. After his place of business was bombed, he received a warning from the Armenian Terrorist Group that 'They were going to assassinate him next'. As he drove home from work, he had to drive by a construction area that required traffic to drive slowly around a particular bend. A single terrorist was waiting for him at this choke point. On May 4, 1982 in Somerville, USA as Orvile turned the corner, the terrorist fired a 9mm hand gun into the driver's window, killing Gunduz. His car rolled to a stop against a fence, where the terrorist then took a .357 magnum and fired a shot off into the ear of Gunduz. He dropped the 9mm and walked calmly down the hill into a waiting car. There is a shop at the bottom of the hill, which had an active CCTV camera, and this captured the terrorist sitting in the shop calmly having a cup of coffee and occasionally looking at his watch prior to the incident being executed. The terrorist had Gunduz's routine down to a predictable pattern.

Gen. Lico Girogieri

The victim, Gen. Lico Girogieri, was assassinated while being driven home in his chauffeur driven vehicle. On Mar 21, 1987 while driving along a dimly lit, narrow street, when two men on a motorcycle travelling behind Gen. Girogieri's vehicle flashed their headlights as though they were going to pass the victims vehicle. The assassins were riding an all-terrain motorcycle and helmets covered their faces. The driver pulled over to the right to let them pass and when his vehicle slowed down, they fired a revolver into the back window of the General's vehicle. They then pulled alongside the victim's vehicle and opened fire into the back of his car. The General was hit in the neck and chest. The victim stopped the car and the two motorcyclists climbed off the bike and fired into the back seat of the car. The time of the attack was approx. 1730hrs and the general was working on the Star Wars project at the time.

Antonio da Empoli

On Feb 22, 1986, four members of the Red Brigade wounded a top official from the Italian Government. As he was being driven to work by his CPO security driver, Antonio, an economic aide, was shot twice in the leg and once in the hand. The shooting occurred as Empoli stepped out of his vehicle to buy his morning newspaper. He bought the paper at a newsstand near his home every morning. As his attackers rushed towards Empoli, his driver/CPO shouted to Empoli to duck and get under a nearby parked car. He sped forwards towards the terrorists, jumped out of his car and returned fire. He killed one of the terrorists, a female in the neck (she was wearing a bullet-proof vest). The other terrorists fled on motorcycles.

Pinochet

Whilst driving home from his weekend retreat in the foothills of Ardenan the motorcade of President Pinochet's was attacked by approx. twelve gunmen who were laying in wait. As the motorcade crossed a bridge, a car with a trailer spun in front of the convoy. Three of the cars in the motorcade were blown up as they sat on the bridge. The gunmen fired at the motorcade with automatic weapons, hand grenades and rockets. The end result was five dead and nine injured. When the attack started, Pinochet dropped to the floor of his Mercedes, covering his 10-year-old grandson. Pinochet's bodyguard's returned fire in what Pinochet described as an 'Intense gun battle'

Sgt Judd

On Apr 3, 1984, at approx. 1700 as he was driving along his mail route, Sgt Judd was shot by two men riding a motorcycle. The shooting occurred while Sgt Judd was delivering mail between the US embassy and Hellinker Air Base on the outskirts of Athens. The attack occurred just six days after the attack on Ken Whitty, head of the British Council in Athens, Greece. The gunmen drove alongside Judd's vehicle and started to fire into his vehicle. Judd was shot in the back and right hand. This gave rise to believe that the gunmen fired too soon without a clear shot at their target. Judd escaped by the mere fact that he kept his vehicle moving and did not stop.

Antonio Somoza Deboyle

On Sep 17, 1980 at approx. 1005 at Ascuncion, Paraguay, Somoza, his driver and financial adviser were travelling towards the centre of town in Somoza's non-armoured vehicle. Driving behind his vehicle was his four CPOs in another vehicle. The attack took place as Somoza's cars passed a house that had been rented one month earlier by terrorists. As Somoza passed the house, a stolen truck pulled out from the rented house and blocked his way. The occupants of the truck fired at Somoza's vehicle. A 2nd group fired at his vehicle from the house. A terrorist in front of the house fired a rocket at Somoza's vehicle. There was an exchange of gunfire with the terrorists and the CPOs in the back up vehicle. The terrorists fled on foot once their objective had been successful.

Two Attacks with Different Outcomes by A. Scotti

Just how important it is for a CP Team Leader/CP Ops Manager to be able to recognise the indicators and warnings associated with various threats and understand the capabilities of potential attackers. The answers can be found by taking a close look at two attacks that took place in 2006 & 2008. One was unsuccessful and not widely publicised whilst the other was successful and made headlines around the world for a short period of time. The two attacks are explained below:

Attack # 1

This attack was against Manuel Diaz Lerma, the Secretary of Public Safety for the Mexican State of Baja, which took place on April 22, 2008 in Mexacali, Mexico. That morning, Secretary Lerma became the highest level Mexican official to be attacked in the on-going struggle between gangs of drug smugglers and Police officials on both sides of the border between the US and Mexico. The attack was launched as Secretary Lerma's two-vehicle motorcade travelled along the route towards his office. Lerma and his security team came under heavy fire from at least ten, and perhaps as many as twenty assailants armed with assault rifles and at least one grenade launcher. The attack continued along a five to six block stretch of route as the motorcade tried to make its way to safe houses of the local State Police facilities nearby.

While Lerma himself was unhurt, three members of his security detail riding in the follow vehicle were injured. Eyewitness reports and the statements given by the security detail show that this was a well-planned attack. If Lerma had not been riding in an armoured vehicle, the attack may just have been successful. As with most attacks, there are indications that trouble was coming Lerma's way both long before and immediately prior to the attack.

Fig. 8.6

During a raid early in 2008, Police in Tijuana recovered a list containing names of Public Officials and State Police Officers that were being targeted for assassination. Manuel Diaz Lerma's name was at the top of that list. This was a serious development, first because no one had ever attempted to assassinate a Mexican Official that high up in the food chain and secondly, because the six men arrested in the raid were believed to be connected with a gang leader that had already claimed responsibility for the assassination of the Director of Public Safety of Beaches for Rosarito. Then on the morning of the attack, members of Mr Lerma's security detail spotted men dressed in military style uniforms, wearing body armour, hoods and carrying assault rifles at various locations along the route they were travelling. It wasn't long after this sighting that the ambush was sprung. During the attack, his vehicle was struck numerous times by large calibre rifle rounds and at least once by fragments from a grenade. Eventually, his vehicle was disabled by a flat tyre forcing the driver to slow the vehicle down in order to maintain control. The driver of the PES vehicle was alert and as soon as he saw the client's vehicle slowing down he manoeuvred his vehicle alongside it to provide additional cover for the client seated inside.

There are a number of lessons that can be learned at the very least, strongly reinforced from this first attack:

- *You Need the Right Tools for the Job.* This is appropriate commensurate with levels of threat at the time. In this attack though, both the target and the attackers seem to have been reading off the same page. Lerma was riding in a heavily armoured SUV capable of withstanding multiple hits from 7.62mm rounds and the vehicle did exactly what it was designed to do – give the driver time to drive away from the 'Kill Zone'. The attackers brought some pretty serious hardware to the fight including large calibre assault rifles and at least one grenade launcher. It's obvious that Lerma and his security team took the threats seriously. Despite the fact that no one had ever attacked a Secretary Level official, Lerma's vehicle offered protection against what some would say was a low probability scenario. Whilst the PES may not have even considered that exact scenario when developing their plan, they were properly equipped to deal with just such an attack.

- *The Attack Begins Long Before the First Gunshot.* The fact that Lerma was on the hit list and that the attack was carried out by a large group who directed most of the rounds at the client's vehicle, are all indicators that the attackers had done their homework. While it is difficult to say for sure, in this case it is entirely possible that the attackers had access to both inside information regarding his security operation and had surveillance in place leading up to the attack. This would have allowed them to know which vehicle the target was travelling in, the route they were taking that morning and where along that route would be the best place to execute their objective.

- *Training, Training, Training.* During the attack, which lasted for minutes, not seconds, the client's vehicle was hit multiple times, at least once by grenade fragments and was partially disabled by a flat tyre. Despite all of this, the drivers of both vehicles did exactly what was needed to be done to ensure the survival of their client. First, they kept the vehicles moving through the 'Kill Zone' and secondly, when the lead vehicle had to slow down due to the flat tyre, the PES driver placed his vehicle – which was not armoured – in a position to provide as much protection as possible for the client. Experience dictates that in a situation like this there is no such thing as coincidence. These drivers were well trained and while they may not have planned for, nor expected an attack this intense, they nevertheless had thought through what they would do if the client's vehicle was ever disabled by an attack. It was probably the actions of both drivers who played a major part in Lerma's survival.

Attack # 2

As mentioned earlier, the second attack was more widely publicised than the incident that took place in Mexico (Lerma), at least for a day or so after the attack. In this case, the successful assassination of the Lebanese Industry Minister, Pierre Gemayel, is similar in at least one aspect to one of the most studied assassinations in modern time, the killing of Alfred Herrhausen, the German Banker with Deutche Bank (***Briefly mentioned in SOP 21)***. In this instance, security was focused on protecting against one specific type of attack and unfortunately, the attackers were able to achieve success by simply launching a different type of attack than was expected.

Pierre Gemayel is not the first high profile, anti-Syrian political figure to be killed in Lebannon in recent years. In fact, he is not the first member of his family to be killed in a politically motivated attack. His uncle, Bashir Gemayel was killed in 1982 shortly after being elected as President and three of his cousins, including Bashir's daughter were killed over the years as well. However, the attack against Pierre Gemayel was unique in a number of ways. Particularly when you consider that his actions prior to the attack indicated he understood that he was a potential target and that security precautions were a necessity. Looking at the attack itself, it becomes clear that this was a deliberate, well-planned attack and executed by an experienced team of assassins.

On the day of the attack on Nov 21, 2006, Mr Gemayel was not riding in the armoured BMW he owned. Instead, he chose to drive a non-descript KIA sedan with tinted windows. He was however accompanied by his personal bodyguard, who was riding in the front seat of the car at the time of the attack. Also in the vehicle was an officer from the Lebanese State Security Services who was riding in the back with Pierre Gemayel when the attack was launched. There are suggestions that Gemayel may have been trying to keep a low profile and blending in with the day-to-day background of daily life in Beirut. As his vehicle moved through a crowded intersection in one of Beirut's busiest neighbourhoods, it was hit head on by a Honda CRV and then in the right rear by another compact car and almost simultaneously by a van directly from the rear. Within just a couple of seconds, the non-armoured vehicle Gemayel was driving was completely boxed in and three gunmen jumped out of the Honda and opened fire at close range. The attackers concentrated their efforts on Gemayel in the driver's seat and his bodyguard in the front passenger seat. The shots fired at Gemayel through the side window were well aimed and it seems obvious that the attackers were practiced shooters who knew exactly where the target would be sitting in the vehicle.

Fig. 8.7

Fig. 8.8

As was the case with the attack against the Mexican Secretary of Public Safety when you sift through the details of the attack it provided some useful information and reinforces some of the lessons learned from previous vehicle ambushes:

- ***Successful Attacks are Intelligence Driven***   Given the timing, complexity and accuracy of the attack, it's obvious that the attackers knew what vehicle Gemayel was in, that he would be behind the wheel as opposed to sitting in the rear and exactly where the vehicle would be at a given point and time. Whilst some of the information needed to formulate the plan conclusively may have come from the inside, this ambush required split second timing, a high degree of familiarity with the surrounding area and a viable escape and evasion plan. Conducting extensive surveillance of the target, the route and the ambush site can only develop this. An insider can give you the who, what, where and when, but what they can't tell you is the best place to stage vehicles or what to expect in an around the ambush site before, during and after the attack.

- ***Expect the Unexpected***   Several sources suggest that Mr Gemayel was concerned that he would be the target of a massive IED, like the ones that killed his uncle and more recently, Prime Minister al-Hariri, and that his armoured BMW made him an easily identifiable target while still leaving him vulnerable to an IED attack. This would certainly explain his choice of vehicle that day. However, just like Herrhausen, whose security was configured to protect against kidnapping and not the roadside bomb that ultimately killed him. Gemayel's attempt to protect against an IED attack by lowering his profile and driving a non-descript vehicle left him vulnerable to the rolling ambush and small arms fire that took his life. Whilst it is virtually impossible to plan for every conceivable attack, those in positions of operational planning should make every effort to find out exactly what capabilities an attacker might have as well as what sort of attack the client might be vulnerable to, despite existing security measures.

- ***High Value Targets are High Profile Targets***   One of the most important lessons to be taken from the Gemayel assassination is that keeping a low profile only works if the client is truly a low profile person. Those who are famous (or infamous) have achieved a certain level of notoriety or are subject to media exposure are not, by definition, low profile. Therefore, they cannot rely on simply lowering their profile to adequately protect themselves against serious threats. Even in Beirut, the sight of a man moving about with two armed escorts would make people take notice, something you want to avoid if you want to blend in.

Conclusion

These two attacks should remind us that those who have a legitimate need for Close Protection are subject to risks no matter where in the world they may happen to live or work. They also remind us that there is no such thing as a risk-free environment or a foolproof security plan. Together, these attacks – one in which the client survived and one in which the attack was successful – also provide some additional considerations for planners to think about. These follow below:

- ***Honour the Threat***   This is the term often used by fighter pilots when discussing aerial combat against multiple targets. What it means is that you must take action to address the most immediate threat first. In the attack on Lerma, it appears that he and his security team did just that. Despite the fact that an attack against someone at his level had never been attempted before, they took specific precautions against the potential threat posed by a well-planned, large-scale attack and in doing so, ensured his survival.

On the other hand, while Mr Gemayel was certainly aware of the risks he faced, he failed to consider that the attackers had the time, resources and capability to launch nearly any type of attack they wished. Because of who he was and his position in the government it was virtually impossible to lower his security profile enough to deter an attack and, when all said and done, his attempt to blend in ended up making him even more vulnerable. Whilst it is true to say that the armoured vehicle he had at his disposal could not protect him against an IED, the un-armoured vehicle he chose when killed couldn't have protected him in a traffic accident, let alone a deliberate rolling ambush. At some point in time, those who intended to inflict harm on him had figured that out for themselves.

- ▪ *If the Vehicle Stops You Lose*   Time and time again it is apparent that when it comes to attacks against someone riding in a vehicle the worst possible scenario is for the vehicle to come to a stop in the kill zone. Even in attacks on an armoured vehicle, once the vehicle is immobilised the attackers have a huge advantage because they have gained control over the movement of the target. Lerma's drivers kept their vehicle moving and in doing so, defeated a well-planned attack. On the other hand, the first step in the Gemayel attack was to stop the vehicle with a head on crash and once that had happened the attackers success was virtually assured.

- ▪ *There Is No One-Size Fits All Solution* Threats are subject to change; often the threat changes in response to new or different security measures. In order to stay ahead of changing threats, the Cp Ops Manager and CP Team Leaders must constantly gather information and intelligence regarding potential threats, the tactics and techniques favoured by certain groups and the security measures that may or may not work against those threats. It must be kept in mind that attackers tend to do their homework as well. In the past it has been proven that various groups study attacks and share their information and lessons amongst themselves, a process that is made much easier by modern communications and computer technology. It is also important to recognise that the attacks and techniques commonly used in Close Protection Operations are not closely guarded or well kept secrets. At this point, literally tens of thousands of people have been trained in the methodology used by the private security sector and quite a few government protection teams and some of these operatives have ended up playing for the other team…

- ▪ *Surveillance Detection is Critical*   In both of the attacks mentioned above, it is apparent that surveillance of the target and the route played a critical role in the attack planning process. In fact, since the mid-60's when Carlos Marighella's Mini-Manual for the Urban Guerrilla was popular reading for leftist groups throughout Latin America and Europe, pre-attack surveillance is something that many groups have relied heavily on throughout their planning process. That is why it is essential for operational planners to learn how, when and where an attacker is likely to conduct surveillance as well as how to plan, manage and conduct effective surveillance detection operations.

> History has shown that in many situations surveillance detection is not just the best protection; it may be the only protection you have.
>
> USE IT TO YOUR ADVANTAGE and NOT THE TERRORISTS
>
> Turn the tide in your favour

Herr Alfred Herrhausen – German Financial Executive

Whilst the events of this ambush, like any others was tragic it caused reverberations across the world but it nevertheless offers a great learning tool to minimise similar incidents occurring in the future. Case studies are invaluable however; they never change the fact that a security team are always one step behind the terrorists. We always try to plug the gap that led to an event-taking place in the first instance. This ambush had all the hallmarks of a well-planned and orchestrated operation that was clinical and well executed. The training of the CP team at the time focused their attention on the standard vehicle ambush, which always seemed to have been the main threat but what they received came as a wakeup call to other CP teams across Europe. The rules of engagement had changed and so must the CP teams in order to mitigate any similar event in the future. This incident has been well publicised across all media formats and the following is a breakdown of how the incident unfolded. This is a learning curve and highlights how easy it is to initiate something and how daring terrorists can be given the right opportunities and circumstances of a soft target.

On November 30, 1989 an event took place that will forever change the way we think about security. Not just personal security but also for those who provide PSD's to HVT. This incident should be something that you will always remember and to take into consideration the wider aspects of a terrorist's skill and mind set. This was the beginning of who we are today. An expectation of the type of training a CPO requires has been addressed in order to better prepare teams to meet these events head-on. Surveillance training is just as vitally important as being trained as a CPO.

On that fateful day, Alfred Herrhausen, chairman of the Deutsche Bank, was travelling to work in his chauffeur driven armoured vehicle. As a creature of habit, his normal routine was to travel in a three-car convoy and would always ride in the second car. He was accompanied by 4 CPOs; two in the lead vehicle (1 minute ahead) and two travelling in the rear vehicle as his PES detail.

After travelling no more than 300 yards from his house in Frankfurt, his vehicle was destroyed by a remote-controlled bomb. The full force of the blast hit the rear door of his vehicle, which literally inverted that side of the vehicle and blasted it across the other side of the road. His CP team were helpless to do anything at that point but the SAP vehicle could have been more alert over the previous weeks. Herr Herrhausen wasn't killed immediately but the blast caused his legs to be severed and he bled to death before the medics could reach him. The RAF (Red Army Faction) admitted liability for the attack. The bomb targeted the most vulnerable part of his vehicle – the door where he was sitting – and required split second timing to overcome the car's special armour plating.

Fig. 8.9   Fig. 8.10

The bomb was detonated when Herrhausen's car broke a light beam generated by a photoelectric cell. Interruption of the beam caused a flow of electricity that detonated the bomb. The bomb consisted of 22lbs of TNT and was packaged into what was to look like a child's backpack. The backpack was affixed to the luggage rack of a child's bicycle that was left alongside some railings. The bicycle here was an important part of the ambush. The terrorists had to make it seem as if it was part of the environment in order not to create any suspicion. Equally, workers posing as construction workers had set up an area some 500 yards from the targets house in order to be the eyes and relay trigger to those who would initiate the device once the lead vehicle had passed through the temporarily inert beam. There is nothing better to get the world's attention and indeed other like-minded people thinking other than having sat next to the target on Monday and then he is assassinated on Wednesday.

RAF Assassination of Alfred Herrhausen
Frankfurt – 30 Nov 1989

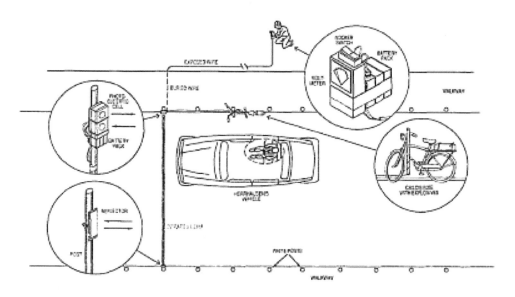

Diagram 8.7

The type of bomb that killed Herrhausen was a roadside bomb comprising of a platter charge (using the Misznay-Schardin mechanism) rather than an Iraq style EFP and it would be detonated as a vehicle drove by. The detonation would cause the platter (a mass of copper) to project towards the car at a speed of nearly 2 km per second, effectively penetrating the armoured Mercedes. Although the type of trigger device had never been used before in a vehicle ambush, it had been used in other ways as an assassin's tool. Until this incident however, most roadside bombs had been unsuccessful. To understand why, we need to look at attacks similar to the one that befell Herrhausen.

Case One – The Texaco Manager

On September 28, 1981 about 1900 hrs, the manager of Texaco Petroleum TN Columbia, John Butler was attacked in a similar fashion whilst travelling from his office to his residence in the northern part of Bogota.

Butler was driving in a two-car motorcade. He was in the lead vehicle, which was armoured and his CPOs were in the follow car (PES). Within 300yards of his home, his car was hit by a powerful bomb that immobilised his vehicle. The bomb, concealed under a vendor's pushcart was remote detonated and activated through a telephone line. A wire coming from a light pole detonated the device.

The terrorist was attempting to detonate the bomb at the precise moment Butler's car drove by the cart but fortunately the bomb was detonated prematurely. The full force of the blast hit the front of Butler's car and although the car was extensively damaged, Butler survived.

The attack on Butler appears to be similar to that on Herrhausen, but actually the two incidents differ significantly. The car breaking the beam detonated the blast that hit the Herrhausen vehicle. The bomb that hit Butler's car was detonated manually and set off prematurely. Although the bomb was initiated early, there is no doubt Butler would have at least been seriously injured and probably killed if he had not been in an armoured vehicle.

Case Two – The Columbian Ministry Of Defence

The terrorists tried again in Bogota. This time they tried to assassinate Guetrero Paz, the Columbian Minister of Defence. On Nov 23, 1989, Paz left the Defence Ministry in a large protective convoy. As the convoy drove by a lamppost, a terrorist detonated a 20-pound charge. Again the terrorist activated the bomb prematurely. It was initiated so early that it didn't even damage the car and the Defence Minister escaped un-injured. The driver drove the armour –plated vehicle back to the designated safe house – The Ministry building.

In both cases, the accuracy of the bomb depended on a person detonating the bomb at precisely the right time. Until the Herrhausen incident, most roadside bombs were inaccurate. The inaccuracy can be explained with some simple mathematics. For a road side bomb to be successful the full energy of the device needs to be focused directly on the intended victim; *It must hit the door where the target is sitting.* For example, if the victim is sitting in the back seat opposite angles to the driver, then the full energy of the blast needs to hit directly on the back door. The bomb that hit Herrhausens vehicle did just that and killed the target but only injured the driver. The terrorist whose job it is to detonate the bomb needs to press the button at the precise moment the car door is adjacent to the bomb. That is not an easy task. A car travelling at 30mph will cover about 45 feet/sec. In a tenth of a second, the car moves 4.5 feet. The average car door is 4.5 feet long, thus the terrorist must be accurate to within a tenth of a second for the device to be effective. These calculations will of course vary from car to car. The speed of the car is important; the faster the vehicle then the less likely there is of a direct hit. Equally, where the bomb hits the vehicle is also important. If the device strikes in an area where the target isn't sitting then the % of a direct hit diminishes greatly. The above really describes where a terrorist has to manually set off the device; the Herrhausen incident was more sophisticated.

Terrorists found a way around the inaccuracies of their devices and the highlighted case changed their thinking forever. The Herrhausen bomb was set off when his vehicle broke a light beam set across the road. The terrorist's ingenuity did not end with using photoelectric cells to detonate the bomb. They also had to ensure that the bomb was detonated at the precise location that would cause maximum injury to their target.

Since they knew the bomb would explode when the nose of the car broke the light beam, it was a simple matter of placing the bicycle carrying the bomb the same distance from the light beam as the door of the car would be from the light beam. The ingenuity continues; they had another problem to solve. Because Herrhausen used a 3-car convoy, the terrorists had to make sure the first car did not set off the bomb when it broke the light beam. Therefore, two switches had to be closed for the bomb to be detonated. One switch would close as the lead vehicle broke the beam and the other by the terrorist. They had to plug the human factor back into the problem.

The terrorist operating the switch had a much easier job than the terrorists in the other incidents described earlier in this document. He or she would have to wait until the lead car broke the beam then close the first switch. When Herrhausens vehicle broke the beam, it closed the second switch and detonated the bomb. The switch operated by the terrorist would not be closed until the lead car had passed. This still required good time keeping. If the cars were moving at 30mph and were separated by 45 feet, the terrorist had less than one second to arm the bomb.

The Herrhausen incident seems to be an example of protecting A when the problem is B. He and his staff appeared to be ready for the classic vehicle ambush, but they were given a roadside bomb. Whilst it cannot be argued that the CP team hadn't afforded the right protection for their client, they should have been more alert to their surroundings. By protecting a HVT such as Herr Herrausen the CP team would've had access to local police and intelligence assets and anything deemed suspicious would be reported in real time. It seems on this occasion, however, that something may have been allowed to slip through the net.

What can be done to protect against a device as sophisticated as the one used in the Herrhausen attack? The key lies in the word sophisticated. Something this complicated takes time to set up. Four weeks before the assassination, a neighbour raking leaves had actually handled the arming cable, yet had no idea what it was and forgot about it. The more sophisticated they become, then the more time they will require to set up. In a vehicle ambush, the terrorist needs to plan and organise the attack. Such planning and organisation requires intensive surveillance on the intended target. The *SURVEILLANCE* is the key to the terrorist's success and detecting surveillance is the best way to foil an attack. Although the technical skill in the Herrhausen incident was impressive, the real key to their success was meticulous planning and surveillance something which a CP team should be able to identify and disrupt in the early stages.

Chapter 9

Understanding Bomb Awareness & Management

1. **Introduction**

To begin this chapter, there was a very well-known and publicised incident that took place in Bad Homburg, a suburb of Frankfurt, Germany on 30 November 1989 involving a high-end corporate financier, Herr Alfred Herrhausen who was at the time the Chairman of Deutsche Bank. He wasn't just Chairman of the bank but he presided over the third largest economic power in the world, even larger than the US banks. As mentioned in an earlier chapter, the technology of today allows terrorists to design smaller devices and whilst this incident occurred in 1989, before the technological revolution, it acts as a reminder of how deadly a small amount of explosive material can cause such destruction. It also lays bare that most of the signs were evident that an incident was pending and was clearly missed by the PSD. In this particular case, only 22 lbs. of TNT, placed in a small holdall on the back of a child's bike and linked to a platter charge exploded and propelled shrapnel through the right rear door, forcing a piece of the armour into Herrhausen and then blowing him across the back seat and into the left door. The force of the explosion that happened to be three feet away from the rear right door threw his vehicle, a 2.8 tonne armoured Mercedes approx. 82 ½ feet across the road. The explosion was so intense that it was heard some 500 metres away at a nearby school where Herr Herrhausen's daughter was attending a social science lesson.

The precision of the explosion is evident in the fact that Herr Herrhausen was the only casualty. His driver suffered only slight injuries and the PSD were unscathed.

This topic is also lengthy in its content, but it cannot be stressed enough that before each PSD are deployed by you that they are fully aware and reminded of what is at stake in the world and what they are up against. It would be negligent of a supervisor, team leader or manager to deploy teams without looking at the deployment risks and managing these whether its through correct recruitment, training or the provision of suitable resources to minimise the chance of a mission failure.

Despite the upsurge in the use of suicide bombers recently, the Improvised Explosive Device (IED) is still the most popular method of attack by terrorists worldwide and is high on the list of criminal extortionists. Syria has seen an upsurge in the use of such devastation that has spilled over to mainland Europe on several occasions. Global terrorists prefer this kind of device because:

- o They are simplistic in their construction with minimal components.
- o Terrorists do not need to be anywhere near the target.
- o If positioned correctly there is a high chance of success.
- o Finding and hitting the right target will create maximum publicity.

Many so-called experts have tried to define the term terrorist and associated meanings but often these lose the impact of what these groups are about. The following are simplified definitions by some internationally respected people:

a.   *Terrorism.*   Premeditated, politically motivated violence perpetrated against non-combatant targets by sub-national groups or clandestine agents.

b.   *International Terrorism.*   Terrorism involving civilians or the territory of more than one country.

c.   *Terrorist Group.*   Any group practicing, or which has significant subgroups that practice international terrorism.

2.   **Types of Terrorist Operations**

There are several types of terrorist operations. The typology employed is based upon the nature of their operation and the categories could typically be:

- Assassination
- Discriminate attack
- Mass casualty attack
- Abduction
- Siege
- Hijacking
- Sabotage
- Mass destruction attack

It must be considered that more than one category of attack may be used in a single operation. For example, a large bomb could be intended to cause both mass casualties and mass destruction, although in practice most large bombs are primarily intended to cause one or the other.

Assassination – An assassination is an attack that is intended to kill a specific person or specific people. The target need not be well known or powerful but the attack must have been aimed at that person or those people in particular. Other people may be killed or injured in the course of an assassination attempt, and then these casualties are incidental or at most secondary targets such as CPO's who have to be eliminated so that the terrorists can carry out the attack on their primary target.

Discriminate Attack – This attack is one where the aim is not necessarily to harm specific individuals, but to kill or injure people who fall within a specific category – be it racial, religious and occupational.

Mass-casualty Attack – This is one in which the aim is to kill or injure as many people as possible with little regard as to who is harmed. To call such an attack indiscriminate would not be accurate as most attacks contain a degree of discrimination with regard to people or objects damaged or the location of the attack. At the very least, terrorists tend to ensure that their own are not injured with the exception to suicide bombers.

Abduction – This is an operation where a person is seized or taken to a secret place where they are held pending their release or death. Such incidents take the form of kidnappings where the terrorists attempt to gain some form of benefit, usually a ransom or the release of prisoners in return for the release of the person abducted.

Siege – Sometimes termed as a barricade and hostage incident, a siege occurs when terrorists seize hostages and then barricade themselves behind cover with the intention of holding them until their demands are met.

Hijacking – A hijacking is an operation where the terrorists seize control of a vehicle, such as aircraft, ship or car often seizing the occupants as bargaining counters with government of high net worth families.

Sabotage – An act of sabotage is an attack intended to cause damage to specific material targets.

Mass-destruction Attack – This kind of attack is intended to cause a large material damage

3. **General Bomb Management**

It is essential that everyone under your command is familiar with and trained to respond where there are incidents involving bomb equipment. The design of a 'bomb' is done in such a way that anyone in close proximity to the blast will be caught out by flying fragments or fire. As experience in N.Ireland and now the Middle East any blast wave is likely to blow limbs off and in the immediate area of the explosion will actually disintegrate a whole body. There are many books that deal with this subject; my inclusion is really to concentrate on the suicide bomber.

Explosions in confined spaces such as vehicles or buildings are even more devastating than in the open. There are several types of bombs. Some examples are shown below:

a. ***Package Bomb.*** This type of device shown in fig 9.1 below is easily identifiable and can also be referred to as a parcel bomb, letter bomb, mail bomb or post bomb. They are generally sent through the postal system or delivered by courier and designed with the intention to injure or kill the addressee once the item is opened. Related threats with this type of device have been known to contain powders or chemicals in a way to spread a disease e.g. Anthrax.

Fig 9.1

b. ***Incendiary Device.*** This can be identified as any firebomb which has been specifically adapted to cause physical harm to persons or property by means of fire and consisting of an incendiary substance or agent and a means to ignite it. Something as small as a cigarette packet or cassette box can be devastating. An example is shown in fig 9.2 below

Fig 9.2

c.   ***Car Bomb (VBIED).*** This kind of device is as popular as the Suicide Bomber. The acronym stands for Vehicle Borne Improvised Explosive Device. They are an effective device and is an easy way to transport large amounts of explosives to an intended target. A car bomb can also produce copious amounts of shrapnel, or flying debris and any secondary damage to buildings or bystanders. They act as their own delivery mechanism and can carry large amounts of explosives without attracting suspicion. The fuel in the vehicle's tanks makes the explosion of the bomb more powerful. A small amount of explosive concealed in or under a car and detonated by a variety of means is intended to demolish a vehicle and its occupants. They come in all colours, shapes and sizes and are dependent on the vehicle being used. The devices may be of the explosive or fire bomb variants. Cars packed with explosives and left in a strategic position will devastate large buildings, or if timed correctly, kill specific targets whilst in convoy; the larger the vehicle, then the greater the visual and destructive effect.

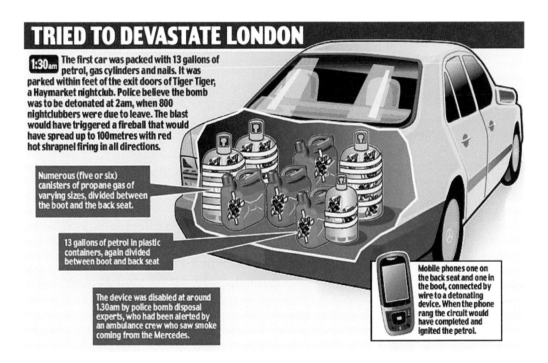

Fig 9.3 A typical car bomb

Fig 9.3 The aftermath of a car bomb

d.   ***Letter or Parcel Bomb.***   An explosive or incendiary material in large or small quantities can be delivered by post or parcel delivery with devastating consequences. They are designed to explode on opening with the intention of seriously injuring or killing the recipient (who may not be the person to whom the letter was addressed). They have been in use dating back to 1764.

e.   ***Bomb Threats***.   A bomb threat is generally defined as a threat, usually verbal or written to detonate an explosive or incendiary device to cause property damage, death or injuries, whether or not such a device actually exists. Many bomb threats are not pranks but are made as part of other crimes such as extortion, arson or aircraft hijacking. Contrary to this is that any bombings for malicious destruction of property, terrorism or murder are often perpetrated without warnings. A bomb threat can have a serious effect on the operation as a whole and the confidence of the client and staff alike. Most bomb threats are delivered by telephone and intended to cause disruption, for revenge, or to play a practical joke, rather than warning of real devices. There are many hoax calls made regarding bombs but care must be taken to evaluate the call and act and respond accordingly. You should always go through the process of completing a bomb-warning sheet that hopefully will cover most things. These checklists have been created over many years from people who have experienced differing calls and as such the checklists have been adjusted accordingly. They should never be taken lightly as there is a real possibility that a device could potentially or actually does exist.

f.   ***Email Bomb.*** This type of bomb has no explosive content par say but its use on the Internet has become popular with activists. The idea here is to send huge volumes of email to an address in an attempt to overflow the mailbox or overwhelm the server where the email address is hosted in a denial-of-service (DOS) attack. There are three methods of perpetrating an email bomb; Mass mailing (sending numerous duplicate emails to same address), list linking (also known as email cluster bomb and designed to annoy rather than cause real trouble) and zip bombing (variant of mail bombing using ZIP archived attachments).

g.   ***Suicide Bomber.***   The first large suicide bombing occurred in the 1980's in Lebanon when 2000Ibs of explosives were used against a US Marine base. Suicide attacks tend to be more deadly and destructive than any other terror attacks. They tend to give their perpetrators the ability to conceal weapons, make last minute adjustments, and because they dispense with the need for a remote detonation there are no needs for escape plans or rescue teams. To understand a suicide bomber, they have been described as a weapon of psychological warfare designed to instil fear in the target population. It is a strategy to eliminate or at least drastically diminish areas where the public feel safe and the fabric of trust that holds society together. Since the 1960's female suicide bombers have been on the increase. It is also not unknown that children have been used as suicide bombers. Diagram 9.1 below shows the increase in the use of suicide bombers since 2000.

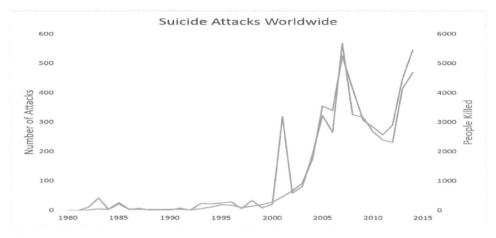

Diagram 9.1

Even with the advent of digitisation, an IED will invariably still have the following constituent parts:

o   A digital timer, a simple circuit board and a means to power the device.
o   A means of detonating and igniting the device e.g. mobile phone, switch.
o   An explosive or incendiary mix. May include additional materials such as nails, glass or metal fragments designed to increase the amount of shrapnel propelled by the explosion.

4.   **Explosives**

A terrorist cell's skill in constructing Improvised Explosive Devices or Vehicle-Borne Improvised Explosive Devices (VBIED) is likely to influence the type of attack it might execute. Bomb makers with only rudimentary skills may be restricted to assembling basic devices. A skilled journey-man bomb maker may have the competence needed to build a range of IEDs from small to large that are highly concealable or have advanced capabilities such as multiple triggering methods, directional blasts, or increased blast effect. *200 kg* of explosives can make:

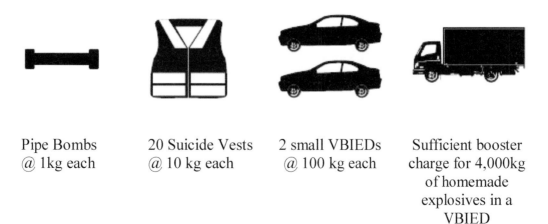

| Pipe Bombs @ 1kg each | 20 Suicide Vests @ 10 kg each | 2 small VBIEDs @ 100 kg each | Sufficient booster charge for 4,000kg of homemade explosives in a VBIED |

5.   **Suicide Bombers**

PSD's along with everyone else in the civilised world are not quite sure how to defend against this new wave of attack. The concept of killing yourself along with others is not a new warfare tactic, nor is it confined to the Middle East. WWII Japanese fighter pilots were suicide bombers as were the 9/11 attackers.

a.   How Would a Suicide Bomber Attack? The most common forms of suicide attacks will likely involve terrorists concealing explosives strapped to their person, carrying bombs in bags or suitcases or delivering explosives by car, van or truck. We can predict with some certainty the type of suicide attacks that can be expected in the West by looking at the long history of similar attacks in the Middle East.

A suicide bomber in Europe would more than likely have been an Islamic fundamentalist, either from al-Qaeda or a Palestinian extremist group such as Hamas or Hezbollah. This can no longer be guaranteed however as several Europeans have begun joining the ranks of terrorism.

The target of a suicide bomber is rarely an individual and would almost certainly be a highly populated space and a well-known public area. When the PSD is out with their client, they should be extra vigilant to spot suicide bombers in the first instance. Prime targets are:

(1)   Underground trains or buses and subways

(2)   Restaurants and casinos

(3)   Shopping centres

(4)   Train or bus stations

(5)   Airport check-in queues

(6)   Sports stadiums

(7)   Cinemas and theatres

(8)   Churches, temples and other religious gatherings

b.   Identifying a Suicide Bomber.   A bomber carrying explosives about his body will need to disguise the bomb, so be suspicious if you see someone wearing a winter jacket on a hot day. Far less obvious are bombers who carry explosives in a bag or suitcase. Witnesses and survivors of attacks have said that they have seen the bombers messing/fiddling with the bags just prior to detonation. Studies of videotapes of suicide bombings show that many of the bombers appeared to be very anxious and apprehensive and that many seemed to be acting suspiciously and drenched in sweat. ***Do not*** merely focus on people from the Middle East, as there is a growing trend of Europeans converting. There is a growing trend that ISIS are now using females and children as suicide bombers. You should remain alert for the following which is not exhaustive:

(1)   People' wearing loose or bulky clothing that is inappropriate for the current weather conditions.

(2)   Robotic walk. Bombers carrying or wearing heavy objects (approx. 40Ibs) under his/her clothing.

(3)   Persons who are sweating, nervous, mumbling or fidgeting

(4)   Persons who are trying to avoid eye contact with any security personnel including the CPO.

(5)   Wearing an inordinate amount of perfume, cologne or other scents that may be used to mask chemical odours.

(6)   Persons who do not look like they belong in the uniform or dress they are wearing, which may be a disguise to elude detection.

(7)   Holding a bag or package close to his or her body.

(8)   Persons who repeatedly pat up and down their body and consistently adjust their clothing.

(9)   Keeping one or both hands in pockets or close to his or her body, possibly holding a detonator switch.

(10)   Having visible wires or an explosive belt protruding from under his or her clothing.

(11)   A person with bulges or padding around the mid-section of the body.

(12)   Appear well groomed but wear sloppy clothing.

(13)   Persons who have a pale face from recently shaving a beard.

(14)   Not responding to direct salutations or authoritative commands.

(15)   Walking in a deliberate, stiff or awkward manner.

(16)   Acting in an unusual vigilant manner.

(17)   Looking straight at the target. Having a blank facial expression, or appearing extremely focused or in a trance.

(18)   Exhibiting unusually calm and detached behaviour.

(19)   Mumbled prayers.

(20)   Lack of response to any shouting.

(21)   Rapid breathing and heartbeat

6.   **Conclusion**

Terrorists will always be one step ahead of authorities and of course any CP team. They control the main parts of a situation; these are target selection, type of attack of where and when. It is therefore paramount that a CP team remain vigilant throughout any deployment to unusual activity; especially where surveillance may be deployed. This is one part where the team can retake control provided you identify this in the early stages. If a team misses this you only make the job more difficult and the odds of identifying anything further on becomes increasingly remote.

It's imperative therefore that surveillance training is implemented as part of any pre-deployment training and that the whole team are aware of the consequences of failure.

When the stakes are high, one moment can change everything. CP teams will nearly always be outwitted by terrorist events. You will never know how, why or when unless you initiate a surveillance detection plan.

None of your teams will be infallible to a determined aggressor but they'll be better prepared to respond if they understand how important surveillance will be in the execution of their duties. Awareness is the key and this key is survival.

SUSPICIOUS ACTIVITY REPORTING CHECKLIST

SUSPECT

Height: _____ Weight: _____ Sex: _____ Hair Colour/Length: _____

Race/Nationality: _____

Clothing (Hat, jacket, trousers, shirt, footware etc): _____
_____

Distinguishing features (glasses, moustache, beard etc): _____

Walks with a limp: _____ Scars: _____ Birthmarks: _____

Other: _____

ACTIVITY

Time of sighting: _____ Location: _____

What was the suspect doing? _____

Any use of a camera, binoculars, telephoto lenses, digital video recorders, SW radio, tape recorder or other devices, note taking, drawing/sketching or hand signals?

VEHICLES

Make & Year: _____ Colour: _____

Index No: _____ 4 door/2 door/Hatchback/Other: _____

No. of Occupants: _____ If departed, direction of travel: _____

OTHER INFORMATION

Did anyone else see the above suspect, vehicle or activity?

YES/NO _____ If yes, who? _____

Full name of person making the report
_____

Signature:_____Print Name: _____ Date: _____

BOMB THREAT AIDE-MEMOIRE

BOMB THREAT
CALL PROCEDURES

Most bomb threats are received by phone. These threats are serious until proven otherwise. It's important that you act quickly but remain calm and obtain as much information as possible with the help of the checklist opposite.

If a bomb threat is received by phone:

1. Remain calm. Keep the caller on the line for as long as possible. DO NOT HANG UP, even if the caller does.
2. Listen carefully, be polite and show interest.
3. Try to engage in conversation with the caller to learn more information and to put them at ease.
4. If possible, write a note to a colleague to call the authorities or, as soon as the caller hangs up, immediately notify the services yourself on a separate phone.
5. If the phone has a caller display, copy the number and/or letters on the window display.
6. Complete the bomb threat checklist opposite immediately. Write down as much detail as you can remember. Try to get the exact words.
7. Immediately upon termination of the call, do not hang up but from a different phone call your security department and authorities.

If a bomb threat is received by a hand written note:

- Call _____
- Handle note as minimally as possible

If a bomb threat is received by email:

- Call _____
- Do not delete the message

Signs of a Suspicious Package:

- No return address
- Excessive Postage
- Stains
- Strange Odour
- Strange Sounds
- Unexpected Item

- Poorly Handwritten
- Misspelled Words
- Incorrect Titles
- Foreign Postage
- Restrictive Notes
- Excessive string or tape

DO NOT:

- Use two-way radios, pagers or mobile phones. Radio signals have the potential to detonate a device.
- Evacuate the building until police arrive and evaluate the threat.
- Touch or move a suspicious package.

BOMB THREAT CHECKLIST

Date of call:		Time of call:	
Time the caller disconnected:		Your phone number where call received	
Length of call:		Call Received By:	

Question the Caller

• Where is the bomb located (Which Room, building, floor etc.)	
• When is it timed to go off?	
• What does it look like?	
• What kind of bomb is it?	
• What will make it explode?	
• Did you place the bomb?	YES NO
• If yes, WHY?	
• What do you hope to achieve by placing the bomb?	
• What Organisation do you represent?	
• What is your name?	

Exact Words Used in the Threat

Information About the Caller

• Where is the caller located? (Background & level of noise)	
• Estimated Age:	
• Is voice familiar?	
• Other Points	

Callers Voice	(X)	Background Sounds	(X)	Threat Language Used	(X)
Accent		Animal Noises		Incoherent	
Angry		House Noises		Message Read	
Calm		Kitchen Noises		Taped	
Clearing Throat		Street Noises		Irrational	
Coughing		Phone Box		Profane	
Crackling Voice		PA System		Well-Spoken	
Crying		People Speaking		Foul	
Deep		Music		Offensive	
Deliberate		Vehicle Engines			
Disguised		Clear			
Distinct		Static			
Distorted		Office machinery			
Emotional		Factory Machinery			
Excited		Local Noises			
Female		Long Distance			
Hoars		Bedlam			
High Pitched		Mixed Noises			
Intoxicated		Trains			

Laughter		Quiet			
Lisp		Voices			
Local Accent		Aircraft			
Loud		Party Atmosphere			
Male		Crockery			
Nasal					
Normal					
Pleasant					
Ragged					
Rapid					
Raspy					
Slow					
Slurred					
Soft					
Stutter					

Action Taken

This document is intended for use within a PSD CP environment whether it be the RST or within the ops room and therefore is worded with that in mind. Recording actions taken is necessary to make sure that all protocols have been followed which will assist with any de-briefing after the event has lapsed.

Police Informed at:		Name of Contact:	
CP Ops Manager informed at:		Name of Contact:	
CP TL Informed at:		Name of Contact:	
Response Team Informed at:		Name of Contact:	
Client Informed at:		Name of Contact:	
Company Informed at:		Name of Contact:	
Evacuation of Property (Yes/No) at:		Authorised by:	
Client to Safe House/Room (Yes/No)		Extracted to:	
Emergency Services arrive at:		Emergcency Services Depart at:	
Time All Clear Given:			

TERRORIST WARNINGS

IMMINENT ATTACK

Possible Characteristics of a Suicide Bomber (Males/Females/Children)	
• Tunnel vision	• Unresponsive to verbal commands
• Profuse sweating, mumbling	• Irregular glances from side to side
• Carrying or adjacent to a large object	• Loose inappropriate clothing
• Nervousness	• Pale from recent shaving of beard
• Repeatedly checks self or adjust clothing	• Inappropriate or lack of eye contact
• Appearing well groomed but wearing sloppy clothing	• Walking in a deliberate, stiff, or awkward manner
• Acting in an unusually vigilant manner	• Having a blank facial expression, or appearing extremely focused or in a trance
• Hands concealed in pockets, luggage bags etc.	• Wearing an inordinate amount of perfume, cologne used to mask chemical odours

On-Going Activities by Terrorists	
Consistently	**Usually**
Supply Acquisition	**Intel Gathering**
• Buying or stealing weapons	• Taking pictures
• Large quantity of similar electronics	• Taking notes
• Buy or steal explosives	**Supply Staging**
	• Abandoned vehicles
	• Concealed packages
	Odd Activity or Indicators
	• Chemical odours/stains
	Criminal Activity
	• **Petty Theft**
	• **Drug related**
Rarely	**Sometimes**
Attack Rehearsal	**Fake Documents**
• Frequently visiting the same site	• Fake ID
• Following the exact pattern repeatedly	• False vehicle plates
Unusual Clothing	**Extremist Writings**
• Bulky/unseasonal	• Pamphlets, booklets, fliers
• Mainly green/yellow	• Graffiti, tagging
Significant dates	**Avoiding Security**
• Event anniversaries	• Purposefully avoiding guards/cameras
• Holy days	**Large cash payments**
	• £50 note for small purchases
	• Using cash for large purchases

Fig 9.4 Potential suicide bomber/terrorist characteristic activities checklist

Green and Yellow are important colours in Islam and are favourites among radicals and extremists.

There is no absolute indicator of terrorist activity. Terrorists are always reviewing and revising their tactics. If you see anything out of the ordinary that may indicate a threat against your client or you have been compromised then report immediately the incident to your Ops Manager without delay and initiate an immediate EXTRACTION to your nominated safe house.

Chapter 10

SECURITY ADVANCED PARTY (SAP)

1. **Introduction**

Every CP novel on the market has a chapter dedicated to the SAP. A SAP is very much an under valued element of a CP operation. Deploying an SAP can be mission critical and is something which a Detail Supervisor or Regional Commander should consider each time a deployment is carried out. This chapter has been included since you are likely to have considered this in the planning phase of the operation and therefore will be a management decision to deploy. They are an invaluable asset and the work they carry out can relieve you of the added burden. The information they bring back can then be used during any planning phase so that all those involved will be up to speed on the event (actual).

The Security Advanced Party (SAP) is generally part of the Special Activities Section (SAS) of a PSD operation and has the role, as the name suggests of going ahead in advance of the main VIP party. The SAP may, if cost is a problem be simply one person but this should be considered less than the minimum required to perform this role adequately. The minimum normal composition is two people. The advance serves two purposes; it makes certain that all the logistical details are prepared and checked to ensure a smooth, hassle-free trip; and it makes certain that all security arrangements are made for the protection of the client and their party.

The primary goal of the advance is to minimise risk, and a well-executed, meticulously detailed advance will have a direct bearing on the probability of avoiding or surviving an attack or preventing embarrassment. Conversely, trips taken without an advance or a sloppy advance are invitations to disaster. Since every advance is unique, not every conceivable situation can be covered in what you are likely to come up against but the principles are the same regardless of where the advance takes place and the nature of the event being advanced.

The thoroughness of the advance is dependent on several factors, among them: the perceived threat level, the number of personnel available for the advance, and the time allocated for the advance. All these will be key to the depth in which you go to obtain the relevant information considered to be necessary for the client's safety, security and comfort.

There may have to be a number of functions/venues to consider but in most circumstances the SAP will be tasked with ensuring that the route the client will be taking, is safe and secure as is the venue to be visited.

Generally, advance personnel should visit every site on a projected itinerary at least twice. The first time will be to conduct a site survey, determine the conditions in which you'll be working and to formulate plans to be used during the client visit. The second time you visit will be to set up the security cordons you planned during the site survey and to execute all other tasks noted at the time. Unless otherwise directed, the SAP will remain on site for the duration of the event. They will continue to assist with the security capability until the CP Ops Manager, Detail Leader, releases them or the 'Drop Dead' time has been reached or other pre-determined conditions have been met.

Wherever possible it is advantageous to include the SAP in the actual mission operation but is not uncommon for a mission to run without them. Some PSD's consist of only two personnel; a PSD (Security Driver) and the PSD (CPO) is all you may have available. This is common in a low threat operation but the fact that no SAP is available should not negate the fact that planning, coordination and other efforts should still be at the forefront of the Detail Leader prior to the mission execution. Where large teams collectively are operating, then it is essential that an SAP is considered an integral part of a mission. Without one then you play into the hands of god or fate. The SAP is the most valuable person in a PSD and he or she will be your insurance to ensure that things are indeed safe for the client to move freely at their venue.

If a mission is protracted and complex, several two-man SAPs may be needed in order to produce the greatest return on the investment of security resources as they will be likely to identify the most likely problem areas, approach routes, choke points and ambush locations. They can also identify the appropriate counter measures most likely to provide deterrence during the mission.

The use of an SAP on some missions is often reserved for the more senior clients but is an invaluable asset where assistance is required on other types of movements too.

2. Responsibilities

The SAP should ensure the following as a minimum requirement. The advance information gleaned will assist the CP Ops Manager or detail leader in confirming the number of personnel to deploy with the client and also to formulate the best plan available given the resources you have at your disposal:

a.   They have up to date location details of current, projected and optional venues. This will include but not limited to:

    (1)   Contact details of the relevant venue manager. It is essential that you never ask for anything that isn't necessary.
    (2)   Floor plan with seating configurations (if applicable). These may be gleaned from the web site of the visiting location.
    (3)   Primary and secondary routes.
    (4)   Map overview
    (5)   Background guide of the venue (if applicable but not necessary for the cinema etc.)
    (6)   Tulip maps if relevant.
    (7)   Physical layout of the venue
    (8)   What security measures already exist
    (9)   Details such as location of entrances, exits, bathrooms and other public areas.
    (10)   Where to park the convoy
    (11)   Location of any safe havens
    (12)   Comms receptive areas or blind spots. (Radio & Mobile phones)
    (13)   All vulnerable areas en-route

b.	The SAP must recee any expected venue that clients are intending on visiting. An SAP checklist must also be completed to ensure that nothing has been overlooked. One is not attached here as there are several on the market which may be of use to the operation and tweaked to your own needs.

c.	They know the scheduled timings of the event.

d.	They have their own mode of transport, which is not in the liking of those being used by the clients and their entourage.

e.	They should dress down where necessary from the client attire unless they are being utilised in a role to assist the PSD.

f.	They should ensure that good comms are established from the outset and throughout the mission.

g.	They should inform the CP Ops Manager of any suspicious activity at any of the arrival points in order for an assessment to be made. If serious, this will be passed to the client.

h.	The escort PSD chase vehicle commander is to be informed of any temporary traffic lights that have been established, rolling roadblocks, which may slow or stop the client convoy.

i.	Be prepared to either travel ahead of the convoy or to secure the visiting location.

j.	Assist the PSD primaries in any arrival routine where necessary.

k.	Leap frog to the next venue if necessary.

l.	Prepare a Tulip navigation map when instructed.

3 <u>Restaurants</u>

Advances to restaurants are fairly simple by design. The SAP should aim to arrive at the restaurant prior to the client's arrival, allowing themselves about 30 to 45 minutes to complete the advance if the restaurant is new to the SAP. If the restaurant is familiar to the advance team then the advance should take considerably less time. You will still need to cover all the relevant points as per previous visits in order to up date the info you have, but since you know the layout already the info can be gleaned in a shorter time without compromise. As soon as the SAP arrives at the restaurant they should notify the LX Ops Room or CP Ops Manager giving the time and distance from the clients start location, best travel route and how they can be reached. This info will of course be passed to the client driver for him to consider the options. At that time, updated information can be given to the SAP on any changes. It is essential that the SAP are notified of the departure of the client so that they are on hand at the front of the restaurant in time for the client's arrival. The table will generally be booked under the name of the person making the reservation and not the client – for obvious reasons.

If the advance is done a day or several days beforehand, the SAP should produce a simple sketch of the restaurant showing the arrangement of the rooms, the tables, the entrances, exits, emergency exits, kitchen and rest rooms. An information pack should be designed by the SAP in which to hold all relevant information. New venues can be simply added in as the event happens to assist in any future visits. This file however must be kept up to date and revisited during the lead-time prior to the client arrival in country. If the file remains un-revised then you can expect to encounter many problems.

An ineffective SAP reflects on the effectiveness of the whole team

Restaurants within hotels, it is easier to work with the Restaurant Manager, Maître d'hôtel, or a hostess in protecting the identity of the client and in arranging in advance for the best, most appropriate for the group and secure seating. In freestanding restaurants (not associated with hotels), it is not always so easy. Provided that the advance is done sufficiently in time, however, most Restaurant Managers will, with a little help, agree to seating. The SAP will of course need to ascertain whether the client has any personal preference for seating before they (the SAP) start their negotiating.

Restaurants, which do not take reservations but seat people as first-come-first-serve, are the worst choice, as there is no control over where or when the client will be seated. In addition to being offered the worst table in the restaurant, the client may be forced to wait in an exposed lobby or waiting area for their table. In the unlikely event that you are tasked to locate and resource such a venue then all aspects of the client's protocol must still remain intact and their confidentiality is not breached by using their name to secure a table.

Restaurants chosen on the spur of the moment usually do not require an SAP as it's not particularly necessary. If no one knows that the client will be in that restaurant, until the last minute then it is hard to do something against him or her. There is generally someone within the group who will use persuasive tactics to ensure an appropriate table for the client.

4. Travel Routes

In picking a travel route, there are several considerations. You must always plan a primary and secondary route to each destination, especially if the client is visiting a publicised event. What is needed is the safest, yet shortest point from start to finish. It is essential where possible to utilise limited access roads (motorways), which will be highly desirable. Motorways (except in rush hour) will move traffic quickly and there are very limited opportunities for anyone to consider moving in on the client's vehicle whilst travelling at speed.

All routes should be driven in advance, preferably more than once. If time permits, it is essential that the SAP map out the distance between locations, plus the time required travelling the route under normal traffic conditions and with heavy conditions also. The SAP must note the proximity of hospitals and safe areas (police stations, embassies etc.,), traffic problems, and potential delaying conditions such as construction, railway crossings etc. All security and travel problems should be noted and others informed.

Chosen routes should be driven at approximately the same time as it is expected the client will travel the route. That is if the actual travel will be done during rush hour traffic, then both primary and secondary routes must be advanced at the same hours. Likewise on the reciprocal, if the route is expected to be travelled at night, then the advance must also be done at night for obvious reasons.

The secondary route should closely parallel the primary so that, if it is used then it can be reached quickly and without problems.

Once both routes have been agreed upon they must be recorded in such a way that they are crystal clear to all drivers.

Technology today will allow you to have up to date traffic reports and alternatives.

5. <u>Hospitals</u>

The advance SAP must identify and locate major full service hospitals and if time permits they must visit them to ensure that they are suitable. The first requirement of course will be to make sure that they accept patients; that is, it is not a military hospital with restricted admittance. Secondly, the hospital should have a 24-hour emergency room or a shock/trauma unit with a doctor on duty 24 hours a day. Ideally, other desirable attributes would include a burn care centre, ample blood supply, well-equipped operating room, good high-tech equipment and rapid access to specialists such as neurosurgeons, cardiologists and orthopaedic surgeons. The clients will have their own desired private hospitals which they will invariably use but the initial need of a localised hospital can never be ruled out in the preservation of life in the first instance and then transferred at a later date.

The primary and secondary routes to hospitals with descriptions as to how to reach the emergency entrances should be mapped out and given to each security detail PSD (Security Driver)

By nature of who the clients are, it will be very rare that we will be apprised of any full medical history of the clients and therefore the treatment we give is very limited but recognition of some major symptoms will be invaluable in the early stages.

In most major cities there are pharmacies that are open 24 hours per day. As part of the advance, the SAP should locate one or more of these pharmacies. This will be particularly useful if the client takes prescribed medication.

6 <u>Fire & Ambulance</u>

If time allows, the SAP should find out a response time for the Fire Department (FD) to the clients property.

Ambulance services may be provided through a hospital, a volunteer service or private and there can be significant variances in the level of care provided. Dialling 999 will take you to a central switchboard and they will try to despatch a medical team from the nearest hospital or mobile unit.

The basic first aid given by a member of a PSD is life sustaining and not advanced, therefore, never try and administer any advanced first aid to your client unless you are fully qualified as an EMT or doctor then you could find yourself at the end of a lawsuit.

7 Police Stations

The SAP should identify local police stations. These could potentially be used as safe houses. It's important that a check is carried out to establish their opening times as some do close after certain hours. Identified stations can be marked on any tulip or route card produced by the SAP.

8 Detailed Briefings

Whilst the SAP are given their instructions by the CP Ops Manager or TL to carry out an advance, they are the ones who will obtain the information required at first hand. They will know whether or not the info meets the clients requirements based on their initial information they were given prior to leaving base. It's important, provided that time is on their hands that they brief all those taking part in the op for that particular event. Those personnel who are not involved in one particular mission can be excluded from the briefing; however, bear in mind that in the event something happens you may need to call upon extra resources to help out.

As the mission moves into its live phase, the SAP should keep apprised all those personnel involved with regular updates.

9 Maximum Use of Checklists

Checklists can be developed to suit any function in which your client participates. Checklists are especially useful for those functions in which a client does not routinely participate because the SAP may have lost, or is not familiar with the details of that particular activity. Checklists are nothing more than forms that can be developed in a 'Fill in the Blanks' or 'Check the Block' type format that SAP can take along with them to the various types of activity or venues. Checklists are created to provide the SAP with a means to record the information developed during the advance. Checklists can be developed for missions where the client will remain overnight, for airport arrivals and departures, for public speaking engagements and any other function or activity in which the client participates.

All those personnel engaged on SAP duties should be encouraged to adapt, expand and modify any checklist that a SAP currently uses in such a away that it enables them to better serve the client. Several quality checklists have been written and published by other experienced professionals and serve as adequate templates for you to be able to create your own.

When doing an advance and speaking with a POC, using a checklist will help keep you from appearing incompetent or unprofessional because you will be able to cover one subject completely before moving on to the next instead of jumping around from subject to subject with no obvious methodology. A checklist will form the basis of the information required by the detail leader or CP Ops Manager in order to formulate his plan. A checklist can also be used as a briefing mechanism but they should be designed as your own and for your use in order to be an Aide-Memoire.

10   Use of 3 x 5 Cards

Instead of having reams of A4 paper folded up and tucked in the inside pocket of your suit jacket or blazer and distorting the shape of your suit then consideration should be given to the use of 3 x 5 cards.   They fit into the inside pocket conveniently. Use one card for general information such as hospitals, police and fire department POC names and contact details if required.

Information regarding other PSD personnel can be on another card as well as venues etc. The point here though is to ensure that OPSEC isn't breached in the event a card or cards are lost. In this modern age of technology, the use of PDA's or blackberry capable phones and other personal computer devices let you carry a wealth of information with you.   You can even download maps, diagrams, reports, spreadsheets and other information you may need as part of your operational requirements. Remember though that these electronic devices are fine in the western world but if you are deployed to a 3rd world country then you may find that you can't find the correct batteries to run the equipment when needed. 3 x 5 cards require no power source and remain a viable tool in this regard.

The point here is to make sure that you have the information you need with you as you work and travel around. When your client asks you a question or the CP Ops Manager requires an answer you should be able to answer it correctly and quickly. It's no good having it written down at the ops room, you need it with you at all times.

11   The Use of Technology

Technology has come along way and has now been introduced into aspects of CP. Consideration should be given to personal and vehicular tracking devices that can be a useful asset when screened in a viable command room situation. Equally, clients can be issued with a tracker if there is a serious risk/threat against them. The use of WhatsApp is becoming ever popular since anything sent is encrypted at one end and decrypted at the other. It is simplicity in itself and teams should consider using this method and setting up WhatsApp groups so that there can be no error that any script will be sent to an unauthorised recipient. This is useful since you can stop and start particular groups.

If you do not have access to trackers then Google maps are useful with drop pins.

Google maps can be useful to give the quickest route to specific locations and can pinpoint restaurants, hospitals, POI etc.

12   No SAP Available

In the private sector it is not always possible to have full support staff and sometimes the CPO has to operate alone, whether it be as a driver, close-proximity security or advance man. This role makes the job so much more difficult and is tempting the gods to say 'Not if but when'.

It's not the end of the world but sometimes a brief advance is all that is possible because of time factors or availability of scheduled personnel, but some action and planning has to be better than nothing at all and arriving at a location completely blind with no knowledge of what to expect could lead to embarrassment on both sides. Depending on the brief, an advance can simply be merely a 'drive by' to determine entrances/exits, parking availability, even down to where the client can debus/ embus.

The advance person has the responsibility for the safe and trouble-free conduct of a VIP squarely on their shoulders. Anything that can be done to make the visit smooth and a clock like operation will greatly enhance the likelihood of a safe trip.

13 <u>Conclusion/Caveat</u>

The SAP, when available are often an under used asset of a PSD's deployment grid but nevertheless serves as an invaluable part of any team. They can make the difference between a smooth and professional mission and a rough-cut and often ill-focused team. Good and thorough advances can be, and are, complex and time consuming especially if required to move from place to place. They are nevertheless worth the time and expense where needed. Only you as supervisors or team leaders will know the true value and it'll be down to you to explain to your potential clients the invaluable contribution they can make in ensuring a secure and comfortable environment.

Where manpower and budgets don't permit such a luxury, those who deploy as a single PSD working alone you may have the time to complete a 2 minute advance survey and will it be worth it – of course it will. It's more knowledge you have gained than you had when you first walked into the building. Never get caught out in not doing your job correctly. You'll find it difficult to recover lost ground when the wheels come off and your client will be looking to you to have some kind of answer to the problem you now both face.

The SAP will augment an existing PSD in the provision of additional security personnel on the ground when required. Its value can never be underestimated. Use it to your advantage.

Chapter 11

Vehicle Anti-Ambush

1. **Introduction.**

As a Manager, Supervisor or Team Leader you will want to be confident that your team are capable of dealing with incidents involving vehicles. This skill should form part of any pre-op training you do. History has shown that the ambush is a very popular terrorist tactic, which has often been employed, both in rural and urban areas with relative success. It is a long established military tactic where the aggressors take advantage of concealment and the element of surprise. The ambush ought to be the most perfect and precise execution of military operations, since attackers have every advantage. It is they who select the place, the time, the choice of weapons and if the situation doesn't present itself precisely to their satisfaction, they are free to decide not to ambush, wrap up for the day and possibly no one would know that an attack was imminent at that time. They just move on as a ghost. Above all else, the element of surprise is strongly in the favour of the attackers and the few moments' delay between the first shots being fired and the response by the escort team may be sufficient for the attackers to achieve their objective. It is important to plan for the worst-case scenario and hope that the outcome will be the best one.

To a PSD, 'Defensive Driving' takes on an entirely different meaning than it has for the average non-skilled driver. Deployed as a Security Driver, there is far more to defensive driving than watching that the other driver doesn't run a red light. Although you must be aware of the everyday dangers present in driving, you must also be knowledgeable in many other areas. The following are some of these areas you will need as a PES driver:

- o Formation Driving
- o Evasive Driving
  - ▪ J-Turns
  - ▪ Y-Turns (2-Point)
  - ▪ Threshold or Cadence Braking
  - ▪ Bootlegs or Hand Brake Turns
- o Running Interference
- o Transfer Car Drill
- o Line of Vision
- o Mechanical Failure (Know your vehicle Characteristics)
- o Ramming Techniques

Some of the above are explained further on in this chapter.

Never Practice the above techniques in traffic or on public streets

Every CPO should have an understanding of what to do in the event an attack is delivered. Drivers are generally the first to be immobilised followed by the security detail so as to make any attempt on the client that much easier. If the PES driver is immobilised, then you as a PPO should be prepared to take over the wheel and continue providing cover to the client's vehicle. Hence why there is a need to ensure that all CPO's are adequately trained in driving techniques for this particular reason alone.

CP courses today only give a brief overview of what is expected and often time is not available for you to practice. Practice is something that is required in this discipline so as to make any reactions instantaneous. It would be beneficial to any CPO to attend a Defensive & Evasive driving course to be able to apply the following. It makes your survivability that much more realistic as without a vehicle, your options are somewhat limited.

2.   **Prevention & Deterrence.**

The over-riding aim of any security operation is to prevent an attack from taking place in the first instance. All the measures we employ in personal security, tactical driving and anti-surveillance are designed to prevent the enemy from being in a position to mount an ambush, and the correct application of tactical driving skills, combined with and appearance of alertness and professionalism will go along way to get the message across that any attack on this client will not succeed. Going back to surveillance, this is all about being aware of your surroundings. The more aware your team are then the more likely it is that they will spot something out the ordinary. If the team can spot something early on then they will have time to assimilate that information and then decide whether it is a tangible threat or not. If it is then they can do something about it based on that actionable observation. The point here is that if their awareness isn't as acute as it should be then there is not a chance in hell that they will be able to initiate the other two (assimilation & action) in order to come out the other end intact.

The information that follows is designed to make you aware of what is required when an increase in threat has been received and techniques of driving will change in a heartbeat. It is not necessary in a low threat assignment to apply hard drills to the detriment of other road users.

In the event an ambush is sprung, there are a number of principles that must be applied:

3.   **Principles of an Ambush**

   a.   *Protect the client*

      (1)   If in the same vehicle, provide body cover.

      (2)   If in PES vehicle, use the vehicle to provide cover on the client's side.

      (3)   If the vehicle is armoured, leave the client in the vehicle unless it is immobilised and you have an exit strategy.

   b.   *Remove the client from Danger*

   c.   *Fast and Aggressive Action.*

(1)   The team collectively are to move the client from the hostile area.

(2)   Use smoke grenades if available to aid an extraction.

d.   *Do not attack the ambush unless you are using the vehicle or you are certain of your outcome.*

e.   *Beware of decoys and double ambushes*

f.   *Use appropriate drills. Don't cuff it.*

Remember: The object is not to fight – it is to flee, however to flee successfully often requires a high degree of aggression and an immediate trained response.

Never involve yourself in a high-speed chase as you seriously increase your chances of serious injury or losing the day.

4.   **Drills**

In 70% of all attacks, the driver will be hit. Of only 30% of those who escape, the driver remains unhurt. As a driver you will need to lower your profile and assume a 'slouch' position but still be able to control the vehicle. Terrorists/criminals will endeavour to stop a vehicle by stopping the driver.

If you are hit from the rear, try and anticipate the impact and brake to lift the rear of your vehicle and prevent locking. Most cars are fitted with an inertial fuel cut-off in the event of such an incident.

In the event of any evasion manoeuvre, all the weight in the vehicle needs to be as low as possible. Avoid being hit at 90 °. Try always to lessen the impact to your vehicle – a broadside hit will lose you control and momentum. You must take into account that the car is a balanced machine and you must know the effects of weight transference and use it to your advantage when making a hand brake turn or power turn by using a pre roll left or right.

Any roadblock or other criminal attempts have been planned with the benefit of surveillance in mind (*See Chapter 10)* as they must know your times and routes etc. Avoid the necessity, when you are able to, of having to apply 'Actions On' drills, which will follow by staying constantly alert to surveillance. This will drain you and impair your awareness and reactive abilities.

Should the worst happen then your actions will depend on the variable factors mentioned above. That is to say that the block may be late, early or perfectly timed and may also be partially blocked, fully blocked and equally the block itself may have been perceived on time or perceived late.

Your drills will either be ***Defensive*** or ***Offensive***.

Defensive   Your options are to escape to the rear but beware of a block to the rear also.

Offensive   These tactics are when ramming will need to take place.

There are three basic drills that can be used with a single car, 2 or 3-car convoy.

a. <u>Ramming or Drive Through.</u>   This drill should be used when the attack comes from the side but the road is clear, or when the road in front is partially blocked by a lightweight vehicle.

    (1) Drive through at best speed if the road is clear.

    (2) If road is blocked, then:

        (a) Slow down as though intending to stop

        (b) Engage first gear or D2

        (c) Apply brakes sharply and as the nose of the car dips accelerate rapidly from about 15 metres in front of the blocking vehicle.

        (d) Strike the blocking car at a point behind the rear axle and, pushing the block to one side, drive on at the best possible speed allowable under the circumstances.

        (e) Don't swerve and drive straight through

        (f) If using a manual gear box, hold the stick so that it doesn't jump out of gear on impact

        (g) Ensure your thumbs are out of the wheel as you could end up breaking them on impact

        (h) ***Never Hit Broadside***

        (i) Break visual contact as soon as possible

A further breakdown and understanding of this technique is discussed further along in this SOP.

b. <u>The Reverse Out.</u>   This drill should be used when the road is blocked to the front by a substantial obstacle such as a fallen tree or a heavy goods vehicle, coach etc. Consider the following depending on the given situation:

    (1) <u>The 'Y' (2 Point) Turn</u>

        (a) If no obvious signs of an ambush, then use the 'Y' turn drill to leave the area.

        (b) Pull in front of the Client vehicle to put yourself between any suspected hostiles and your Client.
            This drill will not cause any undue concern from the client since it is not aggressive.

        (c) Care must be taken when reversing that there is no obstruction to the rear.

(d)   Turn your vehicle inwards at the same time the client's driver turns his so as to afford maximum cover at all times.

(e)   Both vehicles to drive away as normal with the PES resuming its position behind the clients vehicle.

(f)   Beware of the block to the rear suddenly appear

(2)   <u>The 'J' Turn.</u> This drill should be used when there is an intended ambush to the front that has blocked your means of escape in that direction. The vehicles will generally be travelling at speed (between 30-45 mph) in the reverse direction. This movement differs from the bootleg turn as the latter starts in a forward motion.

Note: If you have ABS fitted, you will not be able to use the brake method as it will be impossible to lock the wheels so read through the part below relevant to your car.

(a)   ***Front Wheel Drive, Manual Transmission – NO ABS***

   i.   Hit the brakes hard and select Drive (R)

   ii.   Check mirrors to ensure no block has been put in place to the rear before reversing.

   iii.   Reverse to between 30-45 mph and then;

   iv.   Turn the wheel sharply in whichever direction you have space in which to turn. Place your hands on the wheel as shown in the picture on the next page.

   v.   Ensure you select D as you turn the wheel so as not to fumble later.

   vi.   The PES car will now be facing in the opposite direction.

   vii.   As the driver straightens out the wheel, hit the accelerator to the floor and leave the hostile area.

   viii.   ***Do not wheel spin whilst attempting to reverse.*** Vital seconds are lost when this happens and you ultimate aim is to leave the area and not be a sitting duck.

(b)   ***Front Wheel Drive, Manual Transmission - ABS***

   i.   You won't be able to lock up the front wheels as used in the option above. This means it will be more difficult to select first gear when the wheels are rotating backwards so you will need to do double-declutching.

ii.   To do this, press the clutch in and pop it into neutral, then clutch out briefly. Clutch in again then select 1st gear. This can be done with a rapid series of movements with practice but adds complexity to this manoeuvre.

(c)   ***Rear or 4 Wheel Drive, Manual Transmission With or Without ABS***

i.   It is very difficult to lock up the rear wheels when pulling off a J-turn, so the easiest method is to avoid using the brakes and double-declutch to select 1st gear. Use the method as set out above to double-declutch.

(d)   ***Automatic transmission, front, rear or four wheel drive with or without ABS***

i.   If you have an automatic, this technique can be much easier to pull off. Mid way through the turn, simply flick into neutral then drive away when you're pointing in the right direction. Some autos are more sympathetic and in this case you'll be able to move straight into drive (D).

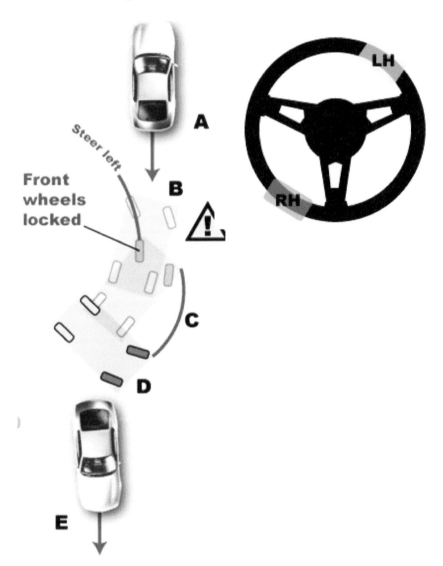

Diagram 11.1

(3)   <u>Evacuate on Foot.</u>   This drill is used when the road is effectively blocked to the front and rear and there is no vehicular means of escape.

    (a)   Vehicle should be stopped in a position whereby maximum cover is afforded by buildings, bushes, walls, trees etc.

    (b)   If PES vehicle is deployed, ensure there is sufficient spacing between the sides of the vehicles to remove the client safely.

    (c)   Use the vehicles as a temporary means of protection.

    (d)   Use smoke grenades if deployed to assist in the extraction.

c.   <u>Bootleg/Hand Brake Turn.</u>   This is a radical type of manoeuvre intended to reverse the direction of travel of a forward-moving vehicle by 180 degrees in a minimum amount of time whilst staying within the width of a two-laned road. The classic bootleg or hand brake turn can only really be effective on cars with a manual transmission and is more easily done with a rear wheeled car as the spinning back wheels will aid in the turn. This is because the manoeuvre is essentially a controlled fishtail spinout. It can easily be adapted for use with an automatic however. If performed correctly, the vehicle will enter a controlled skid, be in the opposite lane and facing in the opposite direction as shown on the following diagram.

(1)   <u>Technique</u>

    (a)   Select a lower gear (usually second) so as not to break the half shaft.

    (b)   Lift the hand brake (to lock the rear wheels only)

    (c)   Turn the wheel in a safe direction, left or right. ***Do Not*** place thumbs inside of the wheel spokes, as you are likely to break them during the violent movement of turning the wheel in the first instance. This drill should now put your vehicle pointing in the opposite direction. Keep your hand on the gearshift so that it doesn't drop out of gear

    (d)   Accelerate away

In a perfect bootleg turn, the car will be at a complete stop at the end of the manoeuvre and ready to accelerate and depart in the opposite direction. It takes practice like most things to perfect a drill.

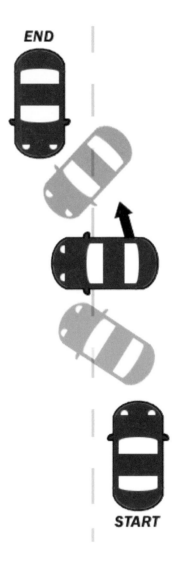

Diagram 11.2

5. **<u>Ramming</u>**

Ramming should only be used as a last resort and in any case where there is a clear and definite exit strategy.

Imagine travelling along a route when you negotiate a bend when several cars pull out and block your path of travel. Behind these vehicles will generally be criminals with hostile intentions. You only have seconds to make a life or death decision; ***Do you reverse or drive through***? Seconds count when in the kill zone and this will be one of the most important decisions in your life.

History shows that the majority of attacks are carried out in and around vehicles. The sole reason for this is that the target is much more vulnerable and the vehicle is easier to penetrate as it is a larger target. Even with state of the art threat detection equipment /procedures along with any pre-planning that has taken place, there will be some degree of vulnerability in the client's daily movement. The assailants will always be on the lookout for your weak spots and this is generally over a period of time. Anti-surveillance should hopefully detect the possibility of being shadowed. Assailants will nearly always have the upper hand, as they will choose the attack point when ready. They will be familiar with the ground and they never play by the rules, therefore, they possess the capability to attack at will.

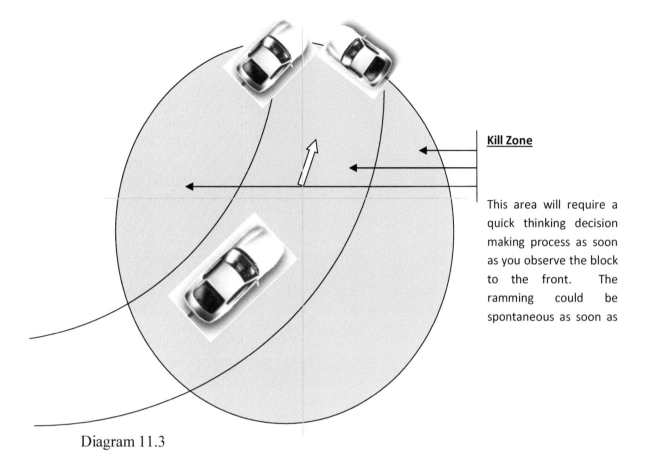

Kill Zone

This area will require a quick thinking decision making process as soon as you observe the block to the front. The ramming could be spontaneous as soon as

Diagram 11.3

A well-trained CP driver understands the value of a vehicle as it is his best weapon and will get the car moving and keep it going until its usage has been exhausted. Just because you are blocked in doesn't mean you can't escape. Ramming the barricade of vehicles is a possibility and should be considered as an option tempered with some reality. You wouldn't ram a lorry, as this will almost invariably immobilise you vehicle and possible cause injury to the car's occupants. Take on what you consider to be a favourable outcome. Ramming should never be considered as the primary means of escaping but only used as a last resort when all else fails.

Ramming your way out of a kill zone could cause damage to your vehicle and generally takes longer than backing up or driving around the barricade. Applying the correct technique could make a difference between success and failure and life and death. The following technique should be considered if you have made an evaluation and considered this as your only option:

    a.   Stop your vehicle short of the barricade at approx.10-15 feet that may briefly imply to the aggressors that you intend to go the other way or give up.

    b.   Put the gear into the lowest selector and hold the gear stick firmly since under pressure it may pop out of gear.

  c. Depress the accelerator (do not cause a wheel spin) but don't let up on the pressure.

  d. Vehicle placement is critical. You will need to place the frame of your car, the most solid part, directly into the axle of the barricade vehicle. Once contact is made you will be able to move the obstruction once your vehicle has built up enough force. What is happening at this point is that the amount of force that your vehicle has generated is being applied to the only part of the barricaded vehicle that is connected to the ground (the tyres).

  e. After you initially hit the vehicle and break the barricade, make sure that you leave the accelerator pedal depressed and not let up. Hesitation will almost certainly move the chances of success into the hands of the aggressors.

To practice ramming in a safe environment first is essential so that you are aware of what pressure to apply to the accelerator, what the picture looks like 10-15 feet from the barricade and what it feels like during the act of ramming. Only when you are confident with the techniques/methods will you have a greater chance of escaping with your life intact and those you have been charged with to protect.

At the height of the moment in real-time, bullets may be flying, adrenaline is pumping and the potential for a mistake is exponentially increased. The only real cure for adrenaline is **Practice** and more practice to the point where it becomes instinctive and without hesitation. The reasoning as to what would be the best course of action takes a nana-second for a trained person rather than the vent becoming a freeze-frame and then all in the vehicle come up with ideas that are conflicting and confusing; **Result – Chaos and mayhem**. If the driver is in control then others will follow his ideology.

The trained driver would hopefully not experience problems caused by judgemental errors, such as:

  a. Slowing down after the initial impact. This is often the first reaction. The car will lose its ability of power and momentum and make it tough to finish the extraction. You don't want to get stuck between two vehicles, as you are likely to find that the aggressors will latch onto this moment. If you do get stuck, shake the wheel but get the pressure applied back to the accelerator and hopefully you will break lose.

  b. If the driver puts in too much speed it will cause the cars to collide at a much greater speed with the potential of causing injury/damage. The object is to escape relatively intact and to get your client to a safe house ASAP.

Using the ramming technique with a newer model of vehicle has the potential of deploying the in-built airbag safety system. As mentioned several times earlier in this section, ramming is to be considered as a last resort where you find yourself in a situation with only one choice. The airbag deploying at the point of the event is the least of your worries. Yes it is a violent explosion and injuries can occur but it beats getting shot or having your client kidnapped. The main problem once the airbag has deployed is that most vehicles become disabled. If this happens then all your efforts will be for nothing because the vehicles computer will need to be reset. The technique for doing this differs from vehicle to vehicle. Before you worry about the computer, step back and analyse the problem. It may not be as bad as you would expect.

First of all the airbag is a supplementary device used to distribute the occupants force more evenly and help the seat belt to stop the occupants more gradually in a frontal crash. Although this force varies, most vehicle manufacturers say that the vehicle has to have an impact that generates at least 7G's before the airbag is released. An example of 7G's would be similar to driving into a brick wall at 9-15 mph. A solid brick obstruction however has no give therefore the airbag will deploy. On the other side of the coin, if the obstruction gives way that would mean that the energy is being spread between the vehicle and the other objects, there would be a chance that the force generated was not large enough to actually deploy the airbag. In simple terms, the air bag is designed to deploy when occupants are in danger of hitting their heads or bodies against the dashboard or steering wheel. Chances are that the airbag won't deploy if the forces generated aren't large enough.

All airbag fitted vehicles use sensors that if their set threshold level is breached would deploy the airbag. Every vehicle has a different setting and each year a more sophisticated model is introduced into the market. A lot of factors come into play which makes the decision making process that much more difficult. Things like, weight of the barricade cars or how much force will it take to move a van vs car. What surface will the attack happen on? Dirt will give a better chance than concrete for the simple reason that it will take less force to break the traction of the barricade vehicle tyres. It is difficult for a CP team to plan a success rate of this technique unless all of these factors are considered prior to deployment. An airbag is a mechanical device and as such there will never be a 100% guarantee that it will deploy when required but nevertheless, what has been mentioned above should still be considered to increase your chances.

Vehicles that initiate the barricade don't follow the rules and they park them in positions that would not be to your advantage. Over time they will have seen historical roadblocks and how successful each were and adapted accordingly. Most ramming techniques show you two cars rear bumper to rear bumper in an inverted manner. This is great for practicing but in reality cars will be front bumper to front bumper also in the inverted configuration. The heaviest part of the vehicle is to the front (engine block) and if you have an option to ram then it won't be at this point. The rear portion of the vehicle is still the best option in order to pivot the vehicle around on its own axis giving you space to extract.

Awareness is still the key to staying alive. It is essential that spatial awareness is considered at every opportunity to maximise your decision making process. The application as to whether or not you should implement ramming is not to be taken lightly, but if you have no other choice, then probably the decision has been made for you…

There are several training schools that can provide modular training on this subject.

6. **<u>Braking Techniques</u>**

Braking a vehicle is not just a matter of applying the foot brake and slowing the vehicle or bringing the car to a halt. It is a technique and a useful skill to master for safety's sake. It may also save the day for you in a given situation. Several braking techniques are discussed further down this SOP and consideration has been given to cars with or without ABS.

Good braking technique is a compromise between the following two factors:

1. If you have locked your front wheels, you lose steering control.

2. The point of maximum deceleration is just before the point of wheel lock.

a. <u>ABS and what is it?</u>

ABS was first introduced in cars in 1978 but has since rapidly increased in complexity and versatility since its inception. By rapidly applying and releasing the brakes in pulses when wheel lock is detected, ABS allows you to both slow down and steer at the same time. In cars with ABS, some of the non-ABS techniques that follow may not be relevant but are provided as an overview in the event you are using a non-ABS vehicle. The ideology behind ABS is to prevent wheels from locking and also slows you down quicker than any manual braking technique, especially on wet or slippery roads.

Hopefully you will never have the need to use any of the following techniques but as part of your anti-ambush driving capabilities you must be knowledgeable and skilled in their application.

The old adage *'Prevention is far better than the cure'* is appropriate in a lot of what being a CPO is all about.

b. <u>What is the best technique for slowing down?</u>

This will very much depend on what you are trying to achieve and the circumstances that you find yourself in at the time. Whatever technique you use, locked wheel braking should be avoided where possible as it does not allow steering control to be maintained.

The four types of braking techniques being discussed in this SOP are:

(1)   Threshold braking

(2)   ABS braking

(3)   Locked wheels

(4)   Cadence braking

c.   Threshold Braking

Threshold braking is by far the best strategy to adopt to gain maximum braking performance on tarmac. The point of maximum braking performance is found before the point of wheel lock and when using this method it is essential that you attempt to try and keep the braking pressure just before this point. In reality however, it is often difficult to know exactly the point at which wheels will lock as many factors will come into play such as tarmac conditions, tyre choice and brake temperature.

d.   ABS Braking

Modern ABS systems are now so good that unless you are a very good driver it can be hard to slow down more efficiently than by using this system. Even if ABS is fitted and it's really good, it's still better to threshold brake and prevent the system coming into play in the first instance. ABS is reactive to a given set of circumstances and is intelligent enough to figure out when it needs to be electronically activated.

e.   Locked Wheel Braking

In some conditions it is more beneficial for the wheels to lock in order to aid the slowing of the car. On loose gravel for instance stopping distances are increased by at least 22%. A locked wheel on gravel allows for a wedge of gravel to build up in front of the tyre, thus aiding braking. A similar issue can occur when driving on snow or in sandy conditions.

f.   Cadence Braking

This method is ideal for use on very low grip surfaces such as an icy road. This method is essentially the applying and releasing the brakes rhythmically in order to get a compromise between steering and braking performance. As you apply the brakes, the wheels will tend to lock up, slowing the car but preventing you from steering. As you release the brakes you regain steering control and can keep the car pointing in the right direction.

Note: Attempting to use cadence braking on a good grip surface at speed will result in weight transfers which can unsettle the car, possibly resulting in over steer. ***This is not a technique to adopt on good grip surfaces!***

Just because a braking technique is not the quickest to bring you to a halt doesn't mean that it shouldn't be used, cornering ability while braking also needs to be considered. Locked wheels do not permit steering so this is only an option when you have a clear straight line ahead of you, however ABS equipped cars and the cadence braking technique both allow you to steer at the same time.

The picture below reflects the braking distances using the 4 methods described above.

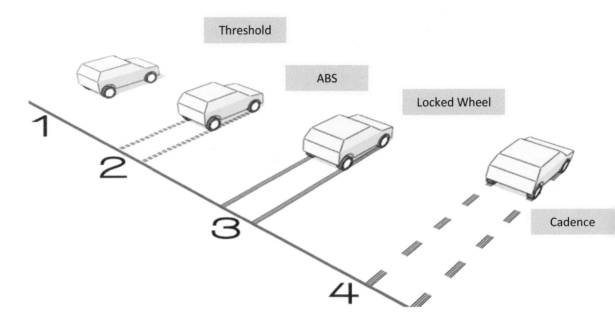

Diagram 11.4 Effects of the different types of braking

7.   **<u>Conclusion</u>**

The response to an ambush has to be rapid and must be constructive. This can only be achieved by constant practice by the PES and client drivers alike. A hesitation, a misunderstanding between client and PES drivers or an inability to recognise the situation, could cost the client their lives.

This chapter is not intended to teach you how to apply the drills but is an overview of what would be expected in a given set of circumstances and qualified and experienced instructors on recognised courses can only do this. There are many courses available which would teach you the skills necessary to become proficient, confident and hopefully provide you with a set of skills to survive the day should you find yourself in such a position.

Constant practice is necessary to perfect the types of driving mentioned in this SOP but initially attending a course would give you the practical experience of how to do the drills correctly. After which, you build on that foundation of knowledge.

No attempt should be made to practice these drills based on the content of this book. This book makes no suggestion that it can provide a level of instruction but merely that it cannot replace the level of instruction/training that a recognised course of instruction can deliver.

Chapter 12

Planning a PSD (CP) Operation

1. **Introduction.**

   The success or failure of a Close Protection operation rests in the planning. As a person in a position of authority/responsibility you may be asked to plan an operation. It matters not how good the members of the team may or not be if the operation is poorly planned. The DPG, SAS and the RMP CPT's are renowned for their meticulous planning of operations throughout the world. It is not practical to develop and promulgate an Operational Oder (OpO) for every small operation but where there are complex issues relating to the op that requires more information than normal then you should be mindful that to convey detailed instructions it might be best to prepare an OpO. The preparation of an OpO could equally relate to low profile (low threat) and high profile (high threat) operations. OpO's can be written for both domestic and international missions. Overseas of course will require more time to construct as you will involve other agencies and if there is a major shift in timings (east or west) then of course this will have an effect on any time lines that have been set which may be mission critical.

2. **Principles.**

   The following principles must be applied when planning an operation:

   a.   Attention to Detail.   This is vital in every aspect of the operation. Check and check again. Make sure it is current, accurate and relevant.

   b.   Accurate Timings.   This whole plan rests on accurate timings. Try and insist on these as early as possible.

   c.   Reconnaissance/Advance.   A recee or advance is necessary very early on and later by team members (if deploying)

   d.   Liaison.   This must be carried out at all levels and with all interested parties. The bulk of information needed to prepare a plan will initially be given by someone close to the family you are assigned to who will also give authority at that time for the recruitment of personnel to fulfil the task. Additionally, any authority needed for financial expenditure will also be given during the initial stages where budgetary constraints are to be implemented.

   e.   Appreciations.   These must be detailed.

   f.   Operational Orders.   The success of the operation hinges on everyone knowing what he/she is doing. A good detailed order is essential. An example is attached to another chapter further in the book.

3.   **Tasking.**

It will be your responsibility to assess the threat and to task a CPT to provide Close Protection to those at risk. Dependent upon the size of the operation, you will also be responsible for organising all aspects of security in consultation with the interested party within the organisation.

Before you can carry out the task, you should acquaint yourself with all relevant factors pertaining to the task to make sure nothing is over looked.

4.   **The Threat.**

As a supervisor you must obtain up to date threat assessments from all relevant agencies and sources within, and if necessary outside your country of operation. The assessment gained will assist you in deciding the level of protection to be provided including the level of resources deployed. Chapter 13 covers threat assessments.

5.   **The Itinerary.**

The expectation of an advanced itinerary is generally a luxury and certainly with any private clients you may be detailed to look after. Corporate ones are more likely to have a structured agenda. One part of the planning process is manpower allocation. If any advance notification of moves is readily available then it is essential that detailed reconnaissance, liaison visits with other agencies providing support and with those involved with any administration is carried out sooner rather than later.

It is far simpler to incorporate the security plan at the initial stages of preparation than to introduce it after all administrative arrangements have been settled. After this it will become chaotic and will often be on a wing and a prayer.

6.   **The Client.**

Before deciding on the requirements of what Close Protection is needed, you must obtain all possible details of the client to be protected. A lot of required information that is often needed to build a client profile such as; blood groups, habits, interests, likes and dislikes together with information on family and personal staff. Some clients may be reluctant to offer this information to you especially if based on religious grounds.

7.   **Planning Sequence.**

The following is an aide-memoir and outlines the sequence of events leading up to the operation. There should remain a degree of flexibility.

a.   Notification of Task. There may be ample warning (3 months) or very little (3 hours)

b.   Threat Assessment. Carry out the seven P's to identify any obvious signs/threats/concerns.

c.   <u>Initial Liaison.</u>

   (1)   Chief Ops Officer (if one exists)

   (2)   Chief Property Officer

   (3)   Logistics Manager in respect of transportation

   (4)   Police

   (5)   Contact with any European security representatives if travel is expected.

   (6)   Any additional Security Managers.

d.   <u>Initial Reconnaissance.</u>   Walk/drive through any expected event programmes or locations to be visited. This will assist in the appreciation phase and identify problem areas early on.

e.   <u>Appreciation.</u> Write the appreciation.

f.   <u>Warning Order.</u>   As soon as notification has been given that an event is to take place then you should notify all those personnel expected to take part. It should be initiated as soon as it has been received from the client and evaluated.

g.   <u>Orders.</u> Write operational orders. If necessary, plans and models may be used if this would aid any familiarisation of the ground.

h.   <u>Team Assembly.</u>   The team should come together and rehearse if necessary or if time permits.

i.   <u>Orders to the Team.</u>   The OpO should be read to the team members taking part. Those not involved should not attend the meeting as it will be classified as Confidential.

j.   <u>Team Reconnaissance.</u>   Whether a single PPO or as part of a multiple team, all members must recee the whole operation if there is time. This allows for instant redeployments in the event of accident, sickness etc.

k.   <u>Team Training.</u>   Ensure that all IADs in the event of a variety of incidents whether on foot or in vehicles is constantly rehearsed and drilled. The procedural work of embus/debus should be practised. Physical fitness should be vital form of pre op training. Every CPO should have a high level of physical fitness.

l.   <u>Final liaison with Relevant Parties</u>

m.   <u>The CP Operation</u>

The time taken to plan an operation can often be long hours. The Plan of Action in all situations must be on the assumption that something will happen. *'Plan for the worst and hope for the best'*. The basic assumption should also be that any evacuation will proceed without difficulty. Contingencies should be prepared and drills practiced. The following intangibles should be taken into account:

a. Travelling time to and from liaison and reconnaissance visits

b. The arranging of meetings at mutually convenient times

c. Programme changes

d. Availability of personnel to form the CPT

e. Availability of appropriate vehicle, radios, mobile phones and any other accessories

The following list should be used to assist when establishing a CPT for either long or short periods:

a. <u>The Threat.</u>

    (1)   Liaison with local and national SB and the security services in London for an assessment of the current and future threat from:

        (a)   Extremist Organisations

        (b)   People with personal grievances.

        (c)   Embassies

    (2)   Is the threat aimed at the appointment of the client, their connection with various organisations or people, their status and wealth or just to the client for what they stand for

    (3)   You must keep the team up to date on any developments as the planning and ultimately the op begins.

    (4)   Receive constant update briefings on the local situation.

    (5)   Any required levels of training to be carried out by the deployed team must depend on the level of threat to the client.

b. <u>The Existing PES.</u>   If there is an existing PES deployed, it is important to consider the following before deciding on any changes:

    (1)   Is the present organisation well rounded and efficient

    (2)   Is it over or under strength

    (3)   Is it loyal, if so to what extent

    (4)   What is the state of its training (individual and collective)

    (5)   Is the present morale good

    (6)   Check on its potential

c.   <u>Proposed Changes.</u>   Before any change is made to the existing team, consideration should be given to the following:

    (1)   The team must be designed to meet the needs of each client highlighting specific skills useful on the op.

    (2)   HR to set up a vetting programme to tighten up the security of the team members

    (3)   The power of selection must be left to the Manager to avoid personal interference in selecting staff.

    (5)   It is important that all team members are up to the physical, mental and educational standards required. It was mentioned in chapter 5 the criteria used in selecting CP personnel.

c.   <u>The Client's Habits.</u>   Outside of this assignment and if the chance exists to obtain information in which to profile the client, then the following should be considered:

    (1)   What are the client's likes and dislikes?

    (2)   What is the image that the client displays?

    (3)   What is the client's preference for means of travel?

    (4)   What kind of protection is required by the client?

    (5)   Does the client accept an escort when attending a private function or during silent hours?

    (6)   What hobbies does the client have?

    (7)   Who are the client's closest friends?

    (8)   Who are regular visitors to the residence?

    (9)   What people make up the family in all respects?

As mentioned earlier, the above information may not be ordinarily available for planning purposes on your assignment.

<u>Residence.</u>   This may be contracted out to a third party but the ideal would be to be manned by the CPT. The following would be useful for planning purposes.

    (10)   How many are there (both domestic and international)?

    (11)   Types of each (town houses, apartments, mansions)

(12)   Present security at each (K9's, static, mobile, electronic)

(13)   Layout of each with floor plans (briefings, rapid interdiction, fire)

(14)   Loyalty of Staff – vetted (including driver)

(15)   Routes to and from with primary & secondary

(16)   Embus and debus points

(17)   Is there an HLS in situ or nearby?

(18)   Are there facilities to establish an ops room at each location?

(19)   Is there any room for improvement at each location?

d.   Finance & Manpower Available

(1)   Regardless of who the client is on any assignment, both points will dictate the size of any PES, support or a single PPO.

(2)   What equipment is available and what may be procured?

(3)   Are there any assisting forces of outside agencies available?

(4)   The level of protection will depend on the manpower that has been authorised by the client that is within the budgets given. Be prepared for some slimming down though.

e.   Administration.

(1)   Is the current admin support up to the standard required?

(2)   Request the use of a separate area/building for offices and stores

(3)   Establish own supply of training stores

(4)   Care and maintenance of equipment

(5)   Reporting sick/Absence

f.   Command and Control

(1)   Set up a security committee with:

(a)   The client's representative

(b)   Other relevant security agencies

(c)   Establish a Chain of Command

g. <u>Training.</u>   In order to function correctly as a team, fitness and skills need to be honed to perfection. The last thing that you need is to be distracted away from the client by the fact that a team member is dragging their heals and can't keep up the pace. It is true to say that the team is only as good as the last man. The skill here is not to have a last man so that you all stand shoulder to shoulder so to speak.

   (1)   All members of the team should be up to a high standard.

   (2)   The CPT must make time to train be it personal skills, group skills or collective skills.

   (3)   Any group or collective skills must be done in secret (away from the public and non-involved personnel). Should also include client drivers in certain drills where there is a desire for them to be on-board.

   (4)   Any training area must be made as secure as possible.

   (5)   Set a high standard so as to ensure that it is maintained.

   (6)   Where possible, training should cover all the eventualities of the client's lifestyle within the limitations that are imposed on your assignment.

h. <u>PES & PPO OpO to Include the following:</u>

   (1)   <u>Discipline</u>

      (a)   Behaviour on and off duty

      (b)   Dress and appearance

      (c)   Chain of Command

   (2)   <u>Weapons & Ammunition (Outside UK Only)</u>

      (a)   Adhere to the participating countries regulations on the storage of both firearms and ammunition.

      (b)   The local procedure for the carriage of weapons on and off duty

      (c)   Maintenance and cleaning

      (d)   Orders for opening fire that must be both clear and concise.

      (e)   Weapon training.

(3)   Vehicles

    (a)   To cover:

        i.   Security (Parking arrangements)

        ii.   Searching (Full or Short)

        iii.   Control of Keys

        iv.   Maintenance (including breakdown procedure)

        v.   Cleaning

        vi.   Refuelling (Where and how. Cash or fuel card?)

(4)   Emergency Procedures

    (a)   Inform only those personnel of other agencies concerned with the client security.

    (b)   Inform the security committee

    (c)   Inform SB or equivalent (if necessary)

    (d)   The client must be moved to a safe house that all team members must know.

    (e)   A security clamp down must be imposed on the release of any information concerning the client

    (f)   The client's representative will decide on any projected move of the clients to extricate from the area. He will notify you in the 1st instance then you can inform the team accordingly.

    (g)   The PPO/PES must have:

        i.   Orders laid down for drills

        ii.   Knowledge of location where to report to in the event of an emergency and what the task will be.

    (h)   Medical

        i.   Static

            (i)   Locate the locstat of the nearest medical facility (static or roaming)

> (ii) Medical conditions may not be notified to the CP team concerning the clients that may hamper any attempts to sustain life.
>
> (iii) If a doctor is with the group then he will probably be on call

ii. Mobile

> (i) Doctor to travel with the client if necessary or in separate vehicle.
>
> (ii) PES (if deployed) and CPO to know advanced first aid
>
> (iii) If available, medical first aid packs must be carried in the vehicle and located at the CP Ops Room.

iii. Procedures for Medical Assistance

> (i) PPO/PES to administer first aid
>
> Doctor/EMT takes over
>
> (iii) Move to hospital if necessary

2. **Conclusion**

There is a lot of work required during the planning phase of the op. The price of failure is high or you may be lucky and just scrape through by cuffing things as you go along. Meticulous planning not only satisfies the planner that everything has been thought about but gives the team members the satisfaction of knowing what is expected of them at any given time. A well-organised team could be mirrored against a well-oiled machine, as all cogs will fit in their respective places. Remember also that should an incident happen there will be an investigation to follow and if you can satisfy the investigators that you covered every eventuality then you can be satisfied that you did the best you possibly could at the time.

Don't be tempted to cut corners as it is guaranteed that an important piece of the jigsaw will be overlooked which may have serious consequences on the outcome of the op. It could be something as simple as Top Hat & Tails for an equine event. Order too late and you miss the fanfare, which means your client will be going on their own. Not a good career move…

Chapter 13

THREAT ASSESSMENTS

1. **Introduction.**

We live in a different world today than we did before 1990 and the need to be mindful of this changing situation is as real as it can be. A Close Protection Operation is normally mounted in response to a particular threat whether deployed as a single PPO or a fully equipped CPT. The assessment defines the current situation, the historic development, the methodology of any extremist groups and ultimately determines in which category the client is to be placed and the expected resources commensurate with that threat category. Every CP deployment must have a threat assessment in order for the team to fully engage in the role they are being employed for. It will be your responsibility as a Team Leader, Detail Supervisor or Ops manager to audit any client threat.

It is very rare that management will be given a comprehensive threat assessment. This may be because there is insufficient intelligence to support an accurate prediction of an enemy course of action. It is impossible to provide an effective shield against every eventuality and it is essential that management be able to conduct their own appreciation of the threat. As Managers, Team Leaders or Supervisors you may find that limitations are imposed due in some part to the nature of the client. These limitations however are personal and not intended as a hindrance to the compilation of the assessment.

A number of sources ranging from the SB, SIS, Local Police, GCHQ and others are available and if you have contacts within any of these departments then they can be invaluable. If you are detailed to a Middle-Eastern client in the UK, then the UAE embassy in London may be a source of intelligence covering local Intel from within his or her own borders. Making contact with these groups however is more of a challenge. It takes time to be accepted by them and once in they are on side and often willing to oblige but with some limitations of course.

The whole object of a Threat Assessment is to try and negate any hostile intent against a client in the first instance. Surveillance covered in an earlier chapter would be a valuable starting point and would make your task a little easier. Whilst there is never a 100% guarantee of success in security it nevertheless goes a long way towards countering an offensive and any defensive strategy applied will be initiated as per your SOP 'Actions On' in a confident, robust and well-rehearsed manner. The outcome will depend on how you react.

A definition of Threat Assessment in CP could be:

'Determine the risks associated with all potential threats and then balance these with the security measures we can take to negate them'

Compiling a threat assessment shouldn't be rushed since areas may be missed or not thought through thoroughly enough, as they should be. It shouldn't be written down on the back of scrap paper either but with a logical approach to what is and isn't required. A locally reproduced template could be the answer to filling in the blanks but they must be constructed in a way so as nothing is over-looked at any time throughout the writing process. They will also need to be revised and up dated over time. Areas or sections within a template could be scored out if it is decided that a particular part has no bearing on the assessment being developed at that point. Whether a client is the President of a Country or a HVT elsewhere, the information required should be no different. It's how you use it to your advantage. The end game is to ensure the safety of your client and others who fall within the threat assessment.

2.   **History of Threats**

Threats typically arise in one of two forms: natural or human. Natural threats are largely unchanged over the course of history; environmental disasters such as hurricanes, earthquakes and tornadoes occur in the same way they always have. Yet population growth and centralisation in large metropolitan areas, as a modern development, raise the impact of those disasters to a much higher level.

Threats posed by human malicious intent have evolved in tandem with the growth of civilisation and the evolution of technology. The oldest social groups on record undoubtedly targeted one another in some fashion, which still occurs in today's social and political landscapes. The tools and weapons available in the current day, however, shape the manifestation of those threats. Advances in technology have been utilised for criminal and inhumane purposes. The advances and evolution of threats driven by human intent necessitate specialised skill to assess and formulate appropriate responses to them. This chapter is introduced to specifically address human threats only.

3.   **Types of Threats**

When compiling a threat assessment it is important to keep in mind the following types of threats that a client may have had or may potentially receive:

a.   *Direct Threat.*   This identifies a specific act against a specific target and is delivered in a straightforward, clear and explicit manner.

b.   *Indirect Threat*   These tend to be vague, unclear or ambiguous. The plan, the intended victim, the motivation and other aspects of the threat are masked or equivocal.

c.   *Veiled Threat.*   Strongly implies but does not explicitly threaten violence. How these threats are interpreted will be how the potential target or assessment team view the message.

d.   *Conditional Threat.* This will warn of a violent act against a person unless certain terms and demands are met.

Many people make threats yet never carry out the actions associated with them. Of those who make a threat and do carry it out, most make a direct threat. Yet those who do consummate their intent make public threats merely 13% of the time. For example, the perpetrators of the 2013 Boston Marathon bombing made no threat publicly or directly to the event planners. The fact that most people who commit targeted violent acts do not communicate their intentions by making threats complicates the process of planning to respond to them.

It is likely that if your client is under surveillance as a pre-cursor to some final act, then no particular threat will be received. It will be down to the PSD (CP) team to identify such interest through anti-surveillance techniques in the first instance.

4.   **Levels of Threat**

Table 13.1

Presumptive Indicators		
Low Level	*Medium Level*	*High Level*
Any threat which is vague and indirect. May be generic rather than specific.	Threat is more direct and more concrete than a low level threat. Clients name, company, associates, family have been named.	Direct, Specific & Plausible
Info within the threat is inconsistent, implausible or lacks detail to have any credibility.	Wording of any threat suggests that the person threatening has given some thought to how the act will be carried out.	Threat suggests concrete steps have been taken toward carrying it out perhaps the person threatening has had the target under surveillance and has info that gives an event some credence.
Threat lacks realism, which would limit the event being initiated.	General indication of a possible place and time (but not a detailed plan).	
Content suggests the person is unlikely to carry it out.	Strong indication that the person threatening has taken preparatory steps, although there may be some veiled reference or ambiguous or inconclusive evidence pointing to that possibility or a vague, general statement about the availability of weapons etc.	
	Specific statement seeking to convey that the threat is not empty and will be executed at a time and place of their choosing.	

The three levels of threat explained in table 13.1 above reflect on the three levels and their significance.

5.   **Aim of Threat Assessments**

The expressed purpose of conducting a Threat Assessment is to identify threats and prepare a plan of action with which to respond to or counter them. A previously completed risk assessment provides the starting point from which to evaluate potential threats, determining whether any of those identified risks are still current or escalating to a pending target. The threat assessment refines the evaluation of risk and tailors the response to account for the ways the threat could be manifested and the severity of impact to client.

The risk assessment process should have resulted in the development of preliminary contingency plans to address the risk.

The threat assessment on the other hand tailors those plans to respond to the now pending threat. Threat assessments, as the final step in developing a security program, cannot be relegated to a shelf. If a threat has been identified in the course of conducting an assessment that threat must be continuously monitored until it has dissipated and is no longer a viable cause of concern

6.   **Purpose of Threat Assessments**

a.   To determine the credibility of that threat and the likelihood it will be carried out.

b.   To identify any person or group posing a threat to the client.

c.   To approximate the means and method by which the person or group would execute their threat, their ability to do so and the timeline on which they might act.

The relevance of interest by a terrorist or criminal group is raised if proposed travel puts a client in a country or region within the borders of a particular group that operates and where the client's profile would fit the groups known target profile. The client on the other hand if they were on home ground then their reasoning for any form of attack would be motivated for financial gain and not political. Whilst abroad, they become symbolic targets through kidnap or assassination where a motive may be to strike at the heart of the Muslim community with a view to changing any political strongholds.

If a threat is non-specific, as a consequence of position, wealth or prominence then there is an all-pervading threat that must be catered for. Note that if a specific threat from a group made many years earlier to the company, its employees and owners; it may become relevant today if a visit to the country of origin is proposed. In this case, a Threat Assessment is looked at in the light of *'Not if but when'*

As the Threat Assessment begins to take shape, it must be bourn in mind that we now need to start being balanced with resources and that *'Security must be commensurate with the threat'*. Once the potential threat has been evaluated, it can then be determined what the appropriate security measures are to be put into place to secure the risk. Such identified risks should be avoided where possible, but if they can't be then efforts must be focused on minimising these risks. Without an appropriate threat assessment the team will be in the dark and have no idea as to the level of protective effort required, nor when, how or where a threat might manifest itself.

The threat assessment should not merely be centered on Criminal or Terrorist activities but should also include fire, theft, accidents, illness, harassment etc. The CPT is there to prevent harm from whatever source befalls the client. If the water in a city is undrinkable, even in a 5* hotel, then such pollution problems should be contained within the Threat Assessment and the client advised accordingly so this particular risk can be mitigated.

7. **Principles.**

The following principles should be applied:

a. Any written or verbal assessment must be clear and concise.

b. The assessment must be logical and constructive in its layout.

c. An accurate assessment that is up to date is vital with as much relevant information as possible for a fair evaluation to be made.

d. It must be relevant to the task in hand and the country of operations and equally to the client being assessed.

e. It must be brief, succinct and clear for all to understand. Over complicated or a jargon infused assessment will kill any enthusiasm an audience may have had.

8. **Method.**

a. Aim. The Detail Supervisor, Team Leader's assessment must not only be to identify the most likely form of attack, but also the most likely place and time for it to take place.

b. Client. Ask the questions; Why may the client be a target? Is it because of his current appointment, previous appointments or because of who he is? Is it because of any connections to organisations that are against some kind of development? See also the seven P's profiling below. It may not be a singular client at risk but also family members who will need to be considered.

c. Identify the Enemy. By knowing the number and nature of terrorist groups or criminal gangs which are active globally it should be possible, from the answer to 3a above, to deduce which group or groups pose a threat to the client. Criminal groups must also be looked into as both groups (Terrorist/Criminals) will have a different agenda and certainly their outcome expectations will differ greatly.

d. Study the Enemy. Once a likely enemy has been identified then a detailed study of the group will be necessary. This should include:

      (1)   Individuals who make up the group (names, aliases, descriptions, histories etc)

      (2)   Favoured Modus Operandi (MO)

      (3)   Present capabilities in relation to any proposed client programme

      (4)   There last known attack of significance

      (5)   Does the group work alone

From this it should be feasible to deduce the most likely form of attack.

e.   <u>Study the Ground.</u>   A study of the ground to be covered during a client move/visit, related to terrorist weapons, traffic conditions, the favoured MO and weaknesses in building, perimeter or vehicle security should now indicate the likely location for an attack

f.   <u>Study Timings.</u>   An examination of movement times will show when the client is going to be present at vulnerable points and when that routine will increase the likelihood of an attack.

g.   <u>Client Profiling (The seven P's)</u>

The following is a list of headings of information that the CPT needs to know about the client when compiling an assessment. On this assignment however a majority of what follows will not be forthcoming but should still form part of the initial assessment and left blank where appropriate.

a.   *People.*   A list of all the clients associates, contacts, family by blood and marriage, friends, acquaintances etc; basically a list of people with whom the client feels comfortable with. This category can also include competitors/opponents and social contacts.

b.   *Places.*   Places where people are born, educated, sport, holidays, previous addresses, work or live all have importance in one way or another to the threat assessment. Geographic implications will often affect the 'risks' if not the overall threat.

c.   *Personality.*   The client themselves should be included in the list of possible dangers especially if they have a poor attitude to security. Some people with a confrontational, arrogant, brash, dismissive, provocative, boastful, vain, ambitious, devious, unscrupulous, fastidious, methodical, mean or abrasive lifestyle often attract problems. Many clients will put their personal security at risk in pursuit of an active social life and expect you to clear up the fall-out.

d.   <u>Prejudices.</u>   Is there a strong religious, racial or cultural prejudice? These potential encounters need to be avoided.

e.   *Personal History.*   If information is forthcoming, then the following basic background information on the client should be obtained. *Do not* expect the release of such information on this assignment.

   (1)   Title, Name and age

   (2)   Place of birth, marital status

   (3)   Previous and current nationalities

   (4)   Languages, military service and any awards

   (5)   Qualifications

   (6)   Previous appointments of influence

   (7)   What title does the client hold

   (8)   Medical history (if available)

   (9)   Levels of fitness, likes and dislikes, ailments, medications, blood groups etc.

   (10)   Convictions

f.   Private Lifestyle.   Is the client;

   (1)   A family man or a philanderer?

   (2)   Drinking, gambling habits or history of drug abuse.

   (3)   Sporting and pastime activities including achievements?

   (4)   Does the client drive or like to be driven?

   (5)   Is the client a workaholic?

   (6)   Does the client keep a low profile despite prominence or does the client seek a profile above their position?

   (7)   What are the client's tastes in food?

g.   Political and Religious Persuasions.

   (1)   What are the client's political views?

   (2)   Do they hold influence?

   (3)   Any published opinions or comments?

   (4)   Membership or association of any political organisation?

   (5)   Practice political faiths?

   (6)   Political ambition?

9. **Threat Categories**.

Having formulated the threat assessment, the Client now needs to be placed in a threat category. The following three broad categories are sub divided. Although the numbering system has been used, it could quite easily be referred to in colours (Red, Amber & Green) or levels (High, Medium or Low).

a. *Category One* (Cat 1)

(1) Cat 1a – The client is in considerable danger

(2) Cat 1b – An attack is suspected

b. *Category Two* (Cat 2)

(1) Cat 2a – The client is in some danger

(2) Cat 2b – An attack cannot be ruled out

c. *Category Three* (Cat 3)

(1) Cat 3a – There may be a threat of some kind

(2) Cat 3b – An attack is a remote possibility

Remember: Cat 1 is in the category of '*Not if, but when*'

Cat 2 is in the category of '*Not when, but if*'

Cat 3 is in the category of '*Could be of interest to someone with ill designs*'

10. **Manpower v Threat Categories**.

Having deduced the category of threat in which to place the client, it follows that in order to provide the level of protection needed to sustain and eliminate a risk, manpower and resources will be necessary. The following should be considered in broad terms:

a. Category 1. The client would get:

(1) A PPO

(2) A PES

(3) Maximum protection of:

(4) Residence (RST)

(5) Places to be visited (SAP)

(6) Use of electronic fortifications

(7)   Armoured vehicle

(8)   Place of work

b.   <u>Category 2.</u>   The client would get:

(1)   A PPO

(2)   A PES

(3)   Some protection of the above as in Cat 1

c.   <u>Category 3.</u>

(1)   The client may get a PPO

(2)   Possible routine search of both place of work and residence.

(3)   PES when needed

(4)   Surveillance awareness

(5)   Security awareness advice given to client

11.   **Conclusion**

The compilation of a threat assessment is merely an information gathering exercise, as it doesn't give any cast iron guarantee that a crisis will be averted or indeed initiate but it will allow you to respond to them effectively when they do arise. The collation and study of intelligence should enable the CPT to reach a reasonable conclusion regarding the most likely form, time and place of an attack. This information will be included in the main appreciation under the heading of enemy courses. Other forms of threat must not be discarded. It must be remembered that a threat assessment can be broad based as simply the political stability or otherwise of a whole country. In every case however, it has many threads and facets that you will need to consider, digest and evaluate accordingly to maintain that sterile environment in which your client requires that freedom of movement.

A threat assessment is an on-going process within a team or group that will need to be addressed frequently. It will be the final, but nevertheless comprehensive development plan for safety and security of everyone.

Above all, it's important that you ensure that the clients are not aware of a threat to themselves about which you are blissfully unaware.

THE THREAT ASSESSMENT PROCESS

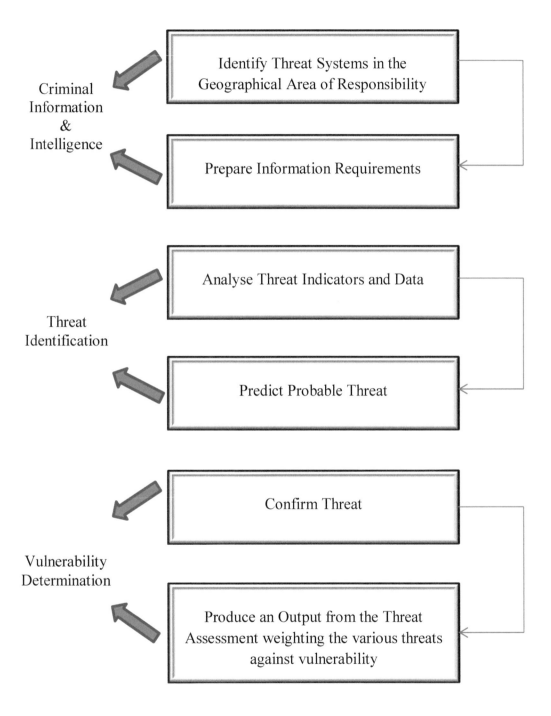

THREAT LEVELS - UK

1. **Introduction**

As of 01 August 2006, information about the national threat level is available on the MI5, Home Office and UK Intelligence Communities web sites.

2. **Threat Level Definitions**

CRITICAL	AN ATTACK IS EXPECTED IMMINENTLY
SEVERE	AN ATTACK IS HIGHLY LIKELY
SUBSTANTIAL	AN ATTACK IS A STRONG POSSIBILITY
MODERATE	AN ATTACK IS POSSIBLE BUT NOT LIKELY
LOW	AN ATTACK IS UNLIKELY

3. **Response Levels**

UK response levels provide a broad indication of the protective security measures that should be applied at any particular time. They are informed by the threat level above but also take into account specific assessments of vulnerability and risk.

Response levels tend to refer to sites, whereas threat levels usually relate to broad areas of activity.

The security measures deployed at different response levels should not be made public knowledge in order to avoid informing those with hostile intent from knowing what we intend to do about it.

There are three levels of response that broadly equate to threat levels above and are shown below:

CRITICAL	EXCEPTIONAL
SEVERE	HEIGHTENED
SUBSTANTIAL	
MODERATE	NORMAL
LOW	

4. **Response Level Definitions**

Response Level	Description
NORMAL	Routine baseline protective measures appropriate to the location. [Passive surveillance]
HEIGHTENED	Additional and sustainable protective security measures reflecting the broad nature of the threat combined with specific geographical vulnerabilities and judgements on acceptable risk.
EXCEPTIONAL	Maximum protective security measures to meet specific threats and to minimise vulnerability and risk.

Terrorism threat levels are designed to give a broad indication of the likelihood of a terrorist attack within the mainland of UK. They are based on the assessment of a range of factors including current intelligence, recent events and what is known about terrorist groups, intentions and capabilities. The information will never be 100% defined and any decisions about an appropriate response must be made with this in mind.

It will be necessary for any supervisor, team leader or manager to be fully apprised as to the country's threat level so that any localised threats can be adjusted accordingly. These threats will all have to be included in the planning phase and any OpO you intend to produce and disseminate.

Chapter 14

Compiling a PSD (CP) Operational Order

1. **Introduction.**

    An Operational Order (OpO), whether oral or written, is no more than a method of conveying the plan to those who must execute it and to those who need to be informed. The OpO requires definite action to be taken and the recipient must be in no doubt of the mission statement and the method by which it must be fulfilled and delivered.

    An OpO will be written from the 'Plan' section of the Appreciation and will normally be issued verbally to all team players. It is often said that OpO's fail on first contact with the enemy as many things tend not to go according to plan. Only when a situation is on-going can a true evaluation of the orders be implemented and the plan tweaked accordingly.

    Whilst the OpO is the orders and op briefing for those taking part, it is also an ideal way to post analyse the op once it has concluded or an incident took place during the live phase. This will allow for the opportunity to establish if all aspects of the operation were considered at the outset and where possible changes need to be made for the future. Planning and appreciations are both integral parts and go hand in hand to formulate the OpO. Miss one and it becomes incomplete. Miss both and the mission is jeopardised. The OpO therefore pulls together these two parts in order to provide the actions to the theory. Each op will historically be different which will require a different response to the compilation of the OpO and its contents, but the routine of planning should never be overlooked for any op no matter how small. The smallest detail in itself can make or break the morale of the team and ultimately affect the outcome and personal commitment to the op, e.g. feeding, pay and accommodation arrangements. These are three of the most important considerations outside of the op in general.

    OpO's are generally prepared by CP Managers and TL's but there may be times when you are an IPPO and solely on your own with no one to turn to but you have additional resources attached who need to know where they fit in the operation. In this case the single PPO will need to routinely plan and prepare the OpO, as this will be an ideal way to communicate their involvement in the operation.

2. **Contents of an OpO.**

    All OpO's comprise of six mandatory sections:

    a. Ground.

    b. Situation.

        (1)   Programme

        (2)   The Client

        (3)   The Threat

        (4)   Enemy Forces

        (5)   Additional Support Agencies

        (6)   Responsibilities

c.   Mission.

d.   Execution.

e.   Op Support

f.   Command & Signal

It may be useful to introduce all those taking part to the programme in its outline stages at the very beginning. It's not essential but it lets them get a feel as to what is likely to be expected of them.

a.   <u>Ground.</u>   Introduce the team members to the area over which they will be operating. Extensive use, where applicable and appropriate, should be made of photographs, models and maps.

        (1)   <u>In Outline.</u>

             (a)   Arrival Point (airports/docks/residence HLS)

             (b)   Towns etc.

        (2)   <u>In Detail.</u>

             (a)   Routes

             (b)   Residencies/Hotels

             (c)   Locations to be visited

b.   <u>Situation.</u>   This paragraph sets the scene for the operation

        (1)   <u>Programme.</u>   If one is available then individual ones can be issued at this stage. This will need to be discussed at this stage.

        (2)   <u>The Client.</u>   It is possible that, due to religious grounds some information will not be available to you, but if you get the chance whilst on the assignment it will assist you in making choices that don't embarrass both parties.

(a)   'Who's Who' resume of background

(b)   Known likes and dislikes

(c)   Medical Profile

        i.   Known ailments

        ii.   Allergies

        iii.   Essential treatments or medications

        iv.   Blood group

(d)   Why is the client a target?

        i.   Symbolic

        ii.   Political

        iii.   Previous appointments

(e)   The Clients family (children, wife, husband, ex partners, parents)

(f)   Members of the Clients Staff (gardeners, drivers, domestic staff, maintenance workers, office staff etc.)

        i.   Names

        ii.   Appointments/function within the household.

        iii.   Are there any staff members who may be targets in their own right?

(g)   Hobbies and Interests and are they regular and at the same place and time?

(h)   The Host (if appropriate)

        i.   Name and appointment

        ii.   Family particulars

        iii.   What requirements are expected from the CP team.

(3)   <u>The Threat.</u>

(a)   <u>Enemy Forces.</u> Who has been identified in the threat assessment as being a likely organisation? This should include names of known terrorists, criminals etc. along with their tactics and capabilities.

(b)   <u>Enemy Courses.</u>   This will be the product of the Threat Assessment and should be the CP Ops Manager and CPTL's estimate of the most likely form of attack and its location.

(4)   <u>Additional Support Units.</u>

(a)   Under Command

(b)   In Support

(c)   Units involved (K9, SB, DPG, SO19 etc)

(5)   <u>Responsibilities</u>

(a)   The CPT is responsible for…

(b)   … is responsible for …

(c)   … who will …

c.   <u>Mission.</u>   This must be clear and concise and should be repeated twice to ensure there is no misunderstanding of what the responsibilities are.   The Mission is obtained from the Aim of the Appreciation.

[Example: 'To protect IA Drill on his visit to ……….. from… to …']

d.   <u>Execution.</u>   This part of the OpO details how the mission is to be accomplished.

(1)   <u>General Outline.</u>   This gives a summary of the plan.

(a)   The operation will be in … phases as follows:

i.   <u>Phase 1.</u>   … from … to …

ii.   <u>Phase 2.</u>   … from … to …

iii.   <u>Phase 3.</u>   … from … to …

iv.   <u>Phase 4.</u>   … from … to …

(2)   <u>Tasks.</u>

(a)   <u>Phase 1.</u>   (and subsequent phases)

i.   <u>PPO</u>

(i)   <u>Name (s)</u>……………………

(ii)   <u>Task</u>.....................................

(b)   PES (if deployed)

        (i)   Names ………………………….

        (i)   Tasks. …………………………

(c)   SAP 1 (if deployed)

        (i)   Names ………………………..

        (ii)   Tasks ………………………….

(d)   Support Teams (if deployed)

        (i)   Names ………………………..

        (i)   Tasks ………………………….

(3)   Coordinating Instructions

(a)   Timings.   Issue task programme

(b)   Order of March (if applicable)

(c)   Routes

(d)   Liaison

(e)   Medical (That which concerns the Client's survival after an attack or in the event of a serious illness)

(f)   Safe Houses

(g)   Baggage Security & Handling

(h)   Guest Lists

(i)   Staff Lists

(j)   Local Security Measures

(k)   Orders for the Use of Force

(l)   Local Security Identity System in force (Pins, tags etc)

(m)   Vehicle Security

(n)   Use of Spare Vehicle

(o)   Use of Helicopters

(p) Emergency Procedures

    i. Action on Increased Threat

    ii. Action on Shooting Attack

        (i) In residence/hotel

        (ii) Whilst mobile

        (iii) Whilst walking

    iii. Action on Bomb Warning

    iv. Action on Discovery of an IED

    v. Action on Bomb Attack

    vi. Action on Kidnap Attempt

    vii. Action on Successful Kidnap

    viii. Action on Traffic Collision

    ix. Action on Breakdown

    x. Action in Event of Programme Changes

(q) Rehearsals

(r) Recees

(s) Conferences

e. Operational Support.

(1) Dress – including any changes necessary

(2) Transport

(3) Weapons & Ammo (if deployed on foreign trips by authorised personnel. To include storage and issue)

(4) Feeding Arrangements

(5) Medical Facilities (local hospitals, medi packs etc)

(6) Refuelling (if applicable and using own hired vehicles. If sub contracted then this responsibility will lye with that company)

(7) Any specialist equipment required (technical) – by phases.

(8)   Any radios/batteries (including spares and breakages)

(9)   Vehicle recovery (if applicable but as (6) above)

(10)   Accommodation allocation (if applicable and known in advance)

(11)   Cash requirements

f.   <u>Command & Signal</u>

(1)   Chain of Command is …………………………

(2)   Ops Room located at ……………………….. (if deployed)

(3)   Telephone numbers

(4)   Liaison (POC)

(5)   Allocation of Equipment

(6)   Spot numbers on maps/Code Words (events)/Nicknames (places/people)

Carry out a time check, scrutinise the task programme to ensure nothing or anybody has been missed or overlooked.

3.   **Military & Civilian Time Designators**

There are 25 integer World Wide Time Zones from -12 through 0 (GMT) to +12. Each one is 15° of Longitude as measured East and West from the Prime Meridian of the World at Greenwich. Some countries have adopted non-standard time zones, usually 30 minutes offset of GMT.

Each time zone is measured relative to Greenwich. There are two designations in use, one by the military and the other by civilians. Civilians use a 3-letter abbreviation (e.g. EST) for most zones. The military however use a single letter from the alphabet (except 'J') and are known by the phonetic equivalent i.e. GMT (civilian) or Z=Zulu (military & aviation).

Timings in any format are crucial but where there are multiple meridian crossovers, the need for a standardised logic is paramount. The writing of an OpO must make use of one of these formats to clarify critical timings across the whole of the document. Generally in CP, the phonetic ruling is used to describe these timings. Only one zone should be used throughout the document to avoid any confusion. The GMT is used as the basis on which to decide which time zone is relevant to the op. If the whole op is in one country then the zone for that country is to be used relative to GMT. Example, if operating in Switzerland then we would use the designator A which is (GMT+1) = CET.

4.   **Conclusion**

The success of a Close Protection Operation can depend on the thoroughness of the OpO. The CP Ops Manager/CPTL must go into great lengths and detail to ensure that:

> b. Nothing is overlooked
>
> c. That all those involved know and understand the plan and their individual role within it.

An OpO should include annexes to support, enhance or describe further the content of the OpO specific to a relevant portion/section within the overall document. Reference must be made within that portion/section pointing the reader to which annex is appropriate. No annex should be included unless it has some relevance and reference to a particular portion/section contained within the OpO.

An OpO, once completed should be marked as **CONFIDENTIAL** and its circulation distributed to only those who have an active part to play or the need to be informed. Anything else will only compromise and jeopardise the operation and ultimately, the Client. Each copy will be marked with a unique number so that it corresponds to a particular participant for control of distribution. All OpO's issued to active operatives will need to return their copy to the CP Ops Manager at the conclusion of the op so that they can be extirpated.   Any documents retained by the Ops Dept. will need to be handled as for sensitive materials and recorded accordingly.

Copy No   of   Copies

File Ref #: OPO/OD/01/XX

Office of the Close Protection Team

See Distribution

Date: Dec XX ⟵▭   Date of Signature

CLOSE PROTECTION TEAM DEPLOYMENT

Country (Location) XX – XX Dec XX   (Phase 1 – if applicable)   Show the appropriate time zone relevant to the AoO

OpO 01/XX (OD) ⟵▭   Sequential OpO #

Time Zone Used Throughout: ALPHA (GMT+1) = CET

References: List all relevant references

A.   Meeting (Surname)/(Surname) (Date when meeting took place)
B.   Meeting (Surname)/(Surname) (Date when meeting took place)
C   Telecom (Surname)/(Surname) (Date when event took place)
D.   Map reference # and title (including scale and sheet #)

1.   **Introduction.**

    a.   General Outline.   During a projected period between the XXth Dec XX to XXnd Dec XX, (client name) and members of her family will be visiting the Swiss Alpine resort of (Location).   (Location) is the ultimate destination for all those who have an interest in adventure sports like skiing and it is famous world wide for its ski resorts. (Location) is influenced by three cultures; those of the German speaking majority of residents, the Romanish speaking population of the Engadine and the nearby Italians. (Location) is both chic and famous with its legendary 'champagne atmosphere' and its sun that shines 322 days of the year.   Train travel is the preferred method of conveyance to (Location) since the weather is unpredictable and road closures are common without notice adding several hours to the journey plans. If the train is not an option for the client, then consideration will need to be made for the route and its security throughout.

    b.   Ground   This can be divided into **six** main areas of concern where Close Protection will be required.

        (1)   (Location) & Airport
        (2)   Train route from Zurich to (Location)
        (3)   (Client) Hotel
        (4)   Movements in and around (Location)
        (5)   Train Route from (Location) to Zurich
        (6)   Zurich Airport

c.   Ground in Detail.

(1)   (Location) & Airport. This airport is aka Samedan (or Engadin airport) and is located in the Engadin Valley of Switzerland at latitude 46° 32' 04"N and longitude 002° 53'02"E with an elevation of 1707m (5600ft). This elevation makes the airport the highest in Europe and prone to weather variations. The airport is located some 5km (3 miles) from the town of (Location). The airport does not have the necessary runway length to facilitate a 747 type aircraft. The town itself lies on the south side of the Alps again in the Engadine Valley at 6000' asl within the Canton of Graubunden. It is on the banks of the Sils, Silvaplana & Champfer lakes and surrounded by the pristine lakes and pine forests of the upper Engadine valley. It is 200km (3hrs) from Zurich by car and 3 ½ hrs by train, 200km (3hrs) from Milano and from Munich it is approx 460km (4hrs). The temperature at this time of year generally fluctuates between 38° F and slightly below 0°. There is a Glacier Express train from and to Zermatt which runs frequently during the winter months. ▮▮▮▮▮ is one of the most luxurious winter resorts in the world and is divided into 2 distinct sectors. Dorf rises into the foothills to the north east and is considered the exclusive area. Bad extends to the west and south along the shores of the lake bearing the same name and offers more suitable areas for the economically challenged. (Location) is 11.1 sq miles in size and has a year round population of around 5600. To put (Location) in perspective as to where it fits in geographic terms, a map is attached at *Annex A* to these orders. Additionally, a town map of (Location) is attached as *Annex B*.

Describe the ground with sufficient information

(2)   Train Route From Zurich Airport to (Location). This route travels through the Grisons to the Engadine with its tunnel turns and viaducts in one of the most interesting and picturesque routes of Europe.

(3)   (Client) Hotel.   The historic palace Hotel was recently renamed as (Client) Hotel. It took four years to complete and was opened in 1896 by ▮▮ ▮▮ as a successor to the resort hotel which invented the cold weather winter resort – the internationally renowned famous Krup Hause. The ▮▮▮ is the first to be built in the world and has distinctive architecture with a Palace Tower making it a landmark within the resort. It is owned and operated by the same ▮▮▮ family, now in its third generation. It is set in six acres of private ground and is located just five minutes walk from the centre of the town. Located on Via Serlas 27, it has 159 guest rooms and 47 suites with views overlooking the Swiss Alps. Its location can be seen on the map at Annex B at accommodation #3.

Describe the Clients hotel

d.   Movements in and Around (Location).   To be confirmed on arrival. A map of (Location) is attached at *Annex X* to these orders for information only. Additional cartography will be available once in situ.

e.   Train Route from (Location) to Zurich.   This will be the reverse of the arrival plans.

f.　　<u>Zurich Airport.</u>　　This airport is aka Kloten Airport and is located in Kloten, the Canton of Zurich, Switzerland. It has an elevation of 432m (1416 ft) at latitude 47° 27' 53" N and longitude 08° 32' 57"E with three runways; (10/28), (14/32) & (16/34). The latter two are capable of accommodating a fully loaded arriving/departing 747. It is located 12km (eight miles) north of Zurich. A terminal and ground plan is attached at ***Annex D*** to these orders.

2.　　**Threat & Risk Assessment**

Compile a threat & risk assessment using country info, FC&O, SS and local crime

a.　　There are no specific threats targeted against any particular member of the family.

b.　　The clients being from an Arabic community and the fact they are members of a Royal Family make them high profile assets.

c.　　Their arrival (by name or department & not status) will be known which would increase levels of interest.

d.　　Nightlife in (Location) is renowned for being the most energetic and expensive of all the alpine ski resorts and the drinking of alcohol is synonymous with this kind of ideology.

e.　　*Crime.*

(1)　　Crime does exist in Switzerland but is relatively low in comparison to other European countries.

(2)　　Crime trends tend to lend themselves to pick pocketing and purse snatching in the vicinity of train and bus stations, airports and some public parks. This kind of crime is on the increase.

(3)　　Where conferences take place and large groups of high profile people gather there tends to be an increase in the volume of undesirables who loiter with intent to gain an ideal opportunity. Violence is often initiated where resistance is met.

f.　　*Terrorism.*　　There have been no recent acts of terrorism on the soil of CH. Although most groups have now dissolved there is still an underlying (low) threat from this quarter given the activities of the most dominant group who has taken the world's stage. Attacks could be discriminate or targeted against groups or individuals anywhere within the borders of CH. These attacks if initiated would be more akin to groups seeking out global media attention rather than being specific in their intentions.

g.　　*Risks.*　Skiing itself is a hazardous sport and should really not be attempted by anyone who hasn't had some level of instruction in the first instance. The clients will have qualified ski instructors accompany them each time they visit the slopes which will limit the levels of risk. Alcohol fuelled crowds pose there own threats with gesticulations, verbal outbursts and outright stupidity.

h.   ***Overall Assessment.***

(1)   <u>Threat.</u>   Based on historical data regarding the visiting location and intelligence updates it is deemed that an assessment can be placed at the ***medium*** level of a ***Cat 2*** but their position and status would warrant a deployment of personnel normally afforded under a ***Cat 1*** assignment. In addition to providing security measures this will also allow the clients to enjoy some aspects of freedom and privacy when needed.

Define an overall assessment and then deploy resources commensurate with the results

(2)   <u>Risks.</u>   Besides the risks faced by everyone on a daily basis, measures are in place to ensure that risks are reduced on the ski slopes by the hiring of qualified and experienced ski instructors so as to ensure that the type of skiing is only done to the level of each individuals abilities. All ski activities will be undertaken using the correct equipment for the task and the wearing of adequate and appropriate clothing to protect against the cold and any minor injuries. There is a moderate danger of avalanches throughout the year in the alpine regions of CH. If an evening outing is scheduled, then additional personnel may need to be utilised to provide a security framework to allow the clients to move freely to and from their agendas. The risks have therefore been graded as ***Low.***

3.   **Situation**

a.   <u>Visit Format.</u>   In broad outline, this will be a holiday break for the family and they will try and blend in as much as possible. It is expected that the following activities will form part of the visit:

Provide an idea of what is available to the clients and expand accordingly with as much info that has been gleaned.

(1)   <u>Skiing.</u>   Most of the children it is expected will attempt the slopes but the following of lots of people will make discretion far more difficult. (Location) has five major resorts in the immediate vicinity with more than 217 miles (350km) of snow covered runs which can all be accessed using a general ski pass. Altitude between these resorts ranges between 5,906' to 10,827' and is fairly snow sure. The Corvigilia-Piz Nair ski area is the most convenient and can be accessed by foot from most hotels. Piz Nair is the highest ski able peak in the area at 10,030 ft and is suited to more advanced skiers and boarders. Corviglia is the most versatile area for all abilities with slopes high up for beginners. (Location) has a ski school which is ranked as one of the top in the world with instructors trained at all levels. All ski slopes are serviced with restaurants, ski huts and snow bars catering for the après-ski. A winter map depicting an overview of (Location) is attached at ***Annex C*** to these orders for information only.

(2)   <u>Shopping.</u> (Location) has many shops catering for many personal tastes selling their highly priced merchandise. Many exclusive boutiques with the latest creations of fashion designers from Paris to Milan can be bought in (Location). Other shops include Swiss watches. The shops line both sides of the main street on the Via Maistra and it is therefore anticipated that this activity will be

something they will partake in. The horrendously up scaled shops and items are in close proximity to the most expensive hotel in (Location), ███████ Palace situated near the corner of Via Serlas. Here you will encounter boutiques for Versace, Prada, Jill Sander, Bulgari and Louis Vuitton as well as other shops for watches and jewellery to befit any royal court. Equally, dining out is something with which the clients are familiar with and this cannot be ruled out. (Location), in line with its promotional tag as being 'On Top of the World' does not lack for a gourmet fare. It offers dining from elaborate restaurants to local taverns and caters for all types of cuisines.

b. <u>Programme of Events.</u>   No programme can be promulgated since this is a relaxed vacation. Some activities (like ski instructors & passes) will require advance notice for the booking of various activities and therefore a certain degree of time line information will be given.

4. **Mission**   To provide Close Personal Protection in its entirety to all those participating Principles on arrival in (Location), during their stay and the routing to the outbound airport on departure during the period (dd – dd Dec (yy).

5. **Execution** ⬅━━━━ Describe here how the op will be implemented starting with the deployment of CP resources through to feeding and accommodation. Include comms, EPs etc

a. <u>General Outline.</u>   In general, the execution will be carried out in **six** phases as follows:

Thu, (dd mm yy)

(1)   <u>Phase 1.</u>   Advance team depart UK for (Location)

Sat, (dd mm yy)

(2)   <u>Phase 2.</u>   Main body of Principles arrive at Zurich airport ex Dubai. Meet up with Swiss Contingent.

(3)   <u>Phase 3.</u>   Vehicle & Train move from airport to location

(4)   <u>Phase 4.</u>   Hotel Security Arrangements

Sun, (dd mm) to Fri, (dd mm yy)

(5)   <u>Phase 5.</u>   Movements whilst in (Location) (including ski slopes)

Sat, (dd mm yy)

(6)   <u>Phase 6.</u>   Train move to Zurich Airport from (Location)

b. <u>Taskings/Groupings.</u> A list of taskings and groupings is attached at ***Annex E*** to these orders however; in general the tasking commitment is broadly outlined below:

(1) **PPO's.**

    (a) <u>UK Contingent.</u> Only the CP Ops Manager and (any other CPO) will deploy from the UK as active operatives. In addition to the CP Ops Manager providing CP to Principle #1 he will also oversee the deployment of the remaining PPO's from the other contingent through the Swiss TL.

    (b) <u>Swiss Contingent.</u> These operatives will provide the bulk of PPO's and supporting resources to implement the strategic deployment of active personnel to fulfil the requirements of this OpO. The Swiss element will join the UK Contingent and the main body of the clients in Zurich and not before.

(2) <u>RST.</u> Provided by the Swiss Contingent as for PPO above. All deployed names will be notified at the start of the op

(3) <u>PES.</u> Provided by the Dubai Police.

(4) <u>SAP</u> Will be used as and when and if manpower allows sufficient flexibility.

(5) <u>Support Teams:</u>

CAT	-	Not Deployed
Top Cover	-	Not Deployed
K9 Unit	-	Not Deployed
HRT	-	Not Deployed

(6) <u>Rear Party.</u> Not Applicable

c. <u>Coordinating Instructions</u> *(All Timings are in CET = +1 to GMT in other words local to CH)*

(1) <u>Timings.</u> (Flights)

    (a) <u>Advance Party</u> **Thu, 13 Dec 07**

        i. <u>Names.</u>

            (i) CP Ops Manager
            ██████████████

        ii. <u>Flight Number.</u> BA 0714

        iii. <u>Departure Loc.</u> LHR (T4) at 1125hrs

        iv. <u>ETA.</u> Zurich Airport 1410 hrs (local)

(2) <u>Baggage Security & Handling</u>. The advance party personnel will be responsible for the security and whereabouts of their own individual baggage and the reclamation at the arriving airport.

(3)   Additional Guests.   It is not anticipated that members of the family will meet other groups whilst on vacation but this cannot be ruled out.

(4)   Local Security Measures

   (a)   Train Route.   The train will be reserved with a set number of carriages and our own security will provide the buffer between them in order to prevent anyone climbing into them as and when the train stops at relevant stations.

   (b)   ▓▓▓▓ Town.   There is a small community police station in the town (Gemeindepolizei) located on Via Quadrellar 7, 7500, ▓▓▓▓. The station is open from 0800-2000hrs daily and is patrolled by officers in cars and on pedal cycles. Their main roles are:

   - Public Order
   - General Transport & Monitoring
   - Special Events
   - Monitoring Restrictive Parking
   - Monitoring the Taxi Industry
   - Management of Dogs
   - Many more duties

   (c)   ▓▓▓▓ Hotel   To be identified by the advanced party. Floor plans to be attached as *Annex F* to these orders.

   (d)   Zurich Airport.   The current security measures comply with all national and international provisions for security. The security organisation at Unique (Flughafen Zurich AG) is a complex system that relies on a comprehensive approach to preventative measures and active intervention. In addition to the airports security staff who are responsible for preventative measures, the airport also has a reaction force made up of airport police and fire fighting services as well as Unique's rescue services. These personnel are on hand 24hrs per day to respond to minor incidents, emergencies and major crisis situations.

(5)   Vehicle Security.   Security of any vehicle is paramount and where it involves Principle vehicles this is taken one step further. Is is essential that if the vehicle cannot be stored overnight in a secure environment then a search will certainly have to be carried out prior to its use. The type of search will depend on various circumstances but one should always be carried out in any case.

(6)   Use of Spare Vehicle/Reserve Vehicle. The spare vehicle allocated to the client should always be readily available along with the clients own allocated vehicle. Its use should be as per SOPs and not for any other reason.

(7)   Emergency Procedures

    (a)   Action on Increased Threat.   In the event that information comes to light that is deemed a direct threat to any member of the family, or the group as a whole, then a re-evaluation with the Doyen, her courtiers & the Chief Ops Officer will have to take place.   Recommendations may include cancelling the holiday and returning back to Dubai or take up phase 2 earlier with a transitional break in the UK.

    (b)   Action on a Shooting Attack.   It's imperative, if possible, to identify where the shot(s) were fired from so that you don't run head on into it and also to allow you to move in to an area which could provide cover for you and the client(s).   This would also assist any forensics follow up.   Our main aim is to provide full body cover given the cultural limitations that are placed upon us.

        i.   At the Hotel.   If a Principle is wounded in the incident then all efforts are to be made to sustain life until emergency services arrive.   Additional body cover is to be applied to protect from any further injuries.   The Principle is our main concern.   If the Principle is not injured then she must be removed, under our controlled conditions with full body cover as quickly as possible to a vehicle nearby and then onto a safe house.

        ii.   Whilst Mobile.   During any period where the movement of a Principle takes place by the use of an assigned vehicle, then any accompanying PES should be confident that any passing vehicle is pretty much safe to do so.   No 100% guarantee can be made though but if a threat is imminent, then the driver should instruct that person to drop to the foot well of the car.   If the Principle is injured, then again the preservation of life is essential and should be driven to the nearest medical facility.   If the car becomes immobilised, then the Principle should be cross-loaded in to the PES vehicle and depart the *HOT zone as* quickly as possible.

        iii.   Whilst Walking.   Walking attracts attention and is a potential problem area especially when the numbers of people involved with the movement of a Principle accompany them.   Maximum body cover should be applied whilst at the same time allowing them a degree of free movement.   If it is seen that one Principle is more vulnerable than the next then additional manpower may have to be deployed.   If an incident takes place and the Principle is injured, then move the injured party to the nearest medical facility.   If no injuries sustained, then move the Client back to a previously identified safe house.

(c) <u>Action on Bomb Warning.</u>

    i.   <u>At the Hotel.</u> Liaise with the Hotel Security Staff/Manager to assess the reliability and source of the call. If it is substantiated, then the Principle will have to be moved to a designated safe house. Consideration should be given to whether or not this has been targeted directly to our charges, against the hotel or any other VIP. There may be other VIPs in the hotel to which any threat may be targeted. If it is against our clients, then the visit has been compromised.

    ii.   <u>At the Airport.</u> Local procedures are in place but to a determined aggressor this poses a mere challenge. It is more likely that any threat here would be against the terminal building and since our charges will land at a separate stand and move outside of the terminal radius under private arrangements. Any warning could nevertheless cause disruption and inevitable delays. The client should be moved as expeditiously as possible to the hotel or a designated safe house.

(d) <u>Action on the Discovery of an IED.</u> It will be more likely that an IED will be placed under a vehicle and if this happens then the visit has been compromised and any one or all the Principle's are legitimate targets. ***Do Not*** touch the device nor vehicle but move the Principle away as quickly as possible and notify the Police through whatever means you have at your disposal. The CP Ops Man/TL is to be notified ASAP.

<u>Action on a Kidnap Attempt.</u> Motives for criminals to engage in this kind of activity are varied but the CPT must be aware of potential scenarios being played out and the following are two possible areas where such an attack may be initiated.

    i.   <u>Whilst Mobile.</u> The weakest areas are at the start and towards the conclusion of travel although, if an ideal location presents itself during the route then this may also be used. Awareness as to how an attack could be initiated could give you valuable time to prepare for a likely ambush. The drivers who will be assigned to our charges will not be qualified security drivers and therefore presents its own set of problems. Anti-ambush drills should be applied to avoid an ambush situation developing and overall awareness as to potential likely areas. Be aware of the block to the front and possible rear coupled with any escape routes.

    ii.   <u>Whilst Walking.</u> If a kidnap attempt is likely then it will invariably involve the use of firearms or a distraction. If our presence looks professional then that in it self can act in our favour and deter an attempt until another day and any weak spots leaves the Principle open to an attempt. Use enough force as immediately necessary to secure the Principle, the legality bits can be sorted out later as we need the initiative at all times. If a situation is likely to be initiated then the Principle should be moved from the zone ASAP to a designated safe house as quickly as possible.

(e)   <u>Action on a Traffic Collision</u>

    i.   <u>Principle Vehicle.</u> Only a small amount of movement around ██████ will be done utilising a vehicular mode of transport. In the event one is used and the Principle is injured, then all attempts are to be made to recover her to the nearest medical facility. Should the Principle be uninjured then the Principle should be moved as safely as possible to the back up car and driven by her own driver (if uninjured). The back up driver will now stay with the old Principle vehicle until recovery is affected.

    ii.   <u>PES Vehicle.</u> This vehicle will generally carry the CPT in support of the Principles in the lead vehicle. Once it has been established that there are no injuries to the crew of that vehicle then the Principle vehicle(s) can continue to their destination. If there are injuries reported then the Principle may decide to wait until the emergency services arrive or if they are satisfied that the crew are in no immediate of danger or medical deterioration she may decide to continue on her journey.

(f)   <u>Action on Breakdown.</u>

    i.   <u>Principle Vehicle.</u> Transfer the Principle to the back up vehicle with her own driver to drive the exchanged vehicle provided he (the back up driver) has local knowledge of the whereabouts of visiting locations. If not the original driver will continue the journey.

    ii.   <u>PES Vehicle.</u> The CPT is to drop back into the spare vehicle (less driver). The driver is to await recovery.

(g)   <u>Fire & Evacuation Procedures.</u> To be detailed during the advance phase of the deployment.

(i)   <u>Action in the Event of a Programme Change.</u> Although no specific programme of events has been formulated and promulgated, the CPT must remain flexible to accommodate any changes that are applied. If the chance arises then suitable recee's should be carried out in advance of any notified visit.

(8) The Use of Force. Attached at **Annex G** to these orders are the legal aspects in which you may use physical and mechanical skills to assist you in executing your duties. Only use the minimum amount of force necessary to allow you to move the Principle away from the hostile zone and to safety. Anything else would be deemed in a court of law to have been excessive and may render you to criminal proceedings. Don't pussy foot around but use your skills in a controlled and positive manner.

(9) Train Move

    (a) Zurich to St. Moritz (Travel Time = 3:21)

        i. Train.

            (i) Zurich – Chur (Intercity)
            (ii) Chur – ▮▮▮▮▮ (RegioExpress)

        ii. Route. The scenic route through the Grisons to the Engadine.

        iii. ETD. TBN

        iv. ETA TBN

A change will have to be made at Chur prior to continuing the journey as there is no direct through train. A schedule is attached at **Annex H** to these orders (Subject to Change)

    (b) ▮▮▮▮▮ to Zurich.

        i. Train. As for inbound journey

        ii. Route. As for inbound

        iii. ETD. TBN

        iv. ETA. TBN

There are complimentary shuttle buses available from the hotels but whether or not the clients accept them will not be known until arrival.

A time table is attached to these orders as prepared by the Schweizerische Bundesbahn (SBB).

All High Value Goods (HVG) will travel by road with additional items carried on the train and secured by the Dubai Police. It may be necessary to provide a member of the Swiss Contingent to provide local security.

(10)   Accommodation

    (a)   Principles.   ▮▮▮▮▮▮ Hotel.

    (b)   PPOs UK Contingent.   To be allocated on arrival.

    (c)   PPOs Swiss Contingent.   To be allocated on arrival.

    (d)   Dubai Police.   To be allocated on arrival.

(11)   Weather – ▮▮▮▮   The climate here is moderate with no excessive heat, cold or humidity.

    (a).   Min & Max temps projected for the period are:

Include the weather as this will allow the team to pack appropriately.

Date	Min Temp (F)	Max Temp (F)	Avg Precip
Dec 15	Avg Low: 9°	Avg Hi: 29°	0.05 in
Dec 16	Avg Low: 9°	Avg Hi: 29°	0.05 in
Dec 17	Avg Low: 9°	Avg Hi: 29°	0.04 in
Dec 18	Avg Low: 9°	Avg Hi: 29°	0.04 in
Dec 19	Avg Low: 8°	Avg Hi: 29°	0.04 in
Dec 20	Avg Low: 8°	Avg Hi: 29°	0.04 in
Dec 21	Avg Low: 8°	Avg Hi: 29°	0.04 in
Dec 22	Avg Low: 8°	Avg Hi: 29°	0.04 in

    (b).   Long term forecast (10 days) is attached at **Annex I** to these orders.

    (c)   Sunrise & Sunset over the period + other relevant data.

Data: Info is as set by the relevant location co-ordinates.

Date	Sunrise Time	Sunset Time	Daylight Length	Twilight Begins	Twilight Ends	Moon Rise	Moon Set	Moon Phase
15 Dec xx	08:25	17:02	8hr 33	07:50	17:37	12:10	22:57	New
16 Dec xx	08:26	17:02	8hr 33	07:51	17:37	12:29	22:57	New
17 Dec xx	08:27	17:02	8hr 33	07:52	17:37	12:46	00:11	1st Qtr
18 Dec xx	08:27	17:02	8hr 33	07:52	17:37	13:04	01:26	1st Qtr
19 Dec xx	08:28	17:03	8hr 29	07:53	17:38	13:25	02:45	1st Qtr
20 Dec xx	08:29	17:03	8hr 29	07:54	17:38	13:50	04:07	1st Qtr
21 Dec xx	08:29	17:04	8hr 29	07:54	17:39	14:23	05:32	1st Qtr
22 Dec xx	08:30	17:04	8hr 29	07:55	17:39	15:07	06:57	1st Qtr

(12)   Personal Equipment.   See **Annex I** to these orders for a suggested list.

(13)   Telephone Call & Texting Costs.   Generally, the cost of a call to the UK from CH through the following networks is as follows. Your own particular contract may differ. Prices shown are less VAT at current rates.

Network	Voice Calls Outgoing	Voice Calls Incoming	Texts Standard
Orange	0.70ppm	0.50ppm	0.30 per txt

Vodaphone
O2

(a)   Dialling Codes.

    i.   <u>UK – CH.</u>   0041 (0)81

    ii.   <u>CH to UK.</u>   +44 (Drop the first 0 of the area code)

(14)   <u>Medical.</u>

  (a)   <u>Switzerland –</u> ███████

    i.   *Klinic Gut* ██████ is a leading hospital for accident care in CH and is located on Via Arona 34, CH-7500. Contact #: 0041 818363434

    ii.   A list of duty doctors and pharmacists in ██████ will be obtained by the advanced team.

  (b)   <u>Switzerland – Zurich</u>   If an incident occurs whilst in Zurich, then the following hospitals can provide a service expected by our clients and are as follows. A map showing both locations is attached at ***Annex K*** to these orders.

    i.   *Klinic Hirslanden.*

      (i)   <u>Contact #:</u> 0041 44 3872111
      (ii)   <u>Location.</u> See attached map.

    ii.   *Im Park Clinic*

      (i)   <u>Contact #.</u> 0041 44 2092111
      (ii)   <u>Location.</u> See attached map.

Whilst this is a small UK contingent deployment, the bulk of the medical responsibilities will rest with the Swiss CPOs but it is essential that all assigned CPO's should be familiar with the following emergencies:

    i.   Traffic Accidents
    ii.   Heart attack or stroke
    iii.   Massive injuries due to explosions
    iv.   Knife wounds
    v.   Bullet wounds
    vi   Fire and smoke inhalation

A small trauma pack should, for basic emergency treatment be carried and include some or all of the following:

Ser	Item	Deployment Priority			Remarks
		Essential	Useful	Consider	
01	CPR Mask	√			
02	Sterile Burnsheet			√	
03	Triangular Bandage		√		
04	Extrication Collar			√	
05	Gauze Sponges (4" x 4")		√		
06	Sterile Water for Irrigation of the eyes		√		
07	Pair of scissors; paramedic type		√		
08	Emergency Blanket			√	
09	Adhesive Tape		√		
10	Oval Eye Pads				
11	Sterile Alcohol Wipes		√		
12	Instant Ice Pack	√			
13	Vaseline Gauze (5" x 9")			√	
14	Air Splint; full arm and full leg		√		
15	Spine Board; stretcher		√		
16	3 pairs of surgical gloves	√			
17	Wound Disinfectant			√	
18	Small Oxygen Tank			√	Restrictions for air carriage
19	Altitude Sickness Tablets	√			
20	Headache Tablets		√		
21	Assorted sizes of plasters		√		

(15) <u>Currency.</u>   The local currency is the Swiss Franc. Euros are also accepted. Approx exchange rates are as follows:

    i.   <u>Euro – CHF</u>   =   1euro = 1.5 CHF

    ii.   <u>UK £ - Euro</u> =   £1 = euro 1.46

(16) <u>Electrical Voltage.</u>   220 volts. An adapter may be available at the hotel reception.

(17) <u>Feeding Arrangements.</u>

    i.   <u>Advance Party.</u>   To be taken at the allocated hotel prior to the arrival of the client's.

    ii.   <u>Main Body.</u>   All meals will be taken at the Principle hotel once they have settled in. It is not to be taken for granted that you can just walk in to the restaurant, wait until you have been invited in. As a general rule, arrangements for breakfast will be different as the client's tend not to use the restaurant in the am. These arrangements are specific to both the UK & Swiss Contingents.

    iii.   <u>Outside Restaurants.</u>   If during the course of your duty you are invited in to a restaurant to eat with them whilst the client is away from the hotel then you are to sit at a separate table once invited to take a seat.

(18)   Fitness Facilities.   If any facilities are available at your own hotel then these may be utilised. Any extras may have to be paid for out of your own pocket. ***Do Not*** use any of the facilities at the client hotels.

(19)   Comms

    i.   Your issued UK mobile Phone.

    ii. Radios will neither be issued nor taken.
Your own charger for the UK issued phone will be needed, however you may be issued with another phone whilst in Switzerland but there is no guarantee that the charger will be compatible with your UK phone.

    iii. Emergency Numbers   Local Numbers

      (i)   Police (Polizeinotrup)   117
      (ii) Fire (Feuermeldestelle)   118
      (iii) Emergency (Medical)   144

(20)   Weapons & Ammunition.   No items of this nature will be deployed on this op.

(20)   Command & Control

    i.   CP Ops Manager.   Overall command of the CP deployment.

    ii. Swiss CPTL.   Responsible for the admin & daily deployments of this contingent both RST & CP Personnel as per directions from the CP Ops Manager.

A command structure is to be highlighted so the team know who is in charge

A Smith
CP Ops Manager
CP Company, London

Distribution: Copy No:

External:

Action:
T Brown   2

Information:

Internal:

Action:

Information:

MD	1
CP File	3

Annexes

A	Geographic Locator Map
B	Vienna Town Map
C	Winter Ski Map
D	Zurich Airport Plans
E	Groupings/Taskings
F	Floor Plans of the ████████ Hotel
G	Use of Force
H	SBB Train Schedules - Various
I	Long Term Weather Forecast
J	Suggested Packing List
K	Zurich Hospitals

Attach annexes to support reference material mentioned throughout the OpO

NOTICE

The issue of this document to CP Operational Personnel is to be returned at the conclusion of the Op to the author for its necessary controlled destruction. All contents within the bounds of this document are to be treated in the strictest of confidence to maintain the integrity of this and any future operational deployments. All information concerning this and the live phase of the op are to be safeguarded at all times. The document is not to be photocopied as each copy has its own unique number issued to the named recipient only.

Chapter 15

Writing an Incident Report/Statement during PSD Operations

1. **Introduction**

During the course of your duties you may find yourself in a situation that you have had to deal with or actually been involved in or maybe just witnessed. Many people will find it difficult to express what they have seen in a written format and therefore the clarity of the situation is a little blurred and begs other questions to be asked so as to avoid any ambiguity. How you record and report the details will be dependant on the nature of the incident. Writing either a report or statement is merely a way of conveying the actual events at the time in order for others to be fully apprised and to follow the events as if they were there at the time. A paper trail of the reported incident is necessary to make sure that you have done everything that would've been required of you. Information may also be either conveyed in a statement or report format dependant on what is the standard at the time. Guidance will need to be sought from the CP Ops Manager or whoever is in charge of your operation as to which type would be appropriate for your particular circumstances. Document writing may include such events as:

- An RTC to support the chain of events and as a supplementary to the accident report required by your company. The people who would be required to make a statement would be:

  o The driver of the security vehicle
  o As a passenger travelling in the security vehicle who may corroborate or otherwise the actions/events of the driver at the time.

- An incident involving a client which may include:

  o Horse riding accident (client only unless a request is made when it involves a friend of the client)
  o Incident whilst away with your client from your assigned location.

- The provision of a witness statement as an independent observer

- A statement to corroborate the actions/events of another team member.

2. **Statement Writing**

Writing a statement correctly and being able to get all the information down in a sequenced and chronological fashion takes practice. Towards the end of this chapter is a template with relevant information that would be required for your statement. Follow those guidelines when preparing your statement. The layouts in terms of the sections are as per any statement you would be expected to give to the police. CPO's are expected to be observant whether on or off duty so writing a report should be relatively easy but some people will find it difficult to pen their thoughts to paper and in a particular set format for others to follow. The basic requirements that would help you are:

a.   ***Place*** (street name and town/city)

b.   ***Date*** (the date the event took place)

c.   ***Time*** (the time in which you event took place)

d.   ***I was*** (explain here what you were doing leading up to the event occurring)

e.   ***I saw*** (explain here what you saw leading up to and during the event. In here you should explain details about the other car if an RTC and what damage you saw on both vehicles. Equally any injuries)

f.   ***I did*** (explain here what actions you took. Any first aid applied, vehicles moved or the police were called etc.)

By following this pattern will allow you to write down everything that happened in a manner, which would be easy for a reader to follow it through in a logical sequence.

An example statement written by a security driver is shown towards the end of this chapter. The statement can be either hand written or typed. However, an official signature will need to be inserted in order to authenticate the document.

Record in writing any conversations made by either party in your presence and not hearsay. This may be useful at a later date.

Statements provided may be attached to any initial RTC report filled out by the security driver in order to expand in greater detail the circumstances surrounding the event. They may be included as exhibits in court or to provide additional information when insurances companies require further details. It will also be attached to any incident report to further expand on the situation. The following will be the necessary parts of a statement:

a.   Part A The Statement

This part requires your personal details and must be completed as part of your statement.

b.   Part B – The Declaration

You will find something similar to this declaration on any witness statement but a police one would bring your attention to the Criminal Justice Act (CJA). A statement provided by you is not governed by the CJA but you will be declaring that the statement's content is an accurate account of the events/actions portrayed therein. You are to sign below the declaration giving your understanding of this. Any statements that you furnish to the Police will be governed by the CJA and liable an offence of perverting the course of justice if found to be false so it is essential that regardless whether it conforms to a CJA or not that your version is an accurate and honest portrayal of events and not a cover story to protect others.

c.   <u>Part C – The Statement</u>

The statement should begin with an introduction about the person writing the statement. If you have any specialist qualifications relevant to your appointment these should also be included at this point. This may include any defensive/evasive driving qualifications or an advanced driving certificate that you hold.

The meat of the statement should follow the listing set out above with no details left out unless not relevant. It should be chronological and structured in how the event (s) unfolded.

Each page should be signed at the bottom left by the person to whom the statement refers from Part A. On the last page of the statement, the person whose statement it is should sign after the last word so that no other words can be inserted thereafter. It is not necessary to sign the bottom left of this last page as was done on the previous ones.

d.   <u>Part D - Conclusion</u>

As the statement should only be written by the individual, then there is a paragraph to insert at the end of the statement.

If you write the statement yourself then include the following paragraph:

'*This statement was self-recorded at <place> on <date> at <time> and is true.*'

Conclude your statement with the following if someone else writes the statement during your presence:

'*This statement consisting of <pages> was recorded at <place> on <date> at <time> and witnessed by <name> <occupation> (if applicable)*'.

3.   **<u>Report Writing</u>**

Writing a report should equally take on the same structure as if you were writing a statement. It still requires the full facts of the event in a structured way. The layout of the document is different from the statement but the content could quite easily be the same. Reports serve as a permanent record of incidents, events, problems etc. There are many types of reports and each of which serves different functions. As a person in a position of responsibility, you may have your own set of guidelines and templates to follow.

Poorly written reports hurt your credibility by making you appear less competent and professional. They can also undermine your goals in a number of ways. In one particular way it could lose the impact on what is trying to be said in which case it would not be clearly understood by the reader and further questions will need to be asked to clarify ambiguities.

Attention should be placed on grammar, punctuation, spelling and word choice. This is also the same when writing statements. Something as simple as improperly omitting a comma can change the meaning of a sentence as can the use of a wrong word. Well-written reports require some effort. Carefully review and edit the report before submitting it to the next level. Make sure it accurately reflects what each team member did if appropriate.

a. ***Good and Bad Characteristics***

    (1)   <u>Common Problems with Incident Reports.</u> The following are some common problems found in incident reports:

        (a)   Confusing to someone who wasn't there. (Report doesn't paint a clear picture).

        (b)   Thoughts not presented in an organised manner.

        (c)   Not enough detail (who, what, when, why and how).

        (c)   Not clear and concise

        (e)   Poor grammar, punctuation and spelling

        (f)   Incorrect word usage

        (g)   Use of terms, abbreviations and acronyms that the reader(s) may not be familiar with.

        (h)   Inconsistency in style throughout the department.

    (2)   <u>Characteristics of a Good Report.</u> The following are characteristics of a good report:

        (a)   Accurate and specific

        (b)   Factual

        (c)   Objective

        (d)   Clear

        (e)   Complete

        (f)   Concise

        (g)   Well-organised

        (h)   Grammatically correct

        (i)   Light on abbreviations

b. ***Who, What, When, Where, Why & How***

The importance of writing a complete report is essential if the reader is to be able to understand what happened. The following are helpful things that you may want to cover when using the title above. The emphasis placed on these questions will vary dependant on the type of incident and how it evolved but hopefully these ideas will stimulate your thinking process:

(1) ***Who?***

    (a) Who was directly involved (who was injured etc)

    (b) Who discovered the incident?

    (d) Who reported the incident?

    (e) Who witnessed the incident? Who saw or heard something important?

    (f) Whom did you talk with whilst at the scene?

    (g) Who responded to the incident?

    (h) Who took what actions?

    (i) Who is the responsible party?

    (j) Who was notified of the incident?

    (k) Whom did you hand over the client to (Hospital – if applicable)

(2) ***What?***

    (a) What happened? (Include type of incident and enough details to paint a picture)

    (b) What property was involved (e.g. name of horse etc.) and to what extent

    (c) What was the client's main complaint of pain/injury?

    (d) What actions did you take?

    (e) What were the results of your actions?

    (f) What was said?

    (g) What vehicle was being used?

    (h) What vehicle was damaged?

(i)   What vehicle must be repaired or replaced?

(j)   What warnings were given if necessary?

(k)   What follow up action is required?

(3)   ***Where?***

(a)   Where did the incident occur?   (Give road names, junctions and grid references if necessary).

(4)   ***When?***

(a)   When did the incident happen? (Include day, date, time & year)

(b)   When was the incident discovered and reported? (if from a third party)

(c)   When did emergency responders arrive on scene?

(d)   When did other agencies arrive?

(e)   When was the incident brought under control?

(f)   When will follow-up activities take place?

(5)   ***Why?***

(a)   Why did the incident occur?   Was it accidental or intentional? What factors contributed to the incident?

(b)   Why did you take the actions you did? (Did you deviate from your SOPs or was it because something out of the ordinary happened)

(6)   ***How?***

(a)   How did the incident occur?

(b)   How was the incident discovered?

(c)   How is this incident related to other incidents? (if applicable)

(d)   How was information obtained?

4.   **Elements of a Complete Report**

The following are other guidelines on things to include. There may be some overlap from early parts in this chapter however it also includes parts not previously detailed.

a.   ***Nature and Extent of Emergency***

Describe the nature and extent of the emergency (especially if it involves a horse riding accident). Provide sufficient details for someone who was not there to develop a mental picture of the incident.

b.   ***Observations***

What did you observe? Don't limit yourself to the incident occurrence itself. What did you see at the point just prior to, during and after the incident? Did you see anything later in the incident that may be significant? Any injury to the horse? (if applicable).

c.   ***Actions***

What did you do to control the scene and mitigate the problem? And what were the results of your actions? Be specific especially where questions may be asked later. Who treated the client? Where was the client taken?

d.   ***Unusual Circumstances***

Note anything out the ordinary particularly if something makes the event non-accidental. Did you notice anything that lead to the incident happening in the first place?

e.   ***Property Damage/Injuries***

Describe what was damaged as well as type and extent of such damage. Describe any injuries by the client or their horse (if applicable)

f.   ***Cause***

Identify the cause if possible and provide specific observations that led to your conclusion. If you don't know the cause then document that also.

g.   ***Statements Provided by Others***

It may be necessary to get other parties (CPO Personnel) to write a statement to concur their observations too. This will provide a strong support for the initial reporting individual.

5.   **General Points for the Writing of Statements or Reports**

The following are general points to be considered when writing either a statement or report. Some may reiterate points mentioned earlier in this chapter.

a.   Make sure the report/statement is completed by the end of the duty or certainly the next AM if a stand down was late on the day of the event.

b.   ***Do not*** give an opinion, just the facts. You may state observations however but not conjecture.

c.   ***Do not*** lie or misrepresent the facts.

d.   Invert quotes when conversations have taken place.

e.   Always assume that the report is going to be reviewed by a third party. All reports/statements are considered *Confidential*.

f.   ***Do not*** share or distribute the report with anyone except authorised persons.

g.   ***Do not*** have anyone write the report for you. ***Do not*** sign a report that you didn't write.

h.   It may be useful to advise your team members to take notes if possible during and after an event. When it's time to write the report/statement they can refer to your notes. These notes however will be original and will need to be kept for evidential purposes.

i.   Ensure that the report is organised into appropriate paragraphs for easier reading. Follow the layout set out above.

j.   If the police attend the scene then make sure your teams take a note of any badge numbers and from which station. They may give them a card with these details on. If any paramedics attend the scene and a client/or member of the group (including any CPO staff) are taken to a hospital, record the name of the hospital and any initial diagnosis.

k.   It may be useful to have a colleague check over the report before being submitted to you.

l.   If the report/statement isn't up to the satisfaction of what is required then the document needs to be handed back to the person involved and to be asked to re-write. It's for an obvious reason and those reasons are as mentioned earlier.

6.   **Conclusion**

CPOs are accountable for everything that they do and we are trusted with a lot of responsibility to complete what we are employed to provide. We are often the first on the scene when an incident occurs and this will be purely down to the nature of our roles. The mould of the CPOs today is different from by-gone years and they are more intellect than the image portrayed by some. We are also more observant, have better communication skills and are able to respond to any given set of circumstances based on the level of our training and to deal with matters head on. When the wheels fall off though, it is essential that an accurate account of what happened is truly reflected and this can be documented in either a written report or statement. The information that has gone previously in this Chapter together with the attached annexes should be a starting point for you to compile such a document. Which document (Report or Statement) to use will be dictated to some degree as to the nature of the event. If in doubt then seek guidance.

CHAPTER 16

OPERATIONAL SECURITY [OPSEC]

1. **Introduction**

Inherent with security, you have an obligation on any assignment to understand and effectively invoke all aspects of OPSEC to your working environment. Unless your team adhere to these practicalities and have a clear understanding of what OPSEC actually covers, then how your day-to-day operations are conducted will be dictated to in some way by OPSEC. If you don't understand the correlation of OPSEC and your responsibilities then it will be that much more difficult to provide effective protection as you would in effect have compromised everything in relation to the mission. By this compromise alone, you would've created unsustainable working conditions for both yourself and other members of your PSD.

Every assignment undertaken is personal and private to each client and they expect any team to respect and protect this. The need for a PSD to share information between other locations is unnecessary and is against the wishes of the client. It is also against the expected Code of Conduct that each and every CPO assigned to a PSD must follow. The only exception to this is to share intelligence information that may have some bearing on other locations/clients. Take pride in your work and protect the client to the full extent of your capabilities and guard against the need to talk to others not associated with your detail. Be discreet in conversation with others and don't talk loosely to friends about what you do. *Think before you speak!!.*

OPSEC unfortunately isn't something taught at a CP academy, it's something you pick up as you go along in the industry. As a team leader you'll need to understand this topic in its entirety otherwise you'll have no credibility in this profession to guard not only your client, but the many secrets they entrust your team with.

2. **What is OPSEC**

A definition of OPSEC can be:

"…a process of identifying critical information and subsequently analysing friendly actions attendant to PSD operations and other activities to:

a. *Identify these actions that can be observed by adversary intelligence systems/personnel.*
b. *Determine indicators that hostile intelligence systems might obtain that could be interpreted or pieced together to derive critical information in time to be useful to adversaries.*
c. *Select and execute measures that eliminate or reduce to an acceptable level the vulnerabilities of friendly actions to adversary exploitation.*
d. *OPSEC protects critical information from adversary observation and collection in ways that traditional security programmes such as information security protect classified information but they cannot prevent all indicators of critical information, especially unclassified indicators, from being revealed.*

    e. In concise terms, the OPSEC process identifies critical information of PSD plans, operations and supporting activities and the indicators that can reveal it and then develops measures to eliminate, reduce, or conceal those indicators"

OPSEC is not only a systems analysis process employing elements of traditional security, intelligence, counterintelligence and deception, but it is also a mindset. By educating yourself on OPSEC risks and methodologies, then protecting sensitive information and activities becomes second nature. (See Page 239 - OPSEC Process)

OPSEC is unique as a discipline, since certain decisions need to be considered when implementing OPSEC measures. Most of these measures will involve a certain expenditure of resources, so an estimate will be made as to whether the assumed gain in secrecy is worth the cost in resources. If the decision is made not to implement a measure, then the PSD will assume a certain risk.

The goal of OPSEC is to keep client and any company critical and sensitive information from adversaries by discovering unguarded (unclassified) pathways that may lead to critical and sensitive (classified or unclassified) information, also known as vulnerabilities and to ensure that all PSD personnel employ such tactics to ensure that OPSEC is maintained. An example of a pathway might be unclassified or classified information being discarded in normal waste receptacles. This collected information could provide an adversary with indicators that could lead to an operation being discovered and compromised. A cost effective counter measure to this would have been to use a cross cut shredder. If a shredder is impractical then it would be ideal to tear the paper into several small pieces before placing in the waste receptacle.

OPSEC is not just for the military or government entities. More and more individuals and corporations are realizing the importance of protecting activities which are personal, private and in some cases secret. Whatever the reason for implementing OPSEC, it can, and will increase the overall security posture. Your position as a member of a PSD requires a full understanding and implementation of OPSEC. You are entrusted with information, details of personalities, activities and locations etc. that must be guarded as much as the client themselves and your profession requires this also. A failure of OPSEC by an individual will make your client vulnerable and you unemployed and you would have broken one of the fundamental rules of being part of a PSD. Not only are you there to protect your client, but also to guard against any adversaries from obtaining information that could be damaging or embarrassing.

Some PSD (CPO's) feel it necessary when compiling their own CV for a potential employer to include the names of those clients to whom you have provided a service in the past or current. This is another breach of OPSEC. *Leave it out!*

3.   **Definition of Critical Information**

"...is information which is important to the successful achievement of PSD (CP) operations, objectives and missions, or which may be of use to an adversary of the UK"

Critical information consists of specific facts about PSD (CP) capabilities, activities, limitations (includes vulnerabilities) and intentions needed by adversaries for them to plan and act effectively so as to degrade any PSD (CP) friendly mission accomplishment. Once this information falls into the hands of others and they act upon it, the compromise of this information could prevent or seriously degrade the capability of the PSD and the mission success outcome.

Critical information can either be Classified or Unclassified. Classified information (Restricted, Secret, Confidential, Eyes Only etc) requires OPSEC measures for additional protection mainly as unclassified indicators can reveal it. Any information you are in possession of which is Unclassified especially requires OPSEC measures because it is not protected by the requirements provided for classified information.

The term 'Critical Information' is a standard usage within the PSD (CP) Department of any company.

4.   **Sensitive Information**

Sensitive Information is information requiring special protection from disclosure that could cause that could cause compromise or threat to a PSD (CP) operation, the clients or your company.

Examples of Sensitive Information include, but are not limited to:

- Unclassified information that requires special handling
- Controlled unclassified information is information to which access or distribution limitations have been applied according to the document/operational requirements.
- Client residential locations (UK & Overseas)
- Photographs whether personal, vehicles, aircraft (Inside or outside of both Rotary and Fixed Wing) or buildings (Including houses) used by clients.
- Telephone numbers of client & PSD personnel
- Vehicle tag numbers of client & PSD personnel
- Lists of names within your company including directors, contractors and sub-contractors. Discretionary release of names of personnel for the purpose of recruiting is permitted.
- Unclassified information for the purpose of "Official Use Only" is a designation that is applied to unclassified information that may be exempt from mandatory release to persons outside of your company. Examples include but not limited to: PSD (CP) strengths, movements, actions-on, readiness data, tactics, techniques and procedures, proprietary information and information protected by copyright and information concerning security deployments (SOPs, OpOs etc).

5.   **Operations Security OPSEC Compromise**

An OPSEC compromise is the disclosure of Critical Information or Sensitive Information that has been identified by the CP Ops Manager or clients that may jeopardise the PSD ability to execute its missions or to adequately protect other team personnel, clients or your company.

Critical or Sensitive Information that has been compromised and is available in the public domain should not be highlighted or referenced publicly outside of your operation as these actions provide further unnecessary exposure of the compromised information.

6. **Why OPSEC**

The world we both live and operate in is increasingly dependent on information. In this world, pieces of information may be assembled in order to form a bigger picture of, not only your client but also you yourself and any organisation that may be connected with the information being pieced together. This information, whether documented or verbal needs to be guarded against falling into the hands of anyone who has no reflection on the departmental operation. You must also realize that being a member of a PSD you are just as likely to be targeted in order to gain information about you or indirectly against your client.

OPSEC is a continuous process and an inherent part of CP operations and as such, must be fully integrated into the execution of all PSD operations and to your private live also when off duty

7. **What are OPSEC Indicators**

An indicator is a 'Piece of Puzzle'. In other words, an indicator is any piece of information that can be exploited to gain further information, or be combined with other indicators to build a more complete profile of operations. Guard against leaving operationally sensitive or personal information in areas where non-PSD personnel are likely to frequent in areas used by the PSD. Equally, **Do not** leave items in your own personal vehicles or hotel rooms where the cleaning maids may see documents.

Your own personal security measures should equally be as high on the list of implementing as those you apply when charged with the security of your client. There has to be a common sense approach here and if you think something isn't quite right with the picture you're looking at then generally there will be.

An example of an indicator could be when you go to work, what you do at work, financial transactions etc. Before releasing any information which may be operationally sensitive or by doing something, take a step back to consider the potential value to any adversaries. They are all around you but often won't be seen until too late.

a. Types of Indicators

   (1) Profile. Activity patterns and signatures that shows how your activities are normally conducted.

   (2) Deviation. Profile changes, which help an adversary to learn about your intentions, preparations, time and places.

   (3) Tip-Off. Actions that warn or shows an adversary of friendly impending activity.

b. Characteristics of an Indicator

(1)   Signature. An identifiable trace or something that causes it to stand out.

(2)   Associations.   Compares current with past indicator information for relationship.

(3)   Profiles.   Other indicators that have not been observed or detected.

(4)   Contrast.   Only needs to be recognised not understood.

(5)   Exposure.   Duration, repletion and timings of exposed indicator.

8.   **Your Responsibilities**

It is essential that all security personnel employed on PSD operations maximize OPSEC in a perfunctory manner. A career as a CPO depends on it and your clients expect it. It is also essential that those in positions of responsibility actually enforce the overall concept for the whole operation to remain intact.

OPSEC awareness and execution is crucial to the success of a PSD (CP) operation. OPSEC is applicable to all personnel and all PSD operations and supporting activities on a daily basis. OPSEC denies adversaries information about your capabilities, activities, limitations and intentions that adversaries need to make competent decisions. Failure to apply OPSEC can result in serious injury or death to PSD personnel or clients and ultimately a mission failure.

Equally, everyone will need to sign a ND form prior to commencing a PSD operation which encompasses not only the current op you are deployed on but passage of information once the op has concluded. Protecting information by not leaking it to others will keep the integrity of the op and if your client is happy with the team and wishes to use them the following year then at least you will know that the security of everyone will be maintained.

You must protect from disclosure any critical information and sensitive information to which you have personal access now and in the future.

You must prevent disclosure of critical and sensitive information in any public domain to include but not limited to the WWW, open source publications and the media.

Do not publicly disseminate, or publish photographs displaying critical or sensitive information as described earlier. Examples include but are not limited to Client properties, client pictures, vehicles, aircraft (inside or outside and fixed or rotary), PSD personnel in operational conditions and any protective measures of client properties.

You must not publicly reference, disseminate, or publish critical or sensitive information that has already been compromised as this provides further unnecessary exposure of the compromised information and may serve to validate it.

Implement all current OPSEC measures.

Actively encourage other members of your PSD to protect critical and sensitive information.

Destroy (burn, shred etc.) critical and sensitive information that is no longer needed to prevent the inadvertent disclosure and reconstruction of this material. This includes all Op Orders, mission sensitive information, serial numbers etc.

It is important to stress to your team that failure to comply with any instructions, policies, orders or directives on OPSEC may render the individual (s) liable to disciplinary action.

9. **What are the Capabilities of your Adversary?**

The unfortunate thing is that you just don't know. There could quite easily be an internal adversary as well as external. Someone within the PSD, Housekeeping, logistics etc. could quite easily fall into this category. You wont be able to determine the full capability of an adversary, so you can only protect your information at your end and be alert to anything you deem as being out the ordinary.

Plan for the worst, hope for the best!

10. **The OPSEC Process**

   a. *Identify Critical Information*

   Without doubt the first step in this process is to identify what information is deemed as critical or sensitive. Critical information is information that would harm the Company, the operation or the client if obtained by an adversary. This information is often the core secrets, personal information, movements, activities, locations, code names, personnel on the PSD, vehicle tag numbers etc. If the information is useful to the way you work and how you go about executing the op then it could equally be useful to an adversary. Any op orders given to you, SOPs, telephone numbers etc. should be secured at all times and treated as *CONFIDENTIAL*. These must not be left in the open for others to see, copy or capture a picture. You must be in the habit at all times to think personal security. Any breach here is against the basic fundamentals of being a member of a PSD and against the profession to which everyone is enlisted in providing a service. Any information that is redundant after the completion of an op or any information associated with the op should be returned to management in order for it to be extirpated without delay. Failure to do so may jeopardise any future op linked to the redundant one.

   b. *Analyse the Threat*

   Once the critical information is identified at 10 (a) above, the next step is to determine the individuals or groups that represent a threat to that information. An op order for instance contains valuable information about an up and coming operation with details of activities, contact numbers, actions on, PSD personnel, movement grids & timings etc. All this is without doubt useful or of interest to anyone outside of the op whether they decide to do anything with such information or not. Common sense plays an important part here and your own judgment as well as those, which others guide you with, are key to understanding what threats are current.

c. *Analyse the Vulnerabilities*

This is an inward looking analysis from the perspective of an adversary. Think about how information (written, mobile phone calls, visuals, general talking) is gleaned by others. Once you understand this then you are able to counter the threat and you then feel safe in the knowledge that you have done as much as you can to limit the risk. Awareness as a PSD (CPO) is crucial at any time in your life whether on or off duty. You must be in the habit of people watching and making your own analysis of vulnerability. Being a CPO is not a game or an easy occupation, it is a serious industry, which can have dire consequences if your teams fail to deliver correctly, or management fails to enforce OPSEC. *Failure can lead to a dismissal from the allocation.*

d. *Assess the Risks*

For each vulnerability the threat must be matched, and at this point each one is assigned a risk level. This is an unmitigated risk level, meaning that any corrective factors are not included in the analysis. The risk matrix is as follows:
- An adversary has demonstrated their ability to exploit an existing vulnerability and the resulting impact would be irreparable; hazard consequence would be catastrophic. **Critical.**
- There is no doubt that an adversary could exploit an existing vulnerability and the resulting impact would be serious enough to consider cancellation of a mission; hazard consequence would be major. **High.**
- It is probable an adversary could exploit an existing vulnerability and the resulting impact would be damaging; hazard consequence would be no higher than major. **Medium High.**
- It is possible an adversary could exploit an existing vulnerability and the resulting impact would be manageable; hazard consequence would be no higher than moderate. **Medium.**
- It is unlikely an adversary could exploit an existing vulnerability and the resulting impact would be negligible; hazard consequence would be no higher than minor. **Medium Low**.
- It is improbable an adversary would exploit an existing vulnerability and the resulting impact would be insignificant; hazard consequence would be no higher than insignificant. **Low**

The risk level assigned to a particular vulnerability helps to 'Triage' the protection of data.

e. *Apply the Countermeasures*

These are developed to protect the activity. Ideally, the chosen counter-measures eliminate the adversary threat, the vulnerabilities that can be exploited by the adversary, or the utility of the information.

PSD personnel are key to the counter-measures and must guard against lose tongues, discarding of material without thinking of the consequences and the nature of the material (whether personal (bank statements) or operational matters). The old adage 'Prevention is better than cure' is relevant here and your contribution goes along way to ensure safety and security is maintained at both a personal and professional level.

Do not:

- Discuss or transmit any critical information over unclassified means; use a fax or email.
- Discuss critical (operational) information with anyone who does not have clearance or 'a need to know'.
- Wear distinctive items (SIA/ID Cards) that identify you or your department/company if this information is critical.
- Leave documents/laptops/storage medias in your vehicle, your hotel rooms or office

Do:

- Safeguard sensitive information the same way you would safeguard classified.
- Practice common sense and self-discipline, which will safeguard you, your position and all others you come into contact with.

11.   **OPSEC Ratings Definitions**

Two sample ratings standards are provided. The first is a six-point scale, the second a five point scale. The associated math is provided with each scale. It is essential to choose the best one which suits your purpose and adjust the definitions to coincide with your circumstances or mission.

Analysis Ratings Criteria (Six-point scale, Low to Critical)

a.   **Threat**

Critical	*An adversary has demonstrated both strong intent and high capability to act aggressively against friendly objectives*
High	*An adversary has demonstrated both intent and capability to act against friendly objectives.*
Medium High	*An adversary has demonstrated intent or capability to act against friendly objectives.*
Medium	*An adversary has demonstrated intent and capability to act against similar friendly objectives.*
Medium Low	*An adversary has demonstrated intent or capability to act against similar friendly objectives.*
Low	*Adversary is not assessed to have intent, or adversary is not assessed to have the capability the capability to act against friendly or similar objective*

b.   **Vulnerability**

Critical	Proven exploitable by multiple collection disciplines requiring virtually no corroboration.
High	Potential exploitable by multiple collection disciplines requiring virtually no corroboration.
Medium High	Potential exploitable by multiple collection disciplines requiring only limited corroboration
Medium	Potentially exploitable by multiple collection disciplines requiring significant corroboration
Medium Low	Potentially exploitable by only limited collection disciplines.
Low	Potential fore exploitation is negligible.

c.   **Impact**

Critical	Deaths or other events that cause postponement of a PSD mission lasting longer than 72 hours loss of critical or classified information that results in the cancellation of a PSD mission or causes catastrophic degradation of a mission success, or compromise of intelligence sources and methods, property loss greater than £1,000,000, catastrophic embarrassment or harm to the reputation of the client or your company.
High	Serious injuries or other events that cause postponement of a PSD mission event lasting longer than 25 hrs., but less than 72 hours loss of critical or classified information that results in the postponement of the mission for more than 25 hours but less than 72 hours or seriously degrades the overall mission success, property loss greater than £450,000 but less than £1,000,000, serious embarrassment or harm to the client or your company.
Medium High	Injuries or other events that cause postponement of the PSD mission lasting longer than 4 hours but less than 24 hours, loss of critical or classified information that results in a delay of a mission for 4 to 24 hours or causes unacceptable degradation of a mission success, property loss greater than £10,000 but less than £1,000,000, major harm to the reputation of your company.
Medium	Injuries or other events which cause postponement of a PSD mission event lasting longer than 1 hour but less than 4 hours, loss of critical information (with no loss of classified information) that causes delay of an operation for more than 1 hour but less than 4 or causes some degradation of a mission success within acceptable levels, property loss greater than £5,000 but less than £10,000, manageable embarrassment or harm to the reputation of your company.
Medium Low	Injuries or other events which cause postponement of a mission event lasting longer than 15 minutes but less than 1 hour, loss of critical information (with no loss of classified information) that delays the mission for less than one hour

	or causes minimal degradation of a mission success, property loss greater than £1,000 but less than £5,000, moderate embarrassment or harm to the reputation of the client or your company.
Low	*No personal injury, no events which cause postponement of a PSD operation, no loss of critical or classified information, no degradation of the mission outcome, property loss less than £1,000, delays to the mission less than 15 minutes, no affect on other operational matters, no embarrassment or harm to the client or your company.*

d.   **Risk**

Critical	*An adversary has demonstrated their ability to exploit an existing vulnerability and the resulting impact would be irreparable; hazard consequence would be catastrophic*
High	*There is no doubt an adversary could exploit an existing vulnerability and the resulting impact would be serious enough to consider cancellation of a PSD mission; hazard consequence would be major*
Medium High	*It is probable an adversary could exploit an existing vulnerability and the resulting impact would be damaging; hazard consequence would be no higher than major.*
Medium	*It is possible an adversary could exploit an existing vulnerability and the resulting impact would be manageable; hazard consequence would be no more higher than moderate.*
Medium Low	*It is unlikely an adversary could exploit an existing vulnerability and the resulting impact would be negligible; hazard consequence would be no higher than minor*
Low	*It is improbable an adversary would exploit an existing vulnerability and the resulting impact would be insignificant; hazard consequence would be no higher than insignificant*

Analysis Ratings Criteria (Five Point Scale, Low to High)

a. **Threat**

Low	*No adversary has demonstrated an intent, or no adversary is assessed to have the capability to act against friendly objectives.*
Medium Low	*An adversary has demonstrated an intent or capability to act against similar friendly objectives.*
Medium	*An adversary has demonstrated both intent and capability to act against similar friendly objectives.*
Medium High	*An adversary has demonstrated intent or capability to act against friendly objectives.*
High	*An adversary has demonstrated both intent and capability to act against friendly objectives.*

b. **Vulnerability**

Low	*Potential for exploitation is negligible*
Medium Low	*Potentially exploitable by only limited collection disciplines*
Medium High	*Potentially exploitable by multiple collection disciplines requiring only limited corroboration of data.*
High	*Potentially exploitable by multiple collection disciplines requiring virtually no corroboration*

c. **Impact**

Low	*No personal injury, property loss less than £1,000, delays less than 15 minutes, no affect on the integrity of other on-going PSD ops, no embarrassment to the client or your company.*
Medium Low	*Minor personal injury (no hospitalisation), property loss greater than £1,000 but less than £5,000, delays greater than 15 but less than 30 minutes, minor embarrassment or harm to the client or your company.*
Medium	*Injuries requiring hospitalization or observation, property loss greater than £5,000 but less than £10,000, delays greater than 30 but less than 60 minutes, moderate embarrassment or harm to the client or your company.*
Medium High	*Injuries requiring hospitalization for treatment for serious, substantial bodily injury, property loss greater than £10,000 but less than £1,000,000 delays greater than one hour but less than 24hours, major embarrassment or harm to the client or your company.*
High	*Death, property loss greater than £1,000,000, delays lasting longer than 25 hours, catastrophic embarrassment or harm to the client or your company.*

d. **Risk**

Low	*It is improbable an adversary would exploit an existing vulnerability and the resulting impact would be insignificant.*
Medium Low	*It is unlikely an adversary could exploit an existing vulnerability and the resulting impact would be negligible.*
Medium	*It is possible an adversary could exploit an existing vulnerability and the resulting impact would be manageable.*
Medium High	*It is probable an adversary could exploit an existing vulnerability and the resulting impact would be damaging.*
High	*There is no doubt an adversary could exploit could exploit an existing vulnerability and the resulting impact would be irreparable.*

12. **The Laws of OPSEC**

1. ***If you don't know the threat, how do you know what to protect.*** In any given situation, there is likely to be more than one adversary, although each may be interested in different information.

2. ***If you don't know <u>what</u> to protect, how do you know you are protecting it***? The 'What' is the critical and sensitive, or target, information that adversaries require to fulfill their objectives.

3. ***If you are not protecting it (the critical and sensitive information), the adversary wins***! OPSEC vulnerability assessments are conducted to determine whether or not critical information is vulnerable to exploitation by others.

In short, Know the Threat
Know what to protect
And then <u>protect it!</u>

12. <u>**Conclusion**</u>.

To preserve the integrity of an operation and a client to whom you have been detailed to protect, it is important to remember that:

a. Never talk about client movements (Pending or Current, and in some cases historical ones). This should also be applied post op also.

b. Never release dates or timings when clients are expected to move/travel or indeed how the movement will be executed. (*Be aware that 'Next Tuesday', 'Next Week' or 'in nine days' time' all constitute releasing dates and are in violation of OPSEC*)

c. Never give specific locations. This can include primary & secondary residential locations, airports in use, and types of vehicles with tag numbers, routes to and from these locations etc.

d. Always practice OPSEC and continue this methodology even when online. OPSEC violations are more prevalent online than anywhere else. Many postings on message boards, social network sites and blogs can easily violate operational security intentionally or otherwise, especially since these postings are usually date and time stamped.

e. Always be aware of pieces to the puzzle. Though you may innocently have released very little information in your last blog or message board post, a quick glance through your history on that site could reveal pertinent information needed to complete a puzzle such as your job, work locations, colleagues etc. and it doesn't take long to build a picture.

It is better to be safe than sorry. If you are unsure whether information you have should be shared, don't share it.

ALWAYS THINK OPSEC!

Acknowledgments

I'd like to thank Paul Andrews for his invaluable input into the surveillance topic. His own background in surveillance whilst working with the government security service has been a great source of information. Paul continues to provide annual three-day bespoke courses for all my personnel prior to deployment. Surveillance is a topic, which is often overlooked by many but is of fundamental importance in CP work.

My thanks also go to Adam Brand for allowing me to use some of his work in writing this particular chapter. His knowledge and expertise in Graphology led me to develop an interest in the subject that has become an invaluable tool in the recruitment for all my personnel.

A thank you is also extended to Tony Scotti from Vehicle Dynamics Institute whose topics and research notes provided some very real analysis of worldwide incidents, which provides a great learning tool for all CP officers.

The research carried out by Atif Ahmad from the University of Melbourne into terrorism activities was also a welcome addition to this book and my thanks are extended to him for allowing me to use some of his work in providing some background information into this topic.

Finally, thank you to Steve and Chris at ShieldCrest publishing.

ISBN 978-1-911090-84-7